THE ORIGINS OF THE WARS OF GERMAN UNIFICATION

ORIGINS OF MODERN WARS
General editor: *Harry Hearder*

Titles already published:

THE ORIGINS OF THE WARS OF GERMAN UNIFICATION

William Carr

LONGMAN
London and New York

LONGMAN GROUP UK LIMITED
Longman House, Burnt Mill, Harlow,
Essex CM20 2JE, England
and Associated Companies throughout the world.

*Published in the United States of America
by Longman Inc., New York.*

First published 1991

BRITISH LIBRARY CATALOGUING IN PUBLICATION DATA
    Carr, William, *1921–*
        The origins of the wars of German unification. – (Origins of modern wars).
        1. Germany, 1815–1871
        I. Title   II. Series
        943.07
        ISBN 0–582–49147–9
        ISBN 0–582–49148–7 pbk

LIBRARY OF CONGRESS CATALOGING-IN-PUBLICATION DATA
    Carr, William, 1921–
        The origins of the wars of German unification/William Carr.
            p. cm.—(Origins of modern wars)
        Includes index.
        Includes bibliographical references.
        ISBN 0–582–49147–9 (cased).—ISBN 0–582–49148–7 (pbk.)
        1. Germany—Politics and government—1848–1870. 2. Germany—History,
    Military—19th century. 3. Prussia (Germany)—Foreign relations—1815–1870.
    4. Schleswig-Holstein War, 1864—Causes. 5. Austro-Prussian War,
    1866—Causes. 6. Franco-German War, 1870–1871—Causes. I. Series.
    DD210.C37 1991
    943'.07—dc20

                                                                90–36318
                                                                    CIP

Set in 10.5/11pt Linotron Times

Produced by Longman Singapore Publishers (Pte) Ltd.
Printed in Singapore

CONTENTS

ABBREVIATIONS

AHR	American Historical Review
APP	*Die auswärtige Politik Preussens 1858–1871*
DPO	*Quellen zur deutschen Politik Österreichs 1859–1866*
GW	*Bismarck. Die gesammelten Werke*
HT	Historisk Tidskrift
HZ	Historische Zeitschrift
JMH	Journal of Modern History
OD	*Les origines diplomatiques de la guerre de 1870/1: Recueil des documents officiels*
RKN	*Die Rheinpolitik Kaiser Napoleon IIIs von 1863 bis 1870*
SF	*Statsraadets forhandlinger 1848–1912*
ZGSHG	Zeitschrift der Gesellschaft für Schleswig-Holsteinische Geschichte

LIST OF MAPS

EDITOR'S FOREWORD

For the ninth volume in the series on the 'Origins of Modern Wars' I have the privilege to present a new work by Professor William Carr. Like the previous volumes in the series, it is valuable both as a work of considerable scholarship, and as a further illustration of the complexity of the general question as to why governments have resorted to the murderous method of warfare in attempts to solve their problems, attempts which were only rarely successful in doing so.

The scholarship behind William Carr's book is immediately obvious, and has enabled him to reduce the Schleswig-Holstein Question, and the no less complicated German Question before 1866, to lucid and convincing accounts. It has further enabled him to give a gripping and fascinating account of the crisis which led to the war of 1870, an account in which Bismarck's own elegant, but untruthful, version is set in its proper perspective.

Bismarck, with his amoral and wholly Prussia-centred policy, exploited, but ultimately by-passed, the ideologues, so far as these wars are concerned. The German national liberals might have fought an ideological war against Denmark over Schleswig-Holstein, and against Austria over the German Question, but Bismarck ensured that no wild ideologies would turn the wars into totalitarian ones. In this sense, a Bismarck in 1914, or in Washington in the 1960s, might have saved humanity much suffering, even though doing good for humanity was not one of Bismarck's preoccupations.

One question which came to the fore in Professor Nish's masterly study of the Origins of the Russo-Japanese War of 1904 is again relevant to the origins of the German–Danish War of 1864: what is the responsibility of the Great Powers who are – and intend to be – neutral, to stop the war from starting? In 1904 Britain and France perhaps did not try hard enough to prevent a war between Russia and Japan, which in human terms was a very terrible one. In 1864 the Danes hoped that the Great Powers – again, Britain and France – would discourage the German Confederation from going to war over Schleswig-Holstein. In Carr's words, 'had the international situation not been favourable, Austria and Prussia would scarcely have gone to war'.

On the vexed question of the primacy of domestic over foreign policy – or *vice versa* – Professor Carr has much to say, 'Certainly,' he writes, 'it is far too simplistic an explanation of Bismarck's foreign policy to attribute it to a conscious attempt to escape the implications of the domestic crisis,' Yet he recognises the 'mutual independence' of the two, and so reminds us that individual political leaders do not ask themselves: 'Am I, at this moment, concerned with domestic, or foreign, policy?'

Bismarck, being all of one piece, did not ask himself such a question. And if he wanted – and succeeded – to limit warfare, it was not for humanitarian reasons but rather because he did not want the military men to gain control. Lest we should think that Bismarck was squeamish about warfare, Carr provides us with a fascinating quote from the young Bismarck:

'German dualism . . . has regularly adjusted relationships in a radical fashion by warfare and there is no other means in this present century by which the clock of development can be made to show the correct time.'

Once again, in this series' study of the causes of wars, the question of miscalculation enters the picture. The Danes in 1864 adopted an aggressive attitude in the belief that Sweden – if not Britain and France – would come to their aid and even when the British and French – and Russian – ambassadors assured them that they were mistaken, they preferred to be optimistic against all the evidence.

And the question of the expenses of war is always present. Governments usually go to war only if they can afford to do so, unless they are blatantly attacked by an aggressive neighbour. In the summer of 1865 neither the Prussian nor the Austrian government could afford to fight another war, and so the Gastein Convention served its purpose as a holding operation. If Bismarck was insincere in signing the Convention, it is also true that the Austrian attitude was reflected in the words of the Viennese newspaper, the *Allgemeine Zeitung*: 'Peace and friendship until further notice'.

On the war of 1870, Professor Carr concludes that it was 'in essence a power struggle fought to determine who should be master in Europe'. But to conceal the truth, what Carr calls 'the ethos of the duelling match' had to be introduced, with 'honour' being 'outraged', 'satisfaction' demanded, and when no 'apology' was forthcoming, war became 'the only "honourable" way of resolving the matter'. The foolish, and totally irresponsible, French foreign minister, the Duc de Gramont, was perhaps alone in believing in

the reality of the duelling match. On Gramont only Shakespeare's
words are adequate:

> 'Man, proud man, drest in a little brief authority
>
> ... plays such fantastic tricks before high heaven
>
> As make the angels weep.'

HARRY HEARDER

PREFACE

It was quite fortuitous that this book was completed at a truly momentous time in the history of post-war Europe. The fall of Erich Honecker, the breaching of the Berlin Wall and the coming together of the peoples of the two Germanies have put back on the political agenda what many of us thought was a remote prospect: the re-unification of Germany. When the story of the reemergence of a united Germany (which does not, of course, include Austria although she was for centuries an integral part of the German Reich) comes to be written it will be seen that the desire of the German people for re-unification – in so far as this can be accurately assessed – was a consequence rather than a cause of what happened with such astonishing rapidity in the winter of 1989–90. It was at best only one of several factors in the total situation. More important have been the momentous changes in the Soviet Union associated with Mikhail Gorbachev; the outcome of the revolutionary upheavals which are transforming the political and economic scene in Central and Eastern Europe; and the desire of the United States and the Soviet Union (two of the Four Powers who defeated Nazi Germany forty-five years ago) to bring about, for sound economic reasons, a substantial measure of disarmament certain to alter profoundly the nature of the Warsaw and NATO alliances and diminish correspondingly the military significance which the continued division of Germany once possessed for these Great Powers. The story of the creation of a (partially) united Germany between 1864 and 1871 also depended upon many variables: the power-political struggle between Prussia and Austria, their divergent economic interests, the military prowess of the reformed Prussian army, and on the political skill of Bismarck as well as on the desire of the articulate middle class for a nation state to protect Germany against French ambitions and to give tangible political form to the growing economic ties drawing members of the German Customs Union closer together. There was nothing inevitable about the outcome in the 1860s any more than there is today in Central Europe. The concepts of Greater Germany and Middle Europe had their supporters just as much as Little Germany. And because the Reich of 1871 was no more a 'national' state than the rivals would have been, the German question has remained on the European agenda in one form or another ever since. In the text I felt it would be pedantic to use the German names of well known Prussian and Austrian rulers. Similarly the anglicized form has been used for the German states. But German and Danish names of organizations are indicated in brackets as the English equivalent does not always convey the exact meaning. In Chapter 2 the Danish term Helstat has been used throughout to avoid the clumsy English 'united monarchy'.

I would like to express my sincere thanks to the Deutscher Akademischer Austauschdienst for a grant and to the Leverhulme Trust for an Emeritus Fellowship which have enabled me to pursue my research in Germany. I am also indebted to the librarian and his staff at the Institute für europäische Geschichte in Mainz for their help and to Professor Erich Hoffman of the University of Kiel for permission to work in the library of the Historisches Seminar. To Longmans and to Professor Harry Hearder I am greatly indebted for their patience in waiting through one deadline after another for the manuscript. And most of all I acknowledge my indebtedness to my wife on whose good nature I have once again presumed during the months I spent grappling with the intricacies of mid-nineteenth-century Germany history. I can only hope that all of them will feel that this volume has some relevance to the present situation.

W. Carr   University of Sheffield

To Kathleen and Mary Louise

xiv

Chapter 1

THE NEW IDEOLOGIES

NATIONALISM AND LIBERALISM

If one were to select a single historical force which moulded the history of Europe in the nineteenth century, without question it would be the French Revolution. This cataclysmic upheaval in the premier state in Europe released a ferment of ideas and fathered political movements which made a lasting impact on the face of the old continent. Liberty, Equality and Fraternity, the watchwords of that revolution, were carried on the bayonets of the French armies to most parts of Western Europe. The old order was shaken to the foundations, thrones tumbled, many ancient feudal privileges were abolished, the structure of government was at least partially rationalized and the accumulated lumber of centuries sometimes discarded virtually overnight.

In the storm and stress of these years two new ideological concepts emerged: liberalism and nationalism. Defining them is no easy task. The historical antecedents of liberalism reach back in time to the English Revolution and the Scientific Revolution of the seventeenth century. Broadly speaking, liberals believed that man was not destined to remain for ever the helpless prisoner of century-old traditions, stifled in his development by the arbitrary actions of all-powerful monarchs. A fundamental tenet of the liberal ideology was the conviction – first proclaimed in the American Declaration of Independence – that all men possessed inalienable rights which preceded the establishment of civil government and which it was the duty of rulers to respect. Indeed, the whole purpose of government was to provide a minimum framework of law and order within which man would enjoy equality before the law, freedom of movement and association, and be able to develop his talents to the full. Secondly, liberals believed that sovereignty resided in the people – a concept Jean-Jacques Rousseau first

1

expressed in imperishable prose in the *Contrat Social* – and that civil government should be conducted in its interests. Generally speaking, liberalism went hand in hand with nationalism.

Historians and political scientists cannot agree on a catch-all definition of this complex and multifaceted phenomenon. Tentatively it may be described as a system of values and beliefs which lead a group of people to become conscious of belonging together because of characteristics such as a common language, common culture or subjection to the same ruler and which are capable of mobilizing the group politically. It is the element of popular participation which differentiates modern nationalism from what is sometimes termed 'proto-nationalism', stretching back over the centuries in many lands. There has been much debate but little agreement in recent years about the earlier forms of nationalism. One can summarize the position by saying that consciousness of the separate identity of a nation preceded the French Revolution but was confined to the ruling élite – the nobility supported by the clergy – and in the late medieval period by the rising bourgeoisie. The mass of the population was, however, scarcely touched by proto-nationalism. In addition, early consciousness of nationality was thickly overlaid by the bonds of universal religion.

The French Revolution marks the turning-point in the growth of modern nationalism. It contributed two new concepts to political philosophy: the secular state recognizing no higher authority than itself and no longer seeking legitimization from the Church; and, secondly, the nation of equal citizens. The latter concept was a mixed blessing. While the state guaranteed to the citizen the enjoyment of certain rights, he was simultaneously placed under certain obligations to serve the community and, if need be, give his life in its defence. Out of this obligatory element grew the power of the modern state, demanding supreme loyalty from its citizens to its institutions. Taken to extremes it produced the totalitarian regimes of the mid – twentieth century which, in theory at least, were not prepared to leave any sphere of life to individual choice.

Why did nationalism emerge as the dominant ideology in Germany and, for that matter, in other parts of Europe in the nineteenth century? For decades Friedrich Meinecke's classic study *Weltbürgertum und Nationalstaat,* written at the beginning of the twentieth century, was regarded as the definitive work on the growth of German nationalism. Nowadays scholars doubt whether the nationalist phenomenon can be explained satisfactorily solely in terms of a marriage between folkish values, the writings of certain poets and philosophers and the material power of Prussia. The missing ingredient which recent studies of nationalism emphasize is the complex process of modernization which was changing the structure of Europe from the middle of the eighteenth century onwards.

The argument runs as follows: the old basis on which the authority of rulers had rested for centuries was undermined by a number of interconnected factors. In an age of declining religious faith and unprecedented social change the 'divinity that hedges round a king' was losing its potency to legitimize monarchical rule. Europe was changing rapidly, most notably in terms of population. In 1750 130 million people lived in Europe; by 1800 the figure rose to 187 million and by 1900 had reached 401 million. In the area which became the Reich of 1871 17 million people were living in 1750; by 1800 this figure had risen to 25 million, by 1850 to 35.4 million and by 1900 to 56.4 million.

Such an enormous increase – for which improved hygiene standards, falling mortality rates and better diet were mainly responsible – presented rulers with massive control problems. This was especially true in rapidly growing urban areas where the inadequacy of the bureaucratic apparatus to deal with problems of employment and social misery, together with the failure of the Church to evangelize the newcomers, had the most disturbing implications for monarchical stability.

Secondly, the advantage which illiteracy had given ruling élites over the masses was waning rapidly. One estimate suggests that whereas only 15 per cent of German adults were literate in 1770, this had risen to 40 per cent by 1830. In Prussia, for example, the numbers at elementary and middle schools increased by 50 per cent between 1830 and 1850. Reading societies were widespread in small towns throughout Germany in the early nineteenth century. Growing literacy made possible a veritable revolution in publishing; the publication of books and periodicals doubled in the first half of the nineteenth century. And as more and more ordinary people learned to read they could enter at last into a kingdom where competing ideologies wrestled for their allegiance, a development which might well undermine traditional loyalties to church and state.

Thirdly, a communications revolution transformed the lives of most people in the nineteenth century. Poor roads had for centuries isolated people from each other, restricted their mobility and tied them to one location for life. Improvements in road building and the introduction of steamships and railways had dramatic effects. For the first time a market economy emerged in which price discrepancies were ironed out as produce moved more quickly across Germany. Better communications enabled people to move out of closed environments, and most of all facilitated the dissemination of ideas and discussion of issues at national level for the first time. As a prominent German radical, Jakob Venedy, remarked in 1835: 'In ten years when all great towns and capital cities are connected by rail, Germany will be another country and the prejudices which

3

have divided the German people so much up to now and which have given our oppressors such easy mastery will cease to exist.'[1] Important, too, was the invention of the telegraph which dramatically reduced the time-lag between events and their reporting. For the first time news of events in Berlin and Vienna could be transmitted within minutes to all parts of Germany.

The pace of change was enormously accelerated by the impact of the Industrial Revolution which affected Germany in the mid nineteenth century. The exploitation of new productive forces dramatically altered the socio-economic landscape. Large urban centres became a feature of the new Europe as country-dwellers moved into towns. New productive relationships developed: a factory proletariat (very small in numbers outside Berlin) and a new industrial middle class *(Besitzbürgertum)* appeared on the scene. In the towns at any rate where dynastic loyalties were crumbling and religious beliefs were fading fast, nationalism – so it is argued – supplied a brand-new social cement to hold society together. Discontented people uprooted from their moorings and plunged into new surroundings where parish-pump loyalties were irrelevant and where their lives were dependent on the activities of thousands of strangers discovered a new sense of community in and through nationalism. Many people, especially lower-middle-class artisans overwhelmed by the social and economic problems of the mid nineteenth century, looked to a new national Reich to redress the grievances which individual rulers had singularly failed to do. Some writers go further and maintain that nationalism in its more extreme forms represented a substitute for organized religion, although the cases of Irish and Polish nationalism suggest that new and old values could co-exist side by side. More will be said later about the ritualism of nationalism. Suffice to say here that flags and songs and the boisterous hurrah patriotism of the mid nineteenth century gave tangible proof to the disoriented and socially deprived of their new place in society and a vision of the Reich to come. Nationalism, incidentally, was a two-edged sword. It was capable not only of comforting the lowly; rulers discovered in it a new legitimization enabling them to assert their authority over this new society and contain within tolerable limits the pressures for political and social change. In this sense nationalism, far from being a democratizing force, supplied rulers with a means of preserving with minimum dislocation the old order, a theme which will figure prominently in this book.

An alternative explanation is offered by Marxists who argue that the creation of nation states is essentially the characteristic expression of capitalist development. The new rising middle class sought national unification primarily to create a unified market in which to dispose of their manufactured goods. However, this interpretation applies much more to the mid nineteenth century when indus-trialization reached the 'take-off' stage than to the first half of the century when such demands played a relatively minor role in the origins of nationalism. Social discontent rather than buoyant capi-talism seems to have given a greater impetus to the growth of a nationalist movement in the 1840s; the *Bildungsbürgertum,* the intelligentsia and government officials – not the captains of indus-try – were the pacemakers until the 1860s.

How useful have modernization theories been in shedding light on the origins of nationalism? It would be unfair to expect precise answers at this early stage before a great deal more work of a comparative nature has been done on nationalist movements.[2] What does emerge pretty clearly is that it is more than a coincidence that the nationalist phenomenon emerged at a time of intense social, economic and political change which could not be accommodated within existing power structures. The frustrations this engendered were certainly a factor explaining the growing demand for a nation state – a strong Reich – to give expression to popular aspirations whether for constitutional freedom, the relief of social misery or economic unification. Beyond this there are more questions than answers. How far was the emergence of nationalism bound up with class structures? Were nationalist leaders invariably middle class? Not necessarily, it would seem – the Polish aristocracy and Irish tenant farmers at once spring to mind as exceptions. How far was nationalism dependent on social tension? How important are the attitudes of foreign powers in moulding the course of nationalist movements? How exactly was the new ideology transmitted to the mass of the population? Did it exert much influence on the coun-tryside until later in the century? How far did the modernization process assist or impede the spread of nationalism? In the German case arguably the partial modernization of some of the larger states discouraged the growth of a national movement in the initial stages, though industrialization altered the balance later. The absence of answers to such questions does not detract from the importance of modernization and communications theories. These are working models which open up new avenues of approach to the problem and are likely to confirm the view that modern nation-alism is closely related to social, economic and political changes. This does not in any way detract from the influence of the Fichtes and Jahns and the Bismarcks. It merely broadens the picture by locating nationalism in a more meaningful sociological framework.

Liberalism and nationalism were associated concepts for most of those who sought political change in mid-nineteenth-century Europe. One of the main reasons why liberals demanded national unification was their conviction that only in a united state could individual rights be effectively protected against arbitrary interference from petty princes. Yet it was already apparent to a few perceptive observers of the political scene that liberalism and nationalism were not necessarily complementary concepts and that the desire for national unification could be exploited in the advancement of illiberal policies. To understand this point properly we must examine a third ideological force which emerged in the early nineteenth century: conservatism.

The origins of conservatism as a political philosophy preceded the French Revolution. Charles de Montesquieu in France and Justus Möser in Germany were already defending the status quo against enlightened princes who were seeking to modernize and centralize their dominions by reducing the power of the local nobility and of privileged communities. What the revolution did was to confer a new philosophical validity on the defence of vested interests. Writers such as Edmund Burke, Vicomte René de Châteaubriand and Comte Joseph de Maistre denounced the universal panacea of the revolutionaries and enthused about the hierarchical structure of *ancien régime* society where the aristocracy enjoyed a privileged position, authority was universally respected, privileges were preserved, law and order prevailed and religion acted as the social cement holding society together. This philosophy had a natural attraction for the landed nobility, a powerful force in post-revolutionary Europe. But it should be remembered that conservatives enjoyed at all times support from other social groups. Even during the Revolution peasants in some parts of Europe – for example in the Vendée – supported their lords. In the course of the nineteenth century other groups were attracted to conservatism. In the 1850s and 1860s master craftsmen *(Handwerkermeister)* turned to the conservatives because they were ready to preserve the ailing guild system which laissez-faire liberals wished to destroy. Later in the century as lower-middle-class groups grew in importance with the development of the industrial system, white-collar workers, perturbed by the growth of working-class organizations, allied with small businessmen and civil servants in supporting the conservatives.

This was not the only reason why conservatism flourished in the nineteenth century. Despite the significant conflict of principle between liberalism and conservatism, in practice conservatives had much less to fear from their liberal opponents. At the beginning of the chapter liberalism was defined as the belief that the object of government should be the protection of individual rights and that affairs of state should be conducted in the interests of the whole people, not of entrenched vested interests. In practice liberals had no desire to shift the balance of power towards the mass of the people. Nor did they seek a monopoly of power for the upper middle class but merely a share in the conduct of affairs, and that by agreement with the sovereign whose powers would be circumscribed in a written constitution. Shocked by the excesses of the French Revolution when rich and poor heads alike had rolled under Madame Guillotine, liberals shared the conservative belief that universal male suffrage – like absolute monarchy – would lead inevitably to tyranny. Only under pressure from below did the liberals agree in 1848 to extend the franchise for the Frankfurt Parliament. And they never lost their taste for aristocratic politics.

The *rapprochement* between moderate liberalism and conservatism in the first half of the nineteenth century was greatly accelerated by the growth of radicalism. Most liberals abhorred violence and confidently expected to change the structure of politics by agreement with the old order. Radicals with a firmer purchase on political reality knew in their bones that monarchs were unlikely to surrender even part of their power voluntarily and would have to be compelled to accept the type of constitutional arrangements favoured by radicals which would vest effective power in a legislature elected by universal male suffrage, and in a fully accountable executive. More extreme radicals advocated the abolition of monarchy and the establishment of a Jacobin-style republic. Nor were radicals content with mere legal equality. Was not the existence of privilege in the form of great wealth a denial of the principle of equality? Consequently radicals were prepared to take steps to correct this imbalance at the expense of vested interests. That posed a direct threat to upper-middle-class liberals totally committed to the defence of property rights.

All over Europe a new 'alliance' of conservative interests was in the making embracing moderate liberals, the new entrepreneurial classes and the old landed nobility. In this 'alliance' the landed interests remained dominant. True, agriculture was a declining sector of the economy throughout the century. That was, however, a slow process so that down to 1914 landed property remained the main source of personal wealth. Aristocrats remained in command of armies, occupied key administrative posts and in general functioned as a public service nobility in many countries. Internal tensions inside the 'alliance' were overshadowed by the joint resolve of aristocracy and middle classes to defend themselves against the 'dark forces' whose power manifested itself fitfully during the June Days of 1848 and again during the Commune of 1870–1.

What connection was there between conservatism and nationalism? It would be far too simplistic to suppose that conservatives were concerned only to exploit nationalism in their narrow class interests; they were, after all, as exposed to nationalist propaganda as any other group in society. Nevertheless, it cannot be denied that one of the consequences of nationalism might well have been that it deflected the attention of the people away from the power of privilege. For nationalism emphasized what people had in common – or, more accurately, what they were alleged to have in common – not what divided them. A common tongue and shared cultural or historical traditions could unite people – if only at a superficial level – and transcend class interests which in the early industrial age might well tear the fabric of society asunder. In one sense what Bismarck and Cavour succeeded in doing was to square the political circle. Unification was brought about by force of arms primarily to serve the interests of Prussia and Piedmont. But by satisfying the demand of the upper classes for unification Bismarck and Cavour effectively cocooned conservative interests in the new states against the threat of political radicalism and conferred on their conquests a new legitimacy which had not been available to rulers such as Frederick the Great.

THE IMPACT OF THE FRENCH REVOLUTION ON GERMANY

The physical impact of the French Revolution on Germany was enormous. Tension soon developed between the new revolutionary government and the Holy Roman Empire. The revolutionaries were suspicious of the counter-revolutionary activities of émigré noblemen in the Rhineland, while West German princes were embittered by the abolition of feudalism in their Alsace estates. With the Girondins in power in 1792 and the new Emperor Francis II eager to do battle with the enemies of monarchy, war was inevitable. In April France declared war on Austria and Prussia, though not until 1793 did the Holy Roman Empire declare war on France. The clash of arms soon revealed the pitiful inadequacy of imperial defences and the moral bankruptcy of the old order. By 1794 France was in control of the Rhineland where she stayed for the next twenty years. The German princes soon abandoned their half-hearted resistance and came to terms with the conquerors. And in the ante-rooms of Talleyrand's office in Paris the princes dispossessed on the left bank of the Rhine joined in an undignified scramble for compensation at the expense of the ecclesiastical principalities.

The territorial settlement of 1803 ratified at the Congress of Regensburg deprived the Empire of its *raison d'être*. On the right bank of the Rhine all but three of eighty-one ecclesiastical principalities were secularized. Only six of fifty-one imperial cities survived; and the imperial knights were mediatized, i.e. their territories – often not more than a few square miles in extent – were placed under the jurisdiction of larger neighbours. Overnight, 112 states disappeared in this gigantic rationalization exercise. The principal beneficiaries were Baden, Bavaria, Württemberg and Hesse-Darmstadt, states favoured by the French who hoped to use them as a counterpoise to Austrian and Prussian influence in Central Europe.

In 1805 Austria once again joined forces with the enemies of France. She was speedily and decisively defeated. This time she had to surrender her Italian possessions to France, the Tyrol and Varneburg to Bavaria, and her remaining German territories were divided between Baden and Württemberg. In 1806 Napoleon simplified the map still further. The remaining imperial cities and smaller territories were mediatized. The Confederation of the Rhine, a loose association of sixteen states excluding Austria and Prussia, was created under Napoleon's protection and pledged to fight for him. On 1 August 1806 Napoleon ordered Francis II to relinquish the imperial crown. On 6 August he agreed and became Francis 1, emperor of Austria. Thus the Holy Roman Empire ended ignominiously after nine centuries. 'There was a time,' commented the historian of the Empire,'when this event would have been thought a sign that the last days of the world were at hand. But in the whirl of change that had bewildered men since 1789 it passed almost unnoticed.'[3] Nor was its demise mourned by the Germans.

Prussia had stood silently by while Austria was defeated. Shortly afterwards, galvanized into action by the growing arrogance of the French, Prussia decided to fight rather than remain a French vassal. At the battle of Jena Prussia suffered a crushing defeat. French troops marched through Berlin while her king sued for peace. Prussia was saved from complete destruction only through the intervention of the tsar, anxious to preserve a buffer state between Russia and France. Even so, Prussia lost all her territory west of the Elbe; this became the kingdom of Westphalia, ruled over by Napoleon's brother Jerome. Most of the Polish territories were incorporated in the grand duchy of Warsaw and handed over to the king of Saxony, one of Napoleon's most devoted allies. Danzig became a free city guarded by a French garrison. In all, Prussia forfeited half her territory; she was saddled with a war indemnity of unknown dimensions and the size of her army was strictly controlled.

Napoleon was now complete master of Germany. When Austria challenged the French in 1809, she fought alone. After the battle of Wagram she was reduced to the status of a second-class power. Her army was reduced in size; she, too, was saddled with a huge indemnity; she was forced to support the continental blockade; and she lost Salzburg and the Innviertel to Bavaria. By this time Napoleon did not respect his own creations. To render the blockade more effective, he annexed Oldenburg in 1810 and the Hansa towns in 1811. No

German state dared resist him. When he held glittering court in Dresden on the eve of the Russian campaign, the rulers of Austria and Prussia waited in attendance on the little Corsican. Although Napoleon was soon to retreat through Germany with the remnants of the Grand Army and deserted by his German allies, his major work was not disturbed. By destroying the fabric of medieval Germany he earned his place as the first maker of Modern Germany.

No less profound was the impact made by revolutionary ideas on the antiquated and semi-feudal structure lingering on in many German states. There were significant regional variations. The most immediate impact was felt in the Rhineland – an integral part of France from 1795 to 1814 – the kingdom of Westphalia and the grand duchy of Berg. In Bavaria, Baden, Württemberg, Hesse-Darmstadt and Nassau the ruling dynasties made extensive use of the new administrative techniques pioneered by the French, whereas Saxony and the Mecklenburgs were little affected. Prussia, outside the Rhine Confederation, was caught up in the modernization process – though for different reasons – whilst the Habsburg dominions were virtually unaffected.

In the more enlightened states the apparatus of government was transformed. The old bumbling bureaucracies were replaced by new administrative structures. The chaotic jumble of local jurisdictions was replaced by more rational divisions, concentrating power in the hands of the central government. The era of ostentatious spending characteristic of eighteenth-century courts was at an end. Princes began to think of themselves as the first servants of the state. Bridges, roads and canals became the first call on the exchequer. The special privileges and immunities of the aristocracy and the corporations were abolished. Uniform taxation systems were introduced. Serfdom ended in the countryside. Trial by jury and a uniform legal system divorced from the administration assured justice for all. The power of the Church was drastically curtailed; church lands were secularized; monasteries were dissolved; and religious toleration, civil marriage and secular education became the norm. Princely armies were remodelled on French lines with conscription and long periods of service with the colours as the distinctive features. The net result of these reforms was that several states, especially in South Germany, attained in the short space of a few years a degree of order and stability which it had taken generations to achieve in Prussia.

However, only in the small area ruled over directly by the French, i.e. the Rhineland, Westphalia and the grand duchy of Berg, was the power of vested interest really broken. For example, only in the Rhineland were the peasants completely released from feudal bondage. Elsewhere reform was carried out by nominally independent princes who, whilst eager enough to centralize their dominions, were not over – anxious to antagonize vested interests too much. Certainly the aristocracy lost some (but not all) of its tax exemptions and its monopoly of high office was broken. But the abolition of serfdom did not undermine its position in the countryside; little progress was made towards the commutation of feudal dues and services, because landowners withheld their consent and peasants lacked the necessary capital. Nor was any attempt made to divest landowners of their very considerable judicial and police powers over their tenants. And in a pre-industrial society the establishment of the principle of legal equality, the career open to the talents and the removal of restrictions on trade and industry did not significantly alter the relationship between a landed aristocracy and a small bourgeoisie composed largely of administrators and lawyers. What the reforms did succeed in doing – and this was their *raison d'être* – was to enable rulers to weld together newly acquired territories into homogeneous and viable entities tightly controlled by the central government.

Turning now to the largest German states: Austria and Prussia. Austria was virtually unaffected apart from Count Joseph von Stadion's reform of the finance ministry and the unification of the chancellery. In Prussia much more significant change took place after the myth of Prussian invincibility died on the battlefields of Jena and Auerstedt. Between 1806 and 1814 a small group of high officials - mostly born outside Prussia – attempted to modernize Prussia. Their immediate objective was to prepare for a war of revenge against France. Their intellectual inspiration came neither from the practice of Revolutionary France nor from the tradition of enlightened absolutism, but from the Kantian model of the independent individual. The Reformers believed that much more could be achieved by relying on the enterprise of free citizens and their active involvement in public life than through the stifling paternalism of the eighteenth-century mercantilist state. To ensure that a reforming bureaucracy would exert decisive influence on the running of the state, the Reformers persuaded the king to establish a ministerial system to assist him in policy-making, an innovation which remained a permanent feature of the Prussian system. At the same time the entire administrative structure of the state was reshaped. To ensure middle-class involvement in local government, Baron Karl vom Stein freed the towns from state control in 1808 and handed over responsibility for municipal affairs (including taxation and police) to elected authorities. Already in 1807 he had abolished personal serfdom, turning peasants hitherto bound to the soil into free men entitled to buy and sell land. His aim was the creation of an independent peasantry capable of standing on its own feet and hopefully applying modern techniques to increase agrarian productivity. Meanwhile, to create free citizens Baron Wilhelm von Humboldt totally overhauled the Prussian educational system. Grammar schools *(Gymnasien)* were founded in which heavy emphasis was laid on the teaching of languages and history, subjects considered ideal for developing a balanced personality. Elementary schools were thoroughly reorganized and training colleges set up to provide a supply of competent teachers. Rowdy students and idle dons brought universities into disrepute throughout the eighteenth century. The situation changed with the founding of Berlin University in 1810 which soon acquired a reputation as an institution where research flourished and students were eager to learn. As war with France was the overriding objective army reform had a high priority. Generals Gerhard von Scharnhorst, August von Gneisenau, Hermann von Boyen and Karl von Clausewitz tried to infuse a new spirit of self-reliance into the ranks: brutal punishments were abolished and able men were at last promoted regardless of social status. In 1814 Boyen introduced a system of conscription which obliged Prussians to serve three years with a line regiment and two years in the reserves followed by several years in the Landwehr, a territorial army commanded by middle-class officers and intended to be an antidote to the feudal spirit prevailing in line regiments.

In fact the power of the landed aristocracy was not seriously weakened by these reforms. Aristocrats still remained in control of the army and had the best prospects of advancement in the administration. After 1820 the number of noblemen in high administrative office, especially as presidents of provincial governments and as *Landräte,* actually increased. In the countryside the emancipation of the peasantry was trimmed back in the interests of the landowners. In return for surrendering their feudal privileges they gained much land. And, once freed of obligations towards former serfs, some landowners transformed their estates into flourishing oases by adopting capitalist techniques. As in Russia, the population explosion created a class of landless labourers and small farmers unable to eke a living out of the soil. Consequently there was much misery and combustible material in rural areas throughout the nineteenth century. Not until industrialization got under way in the 1850s and 1860s did emigration to the towns ease the pressure on the soil.

The last vestiges of the spirit of 'national regeneration' which had fired the Reformers during the War of Liberation disappeared during the reaction of 1819–20 following the murder of August von Kotzebue, the playwright and Russian police spy. But it is important to remember that although reactionaries were in control in Berlin, in the provinces, thanks to a liberal-minded bureaucracy, the reforms already introduced remained more or less intact. The social progress being made in Prussia was obscured by two factors: the failure of the king to give his subjects a constitution, and the often quite arbitrary exercise of their powers by the police, whose duties were wide-ranging and included the monitoring of statutory law.

THE GERMAN ROOTS OF NATIONALISM AND LIBERALISM

The changes wrought by the French Revolution east of the Rhine were so momentous that it is easy to exaggerate French influence upon Germany between 1795 and 1814 and underestimate the indigenous roots of much that was happening in Germany.

Initially many – but by no means all – middle-class writers in Germany were fired with enthusiasm by the news from Paris in the summer of 1789. The creation of the National Assembly and the abolition of feudalism seemed to usher in a new age of reforming monarchy when men would reconstruct civil government in accordance with the principles of pure reason. In Cologne, Mainz, Brunswick and Hamburg popular festivals were held and trees of liberty planted. Friedrich Klopstock's odes on the stirring events in France and the poems of his Göttingen Bund admirers – Gottfried Bürger, Johann Voss and Heinrich Boie – reflected their naive idealism. This period was short-lived. After the execution of Louis XVI and the onset of the Reign of Terror these writers ceased to be Francophile: 'order had come to outweigh liberty', as one authority has remarked.[4]

The ideas which crossed the Rhine were unlikely to be accepted without considerable reservations by that small minority of German people interested in the things of the mind. Conditions east of the Rhine differed substantially from those in France. On the whole there was probably less combustible material awaiting the spark of revolution. Though feudalism was an irksome and often tyrannous system, it does not seem to have borne down on the German peasantry quite so heavily as on the French, possibly because the patriarchal relationship between serf and lord still counted for something. There were angry outbursts in Saxony and in the Rhineland in 1789 but nothing comparable to the *Grande Peur.* And though many territories in the Holy Roman Empire were scandalously and often most tyrannically governed – as a general rule the smaller the territory the worse the abuse of power – several factors combined to protect the Germans from the worst excesses of absolutism: religious diversity, the colourful and chaotic mosaic of conflicting jurisdictions, lingering medieval survivals and the juxtaposition of large, medium and minuscule territories. It was no accident that German writers reverenced historical tradition and were sceptical of the French precisely because of their confidence that the world could be set to rights by drafting the perfect constitution and sweeping away overnight complex and centuries-old relationships. Nor were German writers bitterly anti-clerical like their French counterparts, another factor tempering their attitude.

An extremely important factor explaining the limited attraction of French ideas was the changing attitude of certain German princes towards the practice of civil government. In the first half of the eighteenth century German absolutism was particularly odious and oppressive. Rulers vied with each other in copying the practices of the Sun King. They spent lavishly on ostentatious palaces, theatres and art collections. They ran massively into debt to keep up appearances, their delusions of grandeur in inverse proportion to the size of their dominions. Princes cared little for economic expansion – Prussia was exceptional in this respect – and regarded their subjects as little more than sources of revenue for the maintenance of inflated armies, bureaucracies and courts.

In the second half of the century German absolutism, spurred on by economic development and tempered by the spirit of the Enlightenment, changed in character. Between 1750 and 1800 the population of Europe increased from 140 to 187 million. The consequential increase in demand for food and raw materials stimulated economic growth. Changes in agricultural methods in the Low Countries and in parts of Britain and France increased productivity; substantial food surpluses appeared for the first time; agrarian prices rose steadily; trade expanded; and domestic industry flourished. Germany had a limited share in this economic growth. Merchants, bankers and entrepreneurs in the small towns in West Germany emerged at last from medieval hibernation and basked in the glow of a little unaccustomed prosperity.

On its own this would have been insufficient to undermine the political status quo. In France the bourgeoisie was already a powerful economic force; bourgeois credit sustained successive spendthrift governments; and growing consciousness of the dichotomy between its financial muscle and its political and social impotence created psychological tensions soon to erupt into revolution. East of the Rhine the great age of the German Bürgertum had ended abruptly in the sixteenth century when the trading routes moved to the Atlantic seaboard. The recovery which had occurred by the late eighteenth century was marginal, leaving the German Bürgertum far behind the French bourgeoisie economically.

What the Germans possessed and the French conspicuously lacked were a few rulers who were prepared to try to put their houses in order. Pre-eminent in this small and select band were King Frederick the Great of Prussia, Grand Duke Karl Friedrich of Baden, Duke Karl Wilhelm Ferdinand of Brunswick, the rulers of the small states of Saxe-Weimar, Anhalt-Dessau and Schaumburg-Lippe, and in the Austrian dominions Empress Maria Theresa and – most illustrious of all of them - Emperor Joseph II. There were many reasons for their new-found solicitude for their subjects. Some were seeking to establish their authority over their subjects after the mid-century wars; others – especially in North Germany – were influenced by the pietistic revival which reminded rulers of their Christian duty to subjects; and all were under the spell of the Enlightenment which called on rulers to rule in accordance with the dictates of reason and promote the material and moral well-being of their subjects. Without doubt Napoleon greatly accelerated the modernization process in Germany. But it is equally true to say that it began not with Napoleon but with these enlightened princes.

The fashion was set by Frederick the Great, a child of the Enlightenment, the first ruler to declare that his governing principle was service to the state and not the selfish pursuit of dynastic self-interest – though in some ways he was the least enlightened of rulers, much more a prisoner of the old order than Joseph II. Enlightened princes tried to introduce a note of order into chaotic and overburdened administrative and financial machines. They removed some of the more stifling and irksome feudal jurisdictions, encouraged the growth of commerce and industry, modified the irksome press censorship, built schools, limited the power of the churches, introduced a measure of religious toleration and curbed the extravagant expenditure of their predecessors. Of course, the reforms were frequently half-hearted and limited in effect because these rulers had no wish to compromise their own position by curtailing too drastically the power of those vested interests on which the maintenance of the existing social order depended. Significantly, serfdom in one form or another remained a characteristic feature in most states. Only in the Habsburg dominions was it slightly modified and only in Baden was it abolished.

Nevertheless, monarchy as an institution was stronger on the eve of the French Revolution than ever before. Though there was criticism of the scandalous behaviour of some German rulers, the efforts of the few to respond to the *Zeitgeist* encouraged Germans to believe that in time others would follow the enlightened example.[5]

This attitude is understandable when one examines the origins of the *Bildungsbürgertum* (professional classes). Enlightened monarchs needed trained men to service the burgeoning state apparatus they were creating. Many states, including Austria, Prussia, Saxony and Württemberg, established higher educational institutes to produce the required personnel. The officials, teachers, doctors and pastors appearing in growing numbers in the late eighteenth century owed their position to their own academic ability and enjoyed a privileged status, being exempt from military service and often from taxation. Having grown up in dependency on state and monarch, this new social group did not share the bitter sense of underprivilege and social deprivation felt by their French counterparts. Though politically opponents of old-style absolutism, they mostly remained respectful of princely authority and were content to be excluded from a share in affairs of state. Newspapers and periodicals flourished in German states in the 1780s as abundantly as elsewhere in Europe, but the tone of political debate was muted compared with Britain, France and the Low Countries. The new *Bildungsbürgertum* preferred to find a national identity in the realms of philosophy and literature rather than in politics.

This choice was of crucial importance for it raised Germany out of the intellectual doldrums in which it had lingered since the seventeenth century. Hitherto culture in Europe had been 'locally confined or internationally extended'.[6] Either it was rooted in the rich customs and traditions of thousands of village communities stretching from the Shannon to the Volga and living in comparative isolation from each other, or else it was an exclusive commodity, the preserve of aristocrats and higher clergy able to move easily from capital city to capital city. What the *Bildungsbürgertum* created was a potentially wider cultural heritage which could be enjoyed by people of all classes who were German and literate in an area stretching from Flensburg to Vienna and from Aachen to Königsberg.

The cultural renaissance which blossomed in Germany after the Seven Years' War was the second reason why French ideas, though influential, were unlikely to be accepted uncritically. Between 1770 and 1830 the genius of the German people poured forth in philosophy, drama, poetry and music. The names of Goethe, Schiller, Lessing, Kant and Mozart made the German-speaking world the cultural cradle of Europe for half a century, ending the long dominance of French cultural values.

The German cultural revival was no isolated phenomenon but an integral part of a much broader movement of artistic protest in Western Europe against the rigidity and artificiality of classical values. Young German writers were, however, ahead of their European contemporaries in rebelling against the slavish imitation of French styles by their own rulers. Increasingly dissatisfied with the values of a century which equated culture with the acquisition of knowledge, and virtue with civic pride, they searched for a more profound definition of humanity.

It was in Greek man – rediscovered by German archaeologists – that the classical humanists found their ideal. This was the 'man of independent mind' embodying the values of the *Bildungsbürgertum* to which most of them belonged: confident, self-reliant, sceptical of established beliefs and itching to widen the frontiers of human experience. The philosophy and literature of the period is permeated with the belief that man must rid himself of all cant and prejudice and strive for true independence of mind through the harmonious cultivation of his mental gifts. In this process of self-revelation, passion, sentiment, and imagination played as significant a role as reason. Intellectual self-fulfilment, not the reduction of life to mere conformity with a series of rational formulae, was the true destiny of every educated man and woman. In some ways this was an intensely introspective philosophy, inviting man to attain intellectual satisfaction by averting his gaze from the real world. Not surprisingly very few of these writers were interested in contemporary politics. Those who were, such as the Romantics, had precious little purchase on reality. But in this philosophy of the free individual realizing his manifest destiny lay the seeds of profound political and social change.

Although liberalism and nationalism were manifestly part of a broader movement owing much to American and French experience, both ideologies assumed a specifically German colouration at the *fin de siècle* because of the German cultural renaissance and the reverential attitude of the *Bildungsbürgertum* towards princely houses.

German liberalism owed much more to Immanuel Kant than to the French Revolution. The Königsberg professor of philosophy has been rightly called the founder of nineteenth-century liberal thinking in Germany.[7] In a series of essays in the 1780s Kant outlined his views on the human condition. He was deeply influenced by the writings of the Swiss philosopher Jean-Jacques Rousseau, who broke decisively with eighteenth-century thought patterns when he propounded the revolutionary notion that laws did not derive their validity from principles of abstract reason but were an expression of the general will of the people. It was, however, the philosophical not the political implications of Rousseau which preoccupied Kant. His philosophy was rooted basically in the original idea that the antagonistic nature of man contained the key to human progress. Man could develop his full potential only by engaging in a constant struggle against the anti-social instincts of his nature and the external forces ranged against him. Out of the clash between social and anti-social instincts the highest form of social organization – the state – had emerged. The Kantian ideal was a society of free individuals living under the rule of law. The object of law was not, however, the passage of welfare legislation designed to promote material happiness. All that was necessary to enable men to live in freedom was the establishment of certain minimum requirements including those rights essential for the development of the bourgeoisie: equality before the law, the right to own and acquire property and the right of better-off citizens to share in the making of laws. Here in embryonic form was the prototype of the liberal *Rechtsstaat* in which state intervention was kept to a minimum and the major preoccupation of the citizens would be the conquest of self by regulating their relations with their fellows in accordance with ethical norms.

Kant set his face firmly against the revolutionary implications of this doctrine. Although welcoming the French Revolution, he rejected the Jacobin idea that Rousseau's 'people' should both make laws and exercise executive power: that was the road to a despotism as odious as the tyranny of a prince. The best safeguard against tyranny was monarchy standing aloof above the law and presiding from Olympian

17

heights over man's constant struggle to live up to ethical norms. For the individual the categorical imperative was to struggle for perfection by observing the simple maxim: do unto others what you would have them do unto you. But a people had no right to rise up in rebellion to overthrow a tyrannical ruler; to do so was nothing less than a sin against the Holy Ghost. The only redress subjects had against arbitrary rule was the free expression of opinion which, hopefully, would persuade princes that the critics were right.

German liberals did advance well beyond Kant's non-political stance and in the pre-March period formulated specific programmes designed to curtail the power of monarchs. Nevertheless his highly ethical and individualistic philosophy, with its heavy emphasis on duty and reliance on monarchy as an essential safeguard of bourgeois freedom, continued to exert a profound influence on the German Bürgertum throughout the nineteenth century.

Similarly, the roots of German nationalism were unmistakably indigenous. Whereas the French conceived of self-determination as an abstract right which was activated by a conscious decision on the part of the inhabitants of an area to set up house on their own, those Germans who were nationally conscious were motivated much more by growing awareness of Germany's past history.

Among those writers who contributed to the growth of German national consciousness, Johann Herder has pride of place. For he has rightly been described as the 'intellectual father of the national movement' not only in Germany but in the Slav lands as well.[8] Born to poor parents in East Prussia, Herder initially hailed the French Revolution with enthusiasm. Eventually he turned against it, largely because he disagreed with contemporaries who saw in it positive confirmation of the prevalent belief that history was the record of human progress. History for Herder was a more complex and continuous process in which each epoch had some contribution to make to posterity, including even the Middle Ages, hitherto derided by historians as an age of barbarism. Furthermore, he distanced himself from eighteenth-century writers who regarded the existence of nationalities as tiresome differences and a distraction from the goal of a common humanity embracing the educated classes in all lands. Herder stood this belief on its head, arguing that, on the contrary, nationalities were part and parcel of this common humanity. Every people possessed distinctive and permanent characteristics and each made a special contribution to humanity. As Herder believed that the character of a people *(Volksgeist)* was expressed in language and literature, the preservation of the ancient poetry of each nation was one of his most passionate concerns. But although there were occasionally hints in Herder's writings that he thought German a superior language, nevertheless he remained in many ways a man of the eighteenth century. His concept of nationalism was basically ethical and cultural in nature and his hope was that nations would compete peacefully for the highest crowns of humanity. Modern nationalism with its political and social connotations was an alien concept to Herder.

Around the turn of the century belief in the *Kulturnation* as a symbol of nationhood was very widespread. This is true to a great extent of Ernst Moritz Arndt, Johann Gottlieb Fichte and Friedrich Schleiermacher, members of a group of writers resident in Prussia who figure prominently in nationalist hagiography. Fichte, whose public lectures (Addresses to the German Nation), delivered in Berlin in 1812, were said by the nationalist historian Heinrich von Treitschke to have electrified Germany and earned for him the title of the first German nationalist, was no nationalist in the modern sense. Of course, there were proleptic hints in his demand that the state should be the Sergeant-Major of Germanism *(Zwingherr zur Deutschheit)* responsible for mobilizing the energies of the nation. But the appeal to his fellow citizens was not for a nation state based on the political and social emancipation of the people. 'Cosmopolitanism is the will to attain the purpose of life and of man in all mankind,' he wrote revealingly; '. . . patriotism is the will to attain this purpose first of all in the nation of which we are members and the wish that this light may radiate from this nation to all mankind'.[9] It was to achieve this transcendental goal – not to create a nation state – that Fichte advocated a national education system for German boys and girls. The same is true of Arndt. While he wrote passionately of the need for the nation to rise up in arms to throw out the French, on the subject of how this national spirit was to be encapsulated in a nation state he was silent.

Friedrich Jahn is the exception. His book *Deutsches Volkstum* published in 1810 went much further in proposing concrete political and social reform as the basis for a nation state: the ending of serfdom, the creation of a national army and a popular representative body. True, he accepted monarchy, estates and a hereditary nobility as part of the natural order of things. But for all that, he takes his place as the one writer in this period whose concept of a politically united nation with popular participation (albeit limited) had the essentials of modern nationalism buried in it.

He was also a doer of the word and is remembered as the founder of the gymnastic society *(Turngesellschaft)* in Berlin in 1811. This, the first organized nationalist body, by 1818 had 150 branches, some in South Germany but most in the north. Jahn shared the widespread belief in the late eighteenth century that physical exercise should be part of a national education system. He gave his gymnastic society a nationalist twist by inculcating into young pupils and students something of his own enthusiasm for a united Germany under one prince – he did, in fact, favour the Hohenzollerns. The gymnastic societies were suppressed in

1819 in the reaction following Kotzebue's murder.

German nationalism owed much to the Romantic writers. To explain the philosophy of this, the first literary school so called, would be both difficult and unnecessary. The essential point is that because emotion and imagination moved them more than abstract reason, they were particularly sensitive to the first stirrings of popular nationalism at the turn of the century. Disoriented in a rapidly changing world, young writers such as Adam Müller, Friedrich von Hardenberg (known as Novalis) and Friedrich Schlegel turned to history for consolation. Although Arndt and Fichte occasionally referred in their writings to the medieval Reich, the Romantics can really be credited with the rediscovery of the Middle Ages, dismissed as barbaric by eighteenth-century writers. Whereas Herder remained cool and sceptical about medieval values, the Romantics positively enthused about them. They saw Germany by candlelight; in the shadow of ruined Rhineland castles they conjured up a grotesquely unreal and thoroughly unhistorical picture of an unspoilt society where knights, merchants, clergy and peasants were inspired by a truly national spirit and where the Holy Roman Empire had been the focal point of a Christian-German Europe. At a time when few Germans mourned the demise of that crumbling edifice, Romantic writers ensured that the corpse would live on in an idealized form and become the prototype of the united Germany liberals were seeking to create in the nineteenth century. When the Frankfurt Parliament debated unification the preferred frontiers of the new Reich were roughly those of the Holy Roman Empire in its declining years, not those of a modern national state. This outcome was due at least in part to the lasting influence of the Romantics.

Of lasting importance, too, was their doctrine of the state. Whilst Romantics, like classical humanists, believed passionately in the right of the individual to develop his talents to the full, they differed sharply in their attitude to the state. Eighteenth-century men eyed the state with suspicion as a necessary evil to protect individual rights. Some writers, anticipating Karl Marx half a century later, believed the state would wither away in the fulness of time. The Romantics, however, developed a more positive concept of the state. It arose out of their belief that medieval society formed an organic whole ethically superior to the atomized communities of the eighteenth century. Needless to say, the reality of medieval society, fissured by bitter conflict between church and state, princes and towns and peasants and feudal lords, bore little resemblance to this idealized reconstruction.

Nevertheless, the organic theory offered a promising framework for the creation of a nation state harnessing the energies of the people in a common cause. If the state was indeed an organism bringing the people together in a symbiotic union, then the life of the individual was intimately associated with the growth of the community. So the state was not an imposition from above, an external device allowing princes to interfere in the everyday life of subjects, but, as Friedrich Schlegel put it: '. . . a coexisting and successive continuity of men, the totality of those whose relation to one another is determined by the same physical influence'.[10] It was only a short step to the realization that factors such as language and historical conditions were not anachronistic impedimenta standing in the way of a world republic but part of the Divine scheme of things designed to allow communities to develop their own identities. There was a much darker side to all this. Once the cult of the irrational had entered political philosophy it was perhaps only a matter of time before it degenerated in the case of Germany into the *Blut und Boden* mythology of the Nazis.

THE GERMAN REACTION TO FRENCH DOMINATION

The point has been made earlier that the role of literary figures in the growth of German national consciousness should not be exaggerated. Their appeal was restricted to a reading public. Many Germans became nationally conscious, if only in a rudimentary form, as a result of French occupation of German territory. Initially there was much support for the French, especially in the Rhineland. Some of the Bürgertum had a high regard for Napoleon, the harbinger of much-needed political and social change, while others more to the right politically respected him as the bulwark of law and order holding Jacobinism at bay. Illustrious *literati* such as Goethe and Hegel felt no inhibition in basking in the sunlight beating on the French emperor, the man of destiny and the *Weltgeist zu Pferde*. On the other hand, though pro-French feeling remained strong in the Rhineland after 1812, even there it was diluted by growing resentment of French rule, for several reasons.

Firstly, Napoleon's Continental System. Initially, the exclusion of English imports had favoured the growth of some industries, notably textiles, in the Rhineland and Saxony. But North Germany was adversely affected by the loss of English markets for grain, wood and linen. To prevent widespread smuggling of English goods into Germany, the French were obliged to intervene increasingly in German affairs. To seal off the coastline, French troops occupied parts of Prussia and Hanover as well as the ports of Hamburg, Bremen, Lübeck and Danzig with disastrous consequences for many merchants. Nor were the Germans allowed to trade on equal terms with the rest of Napoleon's Europe. Tariff walls excluded German goods from France,

Italy and Holland, while the French ruthlessly exploited German markets. A second cause of discontent were Napoleon's incessant demands for men to fight in interminable campaigns – one-third of the Grand Army invading Russia was composed of German soldiers. Thirdly, the heavy tax burdens, an inevitable consequence of Napoleon's wars, aroused growing resentment. Finally, the arrogant and tyrannical behaviour of French officials alienated many Germans hitherto well disposed towards Napoleon. The French *chargé d'affaires* had always exercised a virtual veto over the actions of state governments. As Napoleon's difficulties increased after the Spanish Uprising, French officials became even more tyrannical, muzzling the local press and stifling all signs of opposition. The dismissal of Stein from the king of Prussia's service was only one notable example of the iron grip the French emperor had over Germany.

This accumulated discontent led to an outburst of patriotic feeling in 1813. The story told by Little German historians in the late nineteenth century is a familiar one. As Napoleon retreated from Moscow in December 1812 and the tsar announced his intention of liberating Europe, Prussia roused herself. At first King Frederick III hesitated to break with Napoleon and dismissed General Hans Count von Yorck, commander of the auxiliary army, when he signed an agreement with the Russian commander promising not to resist the Russian advance. Public opinion expressed in the form of anti-French demonstrations changed the king's mind. In February 1813 Prussia signed a war alliance with Russia.

Symptomatic of the new mood of confidence gripping the educated classes was the removal of all exemptions, making universal conscription a reality at last, and the creation of a new award for bravery: the Iron Cross. Volunteer units, the Free Corps, were established and quickly attracted several thousand citizens. The most famous was the Lützow Corps whose members – over one-third were students, many from other German states – swore an oath of allegiance not to the king but to the fatherland. Incidentally, the Corps' black uniform with red stripes and yellow piping may have been the origin of the German national colours. Enthusiastic townsfolk also contributed a staggering six and a half million talers for the war effort. Carried forward on this patriotic wave – so the story goes – Prussia declared war on France in March 1813. The next day the king called on the people to sacrifice themselves in the struggle for independence in the name of king, fatherland and honour.

Though the 'spirit of 1813' became an important ingredient in the mythology of German nationalism, modern research has shown that it was greatly exaggerated. For one thing, the 'spirit' was confined to Prussia and Westphalia. In the rest of Germany, despite resentment at heavy taxation and the arrogance of French officials, there was still much residual sympathy for Napoleon. The Saxons fought side by side with the French against the Prussians in 1813. General Yorck, the hero of nationalist accounts, was in fact forced into his 'self-sacrificing' deed by pressure from his own officers who were ready to join with the Russians. Prussian enthusiasm for the war was strictly limited. Rural communities, forming 75 per cent of the total population, were virtually untouched. Basically support for the war was an urban phenomenon; 12 per cent of the volunteers who flocked to the colours were students and officials and 41 per cent craftsmen – this may perhaps have been due to the introduction of freedom of entry into trades *(Gewerbefreiheit)* in 1810 which had permitted journeymen apprentices to set up in business on their own and gave them a positive incentive to fight. As for the much-publicized Lützow Free Corps, it was kept away from the front line – whether because the king was suspicious of its social composition or, more likely, because it could not in the nature of things be an effective fighting force is an open question. It operated as a flying column – *brigands noirs* as the French called it – harrying the enemy, and was finally disbanded allegedly for breaking the armistice.

What is of particular interest about the War of Liberation in terms of the development of nationalism are the pseudo-religious overtones creeping into nationalist writing. In practice, far from being a secular ideology, nationalism has invariably employed the imagery and language of religion. Thus Theodor Körner spoke of the coming battle as 'not war as crowns know it, it is a crusade, it is a holy war'.[11] In other words, this was not to be an old-style campaign waged by professional armies but a total war waged by a people in arms inspired by a love of fatherland of quasi-religious intensity. Arndt and Jahn in a fit of xenophobic nationalism claimed that the Germans were superior to all other peoples – because of the alleged purity of their language – and destined to play a leading role in European affairs. The patriotic mood of 1813 was bitterly anti-French. In the most famous of all patriotic songs, *'Was ist des deutschen Vaterland'*, Arndt appealed to Germans to create a fatherland out of all the territories where German was spoken and where 'every Frenchman would be an enemy'.[12] 'Unity of hearts be your church, hate against Frenchmen your religion. Freedom and fatherland be the saints you pray to' was another piece of advice he offered his readers.[13]

The fact that the poems and songs circulating during this war ran into hundreds of thousands of copies indicates a wide readership. But at this stage, before socio-economic changes had begun to alter the material base of society, nationalistic outbursts, however intense, simply could not survive into peace-time.

It was the professional army, reformed by Scharnhorst and Gneisenau, and not Free Corps which helped turn Napoleon out of Germany. Even so, Prussian military efforts alone would not have sufficed. In May 1813, with a hastily recruited French and Rhine

Confederation army, Napoleon defeated the Russians and Prussians at Grossgörschen and Bautzen. Then he blundered; instead of driving home his advantage he played for time, offering his enemies an armistice. His attempts to detach Russia from Prussia and to prevent Austria joining them were, however, frustrated by the brilliance of the Austrian chancellor's diplomacy. Prince Klemens von Metternich delayed a decision until Austria was ready to fight. During the negotiations with Prussia he persuaded the king to abandon the revolutionary programme contained in the Proclamation of Kalisch. In this statement of allied war aims the Russian commander, under the influence of Stein, agreed to press for the restoration of the rights and independence of the princes and peoples of Germany and Europe, the dissolution of the Rhine Confederation and the creation of a new united German Reich. Princes who hesitated to abandon the Confederation were bluntly threatened with the loss of their thrones. But by August 1813 when Austria allied with Russia and Prussia, the Kalisch programme had been superseded by a commitment to restore a balance of power in Europe and guarantee the independence of the German princes. All hope of a united Reich was thus effectively sabotaged. This time Napoleon was defeated at the battle of Leipzig and forced to retreat across the Rhine. In May 1814 Paris was occupied and Napoleon was forced to make peace.

When the Congress of Vienna met, scant attention was paid to the agitation of a handful of Prussian patriots for a united Reich led by Prussia, or to the pleas of others such as Stein for the restoration of the Holy Roman Empire. Power-political considerations and wartime commitments to the German princes, coupled with an overwhelming desire for peace and stability, were decisive. If Central Europe was to become a bulwark against renewed French aggression in the west and Russian expansionism in the east – and such were the aims of Metternich and the British foreign secretary Viscount Stewart Castlereagh – the principle of legitimacy had to go out of the window and the petty princelings could not be restored. To that extent the clock could not be put back. On the other hand, the peace-makers had no desire to create a powerful united German Reich likely to upset the balance of power too much. In the end, as Austria and Prussia could not agree on any intermediate solution, the Congress settled for the creation of the German Confederation *(Deutscher Bund)*, a loose grouping of thirty-nine states presided over by Austria.

The Confederation was reviled by Prussian patriots at the time and denounced by later Prussian historians as an obstacle to the creation of Little Germany. Given the power configurations of 1815 and the weakness of national feeling, this was the only possible solution. More recently revisionist historians, lamenting the post-war division of Germany into three states, have looked back nostalgically to the Confederation. It did at least enable the Germans to remain at peace for half a century, a better record than the German Empire's forty-three years and certainly better than the twenty years' peace Germany had between the two world wars. Given time, so these historians argue, the German Confederation might even have developed into a nation state – a contention we will return to later in this book.

NATIONALISM AND LIBERALISM 1815–60

The growth of liberalism and nationalism in the first half of the nineteenth century has been described many times. To repeat it here would be superfluous. However, to understand the origins of the wars of 1864, 1866 and 1870 it is necessary to explain the changing relationship between these new ideologies and the old power structures in Germany.

Before 1840 liberalism and nationalism remained relatively weak ideological concepts supported by a small minority of educated people: a handful of writers, a few merchants in the Rhineland, some state officials and a few (but by no means all) university professors. Given the regionalism of the German-speaking parts of Europe and the obvious difficulties of determining 'national' frontiers in Central Europe, it is hardly surprising that German nationalism remained an open-ended concept in these years, shrouded in a cosmopolitan haze. Early nineteenth-century nationalists wanted a strong Reich not because they wanted to dominate Europe by force or to demonstrate a mystical sense of folkish solidarity, but only as a vehicle for expressing humanistic values. Germany's mission, so they argued, was to draw the peoples of Europe to her to share in her great cultural heritage. Those who harped on specifically 'German' characteristics, as did members of the student societies *(Burschenschaften)* with their long beards, way-out clothes and preference for long German rather than short French words, were dismissed as 'unGerman' by all right-thinking nationalists.

Typical of the cosmopolitan attitude of most nationalists was the argument of Friedrich Dahlmann, then professor of history at Kiel University and later a prominent figure during the 1848 Revolution, that if Denmark were given German territory to compensate her for the loss of Norway, this would be positively beneficial for the Confederation; the presence of Danish troops on German soil, far from being a symbol of subservience to a foreign power, would be welcome proof that Germany was free of the xenophobic nationalism characteristic of the hated French invader. And when the Frankfurt Parliament debated the national issue in 1848 it favoured frontiers for the new Reich which were not 'national' by modern standards, i.e. the frontiers of the Confederation extended to include Prussia's eastern possessions plus the duchy of Schleswig. The ready acceptance by nationalists that Poles, Czechs and Danes could be part of a German Reich indicates that nationalism was still largely a cultural concept rather than a political one, even in the late 1840s.

The appeal of nationalism was limited for another reason: the overwhelmingly agrarian nature of German society from the Rhine to the Oder. All over Europe peoples were solidly rooted in their localities. Parish-pump loyalty *(Kirchenturmpatriotismus)* was the dominant sentiment. This was coupled in many cases with a sense of loyalty and even affection for the ruling dynasty, largely because the reforms carried out by some princes had enabled them to weld their territories into homogeneous states. Regional patriotism, especially in Bavaria and Württemberg, was acquiring deep roots in the rural population, a point we will return to presently.

Liberalism, too, was very much a minority ideology appealing to much the same people as those who wanted a 'national' Reich. The fact that German princes reacted violently to isolated incidents such as the murder of Kotzebue in 1819, the Hambach Festival in 1832 and the abortive attack on the Frankfurt arsenal in 1833 was much more an indication of the psychological insecurity of princes than a measure of the popular support enjoyed by 'revolutionaries'.

As a movement pre-March liberalism was weak and divided. Liberals worked in isolation, concentrating their efforts on trying to secure constitutions in their own states. Only very occasionally did a liberal cause arouse wider interest, as in 1837 when seven Göttingen professors were dismissed for refusing to swear the oath of allegiance to the new king of Hanover who had abrogated the 1833 constitution. It is frankly impossible to generalize about the nature of German liberalism, so wide were regional variations. At one end of the spectrum were liberals who had more in common with conservatives in their attempts to revive the remnants of medieval estates lingering on in some places, while at the other end, notably in South and West Germany, liberals were much more attracted by foreign models, especially the French constitution of 1830. In some states, especially in Baden, Württemberg and Hesse-Darmstadt, local liberals enjoyed some popular support largely because they were able to voice the grievances of, for example, lower-middle-class artisans in the consultative assemblies set up by South German princes. But despite occasional angry clashes with sovereigns, the administrative officials who represented the liberal cause in these states were content to remedy local grievances and had no desire to alter the political status quo.

There were admittedly signs in 1830–2 that the desire for a united Germany could arouse interest outside a small élite. The Hambach Festival of 1832, organized by the newly formed Press and Fatherland

Society, was a case in point. It attracted at least 25,000 people ranging from middle-class elements, students and merchants to artisans and even some farmers. Significantly most came from the Rhineland Palatinate, for the centre of the national movement had shifted after 1819 from Prussia to South and South-West Germany where some (limited) constitutional progress was being made in the local estates. Even so, Hambach was very much a flash in the pan. Not until the 1840s did liberalism and nationalism begin to win wider support in Germany.

The new decade opened with the Rhineland Crisis of 1840. This crisis was marked by an upsurge of national feeling which for the first time, if only temporarily, seems to have gripped all classes. Attention was again focused on Prussia because her geographical proximity to France made her the natural guardian of the Rhineland against French aggression. Consequently Prussia was seen increasingly in the 1840s as the power most likely to take the lead in creating a strong Reich. This feeling was strengthened by the accession in 1840 of King Frederick William IV, widely acclaimed as an idealist sympathetic to the national cause as well as an opponent of reactionary domestic policies. Once it was apparent that hopes of significant reform were misplaced, interest in the creation of a strong Reich to solve the political and social problems which individual states were manifestly incapable of doing increased still further.

Consequently national consciousness did not evaporate after the 1840 Crisis as it did fairly soon after the War of Liberation. Sustained by the discontents in society, the National Liberals, as they were called in the 1840s, were able to establish organizations which gave institutional form to the new ideology. These were principally the gymnastic societies *(Turnvereine)* and glee clubs *(Sängervereine)*. Once the ban had been removed in 1842 gymnastic societies sprang up all over Germany, principally in Saxony and the south-west; on the eve of the 1848 Revolution 300 societies with over 90,000 members were in existence. Perhaps more important still were the glee clubs; 1100 with 100,000 members had been established by 1847. Both societies actively promoted nationalism, principally through regional festivals and in the case of the glee clubs through national festivals. Three such festivals were held, the first at Würzburg in 1845, attended by contingents from glee clubs chiefly in Bavaria, Württemberg and Baden, the second at Cologne in 1846 and the third at Lübeck in 1847. These festivals, which were attended by thousands of Germans, certainly played an important role in disseminating nationalist propaganda on a regional basis. The gymnastic displays or glee sessions were preceded by solemn ceremonies and interspersed with entertainments, fireworks and political speeches delivered by prominent National Liberals awakening at last to the need for contact with the mass of the population. The flags, the emblems, the songs and

27

the political speeches helped to imbue those Germans coming together from different areas with a new sense of solidarity. But attendance was restricted in the main to middle-class citizens. However, as the decade moved to a close the lower middle class was increasingly involved: clerks, shop assistants, elementary school teachers and artisans. With the exception of Baden and the Palatinate the rural population was little affected.

The modernization of Germany facilitated the spread of nationalism in this decade. For example, the improvement in communications clearly assisted in the staging of festivals whilst the growth of the press and the proliferation of newspapers and periodicals stimulated the emergence of political groupings. There were already signs of a significant bifurcation of liberal opinion during the 1830 Revolution which was marked by uprisings in Brunswick, Saxony, Hanover and Electoral Hesse. Upper middle-class liberals, supported by the new manufacturing élite and by higher officials in states such as Prussia and Bavaria, were seeking orderly constitutional change within a monarchical framework. Lower middle-class elements such as artisans and students, who had manned the barricades in 1830 and attended the Hambach Festival in great numbers, were demanding a national state with democratic and republican features. This process of political differentiation was accelerated on the eve of the 1848 Revolution. In October moderate liberals met at Heppenheim to draw up a programme for political change, having been galvanized into action by the meeting of radicals in September in Oppenheim which formulated demands for a democratic constitution.

During the initial stages of the 1848-9 Revolution liberalism seemed to have triumphed over princely power. This was all illusion. The liberal victory was due not to the persuasive power of their ideology but to revolutionary pressures in town and countryside over which liberals had no control. Accumulated social discontent erupted into violence, forcing the princes to retreat temporarily and allowing the liberals to occupy the centre of the stage by default. The illusion of power was fostered for some time by the moral authority enjoyed by the Frankfurt Parliament. By the autumn the princes had recovered their nerve and regained their old authority. The liberals were unable to resist the restoration partly because they lacked material force but also because, fearing the spread of radicalism as much as the excesses of princely power, they sided with rulers against the radicals after the June Days.

Whilst the Revolution did not lead to any permanent alteration in the balance between the new ideology and the old power structures, two significant changes had occurred. Firstly, a much wider section of the middle class had become politically conscious. In political clubs *(Bürgervereine)* all over Germany constitutional issues and the problem of national unification had been regularly debated in 1848–9.

This new political awareness remained a permanent feature, so that at least in middle-class circles a groundswell of opinion favourable to political change came into being in the course of the 1850s. This was a phenomenon to which Austria and Prussia paid some attention, for the contest between them was not simply a military and economic struggle but had a significant public-relations dimension as well.

Secondly, the Revolution administered a profound psychological shock to ruling élites all over Europe. What the ruling classes remembered about 1848-9 was not the studied moderation of Ludolf Camphausen and Heinrich von Gagern but the radicalism of Friedrich Hecker and Gustav von Struve, whose naïve attempt to overthrow the princes by force had failed at the outset of the Revolution. Although radicalism suffered a decisive defeat in 1848–9, when liberalism revived in the 1860s princes – for whom radicalism and liberalism were synonymous terms – supposed that their thrones were once more in danger. Objectively speaking, there was little threat of social revolution at a time when the industrial proletariat was still in its infancy. All the same, the conviction of ruling élites that the danger existed is a factor of considerable importance in understanding the attitude of the Prussian government and court circles during that decade.

Finally, the 1860s, a decade which was deeply coloured by the upsurge of German national feeling in 1859 during the French attack on Austria. This was deeply anti-French in nature because many Germans feared that if France won in Northern Italy she would then seize the Rhineland. The failure of Austria and Prussia to combine against this threat exposed very clearly the military weakness of the Confederation and strengthened the growing feeling that a strong Reich was a categorical imperative to enable Germany to resist the hereditary foe. This anti-French mood was reinforced in 1860 by Napoleon's acquisition of Savoy and Nice. In this age of Realpolitik, liberalism was changing in nature. The events of 1859–60 confirmed the conviction that satisfactory constitutional arrangements were secondary to the achievement of national unification, which was increasingly seen as Prussia's task by many Germans. The creation of the kingdom of Italy in 1860–1 was an additional spur; what the Italians had achieved must be achieved by the Germans without further delay.

This decade was marked by a significant proliferation of organizations working for the creation of a united Little Germany under Prussian auspices. Basically this arose out of the industrial and commercial expansion of Germany in the mid nineteenth century. Businessmen and professional people, increasingly irritated by restrictions on economic activity and convinced of the benefits which would flow from unification, set out to create a groundswell of opinion favourable to the creation of a strong Reich. In 1858 the Congress of

German Economists *(Congress deutscher Volkswirte)* was founded, a body which met annually and attracted support from civil servants, journalists and academics as well as merchants, financiers and industrialists. The aim of the Congress was to promote tariff reform and the removal of restrictive legislation, which could be achieved – so it was argued – only in a united Germany. In 1860 the German Jurists Congress *(Congress deutscher Juristen)* was founded to promote reform of the legal system. In 1861 the chambers of commerce springing up all over Germany founded the German Commercial Association *(Deutscher Handelstag)* to agitate for a reformed commercial code. Out of the inaugural meeting at Heidelberg came initiatives which led to the creation of the National Society *(Nationalverein).* This body – taking its name significantly from the Italian society which harnessed middle-class opinion behind Cavour – was established to coordinate liberal political activity. It was a sign of the times that radicals joined with moderate liberals in the National Society, so strong was the desire for a powerful Reich able to stand up to the French. Although it had only 25,000 members at its height, the Society played a significant role in creating, especially in North Germany, a steamhead of opinion favourable to the creation of Little Germany. Through local branches the National Society even enjoyed some lower middle-class support. But the upper-class leadership never sought to build up a mass membership, partly because of a fear of the lower orders but also, in fairness to the National Liberals, because they supposed governments would in the end be persuaded by the power of superior (middle-class) arguments alone.[14]

Commencing with the celebrations of the centenary of Schiller's birth in November 1859, popular festivals blossomed in the next decade. In 1861 the German Sharpshooters' League *(Deutscher Schützenbund)* was founded and in 1862 the German Glee Singers' League *(Deutscher Sängerbund).* Both were highly nationalistic organizations actively encouraged by the National Society. Thousands were attracted to the annual meeting of these bodies; for example, 16,000 singers attended the German Glee Festival at Dresden in 1864 and 20,000 gymnasts appeared at the Leipzig Gymnasts' Festival in 1863. But membership was still fairly limited; there were only 11,000 members of the Sharpshooters' League in 1862 and these were largely from the middle class. Only among the gymnasts was a lower-class element present, especially in South and West Germany. And as in the 1840s, rural areas were still largely unaffected.

Yet in their totality all these organizations, from the Congress of German Economists to the Sharpshooters' League, contributed to the creation of an opinion favourable to unification. Furthermore, they had interlocking directorates and overlapping memberships. 'The same liberals,' says one authority, 'who supported the Progressive Party joined the *Nationalverein,* attended the sessions of the Congress of

German Economists, and addressed the meetings of gymnasts and sharpshooters'.[15] Whilst it would be most misleading to suggest that national liberalism modified in any fundamental sense the policies of Austria and Prussia in the 1860s, nevertheless the existence of a steamhead of middle-class opinion favouring unification was an objective factor of considerable psychological importance which both powers tried to exploit. To this extent power structures in Germany had become more responsive to ideological forces.

Reference was made earlier to the contrast between the weakness of nationalism in the first half of the nineteenth century and the strength of local feeling. In many states, such as Bavaria, Württemberg and Baden, rulers had successfully welded their territories together on the basis of administrative measures and had brought into being a very genuine state patriotism. It is well known that the Little German historians dismissed regional patriotism with contempt as narrow-minded 'particularism' which served no purpose other than to oppose the realization by Prussia of her 'historic' mission to create Little Germany and oust Austria from Germany. More will be said later about present-day reactions to this sweeping condemnation of regional patriotism. But it is important to understand that regional patriotism had its philosophical defenders. For example, writing in 1833 the editor of the *Politisches Wochenblatt* commented that:

> . . . the German fatherland has its very own principle of existence precisely in that legitimate variety which is to be sacrificed to the deceptive picture of a false patriotism . . . . Do not let us chase after castles in the air, let us allow the French their levelling-down concept of equality, their departments, their centralization and their vanity and let us preserve the true knowledge that on the contrary Germany's unity consists precisely [in the fact] that in each part of the German fatherland, even in the smallest part, special life impulses are beating which give nourishment to the heart'.[16]

Behind these remarks lay a conservative philosophy of nationalism which differed profoundly from liberal theory. The starting-point was not the will of a people to assert its independence but the belief that the deep-rooted customs and traditions of the Germans in what was an intensely regional land were all equally valid manifestations of a common *Volksgeist*. There was, therefore, not one German nation as the liberals maintained but several, each with a right to an independent political existence. In practice only the larger states – Austria, Prussia, Bavaria Württemberg, Saxony, Hanover and perhaps Baden – were strong enough politically to think of themselves as separate German nations within the larger political entity of the German Confederation. But should one of these states expand at the expense of the others and disrupt the existing status quo, then the conservative philosophy – unlike the liberal theory of nationalism – opened up the possibility that the aggressor would not forfeit its German character. That is what

Bismarck had in mind when he observed four years before he came to power that 'there is nothing more German than Prussian particularism properly understood'.[17] The way was opened up for a marriage of convenience between this form of nationalism and the creation by force of arms of Great Prussia.

NOTES AND REFERENCES

1. Quoted in Dietrich Eichholtz, *Junker und Bourgeoisie vor 1848 in der preussischen Eisenbahngeschichte* (Berlin, 1962), pp. 7–8.

2. E. G. O. Dann (ed.), *Nationalismus und sozialer Wandel* (Hamburg, 1978).

3. J. R. Bryce, *The Holy Roman Empire* (London, 1941), p. 410.

4. G. P. Gooch, *Germany and the French Revolution* (London, 1965), p. 52.

5. The Swiss historian Johannes Müller, then in the service of the elector of Mainz, while writing enthusiastically in August 1789 about events in France went on to say '. . . what is occurring in France does not inspire a desire for imitation; and people would rather retain the good or the tolerable than buy the better too dearly'. Quoted in G. P. Gooch, op. cit. p. 48. Cf. Schlözer of Hanover, another supporter of revolution in 1789: '. . . no such revolution is in store for Germany. Abuses will be abolished by reasonable inquiries, not by gunpowder': ibid. p. 75.

6. James J. Sheehan, 'What is German History? Reflections on the Role of the Nation in German History and Historiography', *JMH* 53 (1981), p. 7.

7. A. Ramm, *Germany 1789–1919: A Political History* (London, 1967), p. 113.

8. R. Aris, *History of Political Thought in Germany from 1789 to 1815* (London, 1965), p. 235.

9. Quoted in R. Aris, op.cit. p. 353.

10. Ibid. p. 284.

11. Quoted in D. Düding, *Organisierter gesellschaftlicher Nationalismus in Deutschland (1808– 1847)* (München, 1984), p. 107.

12. Quoted in J. S. Nollen, *German Poems 1800–1850* (Boston, USA, 1912), p. 33.

13. E. M. Arndt, *Geist der Zeit,* Teil 3 (Altona, London, Berlin, 1814), p. 430.

14. A. L. Rochau, editor of the *Wochenschrift,* the organ of the National Society, rejected a proposal for the production of a cheap paper to reach the lower classes as 'nonsense . . . these are not the classes which make politics and history in Germany'. Quoted in Lenore O'Boyle, 'The German Nationalverein' *J. Central European Affairs,* 16, 1956/7, p. 337.

15. Theodore S. Hamerow, *The Social Foundations of German Unification 1858–1871: Ideas and Institutions* (Princeton, 1969) p. 358.
16. Quoted in Peter Alter, 'Nationalbewusstsein und Nationalstaat der Deutschen', *Aus Politik und Zeitgeschichte*, B 1/86, 4 January 1986.
17. *GW* 2 no. 343, March 1858, *Einige Bemerkungen über Preussens Stellung im Bunde*, p. 317.

Chapter 2

THE WAR OF 1864

SCHLESWIG – HOLSTEIN BEFORE 1863

For over a quarter of a century the affairs of the duchies of Schleswig and Holstein on the periphery of the Teutonic and Scandinavian worlds occupied a special place in the story of German unification. Neither duchy was of any great economic significance; no mineral resources lay hidden beneath its soil to attract predatory powers. Strategically, however, they were of some significance. The Helstat or united monarchy (the term used to describe all the possessions of the Danish crown) still had a role to play as guardian of the Sound, while towards the end of the nineteenth century the Kiel Canal linking up the Baltic and North Seas conferred special strategic importance on Holstein. And a glance at the map reveals the significance of the duchies as an arrondissement to Prussian territory once that power embarked on an expansionist policy. But the continued interest of the German and Danish peoples in Schleswig-Holstein from 1846 to 1866 was due not to its strategic importance for Prussia but to the fierce clash between German and Danish nationalism in the flat land between the Eider and the Kongeaa rivers and its repercussions in Germany.

Despite the hyphenated name Schleswig-Holstein, the duchies differed in various respects. Holstein, with approximately 500,000 inhabitants in 1860, was completely German-speaking, had been a member of the Holy Roman Empire and was admitted without question to full membership of the Confederation in 1815. The king of Denmark, as duke of Holstein and Lauenburg (the latter a duchy acquired by Denmark in 1815), had a seat in the Federal Diet as had the British monarch in respect of the kingdom of Hanover (until 1837 when Queen Victoria came to the British throne) and the king of the Netherlands in respect of the grand duchy of Luxemburg. Schleswig, with approximately 400,000 inhabitants in 1860, had never been in the Holy Roman Empire and was not in the German Confederation. The Federal Diet had no direct jurisdiction over this duchy which was subject only to the authority of the Danish king. Secondly, at least half the population spoke a Danish dialect until well into the nineteenth century although the language of state there, as in Holstein, was High German.

The duchies had been associated with each other since the late Middle Ages when the council of the local nobility, anxious to prevent fresh partitions of the duchies, agreed to elect as their ruler Christian of Oldenburg, the king of Denmark. Before becoming duke of Schleswig and count of Holstein and Stormarn (the title was consolidated in 1474 into duke of Schleswig-Holstein) King Christian recognized the privileged position of these powerful local magnates. In the charter of 1460 he solemnly affirmed that he was ruler not by hereditary right but by election; acknowledged that only his male heirs would be eligible for election as duke; and promised that the close association between them would remain unimpaired, that only residents of the duchies would be appointed to high office in either duchy, and finally, that the local estates would be consulted before taxes were levied or war waged.

Had history taken the course it did in Britain, Sweden and Spain, Christian's successors would have ignored promises squeezed out of them by ambitious local magnates. In the normal course of events the duchies would have been assimilated into the Danish kingdom and in all probability no more would have been heard of the 1460 Charter.

But in the mid sixteenth century the brothers of the reigning monarch partitioned the duchies and ruled over their shares as virtutally autonomous territories. So for the next two hundred years, when other European monarchs were consolidating their dominions the Danish kings were struggling to reassert their authority over the duchies. This was no easy task. Only in 1720 did Denmark recover the Gottorp parts of Schleswig at the end of the Great Northern War. Not until 1773 did she recover the Gottorp possessions in Holstein. That was because the duke of Holstein-Gottorp, fighting a rearguard action against the loss of his Schleswig possessions, was able through his marriage to a Russian princess to enlist the support of Russia in his struggle. When Peter III, a Gottorp prince, became tsar of Russia, war with Denmark seemed inevitable. It was averted by his death, for his successor, Catherine the Great, bent on expanding at the expense of Poland and Turkey, was ready to abandon the Russian claim to the Schleswig territories and surrender the Gottorp parts of Holstein in return for the grand duchy of Oldenburg acquired by the Danes in 1699.

Because the Danish rulers had not been able to incorporate the duchies into the Helstat at an earlier point, they retained their distinctive political and social structure despite the three-hundred-year-old association with the Danish crown. Their special status was recognized in Copenhagen where their affairs were handled by a separate administrative body – the Schleswig-Holstein chancellery – run by German officials. In the kingdom of Denmark the power of the crown had been unlimited since 1665. The status of the nobility had been much reduced, the remnants of the elective machinery of medieval times swept away, the towns subjected to royal control and a uniform legal system introduced. In the duchies, on the other hand, strong local traditions lingered on well into the nineteenth century. The small farmers who owned 75 per cent of the land in Schleswig and West Holstein shared in the administration, appointed minor parish officials and elected assessors to the lower courts. And in the few towns strung out along the east coast the citizens elected the members of the local councils. Economically the duchies looked not to Denmark to dispose of their cattle and agrarian produce, but to the south. Hamburg, gateway to the English market, exerted a greater influence on them than Copenhagen.

Geographical remoteness conspired with historical accident to guarantee the duchies' semi-autonomous status. The Baltic separated them from Copenhagen, and the fiord-indented east coast discouraged travel between Scandinavia and Germany. Even in the duchies contact between west and east coast was minimal because of the inhospitable moorland in the centre and almost ceased during the winter months. Not until the 1830s was the first metalled road built and the first railway laid, significantly between Kiel and Altona, consolidating still further the link with Hamburg.

Despite the looseness of the political and economic links binding the duchies to Denmark, loyalty to the Danish crown was strong enough to enable the Helstat to survive the trauma of 1814 when Denmark, the ally of Napoleon, suffered defeat. King Frederik's German subjects remained as loyal to the crown as his Danish subjects. And the educated classes – the German pastors, teachers and officials, who exerted much influence in Copenhagen as well as in the duchies – prided themselves on being 'brave Danes' during the English bombardment of Copenhagen in 1807. They were 'German' only in the sense that they shared in the rich cultural heritage of the German fatherland.

Not until the 1840s did national animosities seriously affect relations between Germans and Danes. Schleswig was at the heart of the dispute.

In ancient times Danish was spoken down to the Eider river. But in medieval times German knights, merchants and artisans extended German influence along the northern, eastern and south-eastern frontiers of the Holy Roman Empire. By the fourteenth century Low German had superseded Danish as the common tongue in

South Schleswig and made significant inroads in the centre of the duchy in the so-called 'mixed districts'. Even so, at least half the inhabitants of Schleswig still spoke a Danish dialect, although German officials and pastors spoke German in the courts, schools and churches.

In the 1830s a small group of dedicated activists launched a campaign to arouse in the local people in North Schleswig a sense of awareness of their Danish cultural heritage. In 1836 the Danish liberal movement gave its blessing to these activists. Since 1831 when the king had established consultative estates – two for the kingdom and two for the duchies – a vigorous liberal movement had developed north of the Kongeaa. Encouraged by this development, and working through the Copenhagen-based Freedom of the Press Society (*Trykkefrihedsselskabet*), Danish liberals raised their sights and began to agitate for fully responsible government. In supporting the Schleswig activists, especially their demand that Danish be introduced into the courts and schools of North Schleswig, Danish liberals were originally inspired not by national sentiment but by the belief that every people had a natural right to use its own tongue in administrative matters.

Nor when the new king, Christian VIII, decreed in 1840 that Danish was to be used in the courts, churches and schools of North Schleswig was he inspired by nationalist, much less liberal, sentiments but simply by a perfectly understandable wish to preserve the Helstat intact in a changing world. By giving limited recognition to the Danish movement in Schleswig the king hoped to retain the loyalty of that duchy. And through the Holstein association that duchy, too, would remain loyal to the Danish crown. A long-overdue modernization – which he pursued energetically in the 1840s – would then cement the relationship between all parts of his kingdom.

However, the Schleswig estates, which were dominated by German officials and landowners, denounced the new regulations and demanded the re-introduction of German as the only official language. In 1842 when a prominent North Schleswig deputy suddenly insisted on speaking in Danish, the Germans refused to let him continue. As so often in confrontational situations, exaggerated fears inflamed passions on both sides. The Germans were convinced that the king and the Danish liberals were plotting to separate Schleswig from Holstein – which was not the king's intention nor that of most liberals at that time – while Danish liberals assumed – wrongly – that because the Germans would not concede to Danish equality of status with German, they wished to separate the duchies from Denmark.

On its own this local quarrel would not have had a permanent effect on relations between Germans and Danes in Schleswig. For in the end the estates, though refusing in principle to allow those able to speak German fluently permission to use Danish, made exceptions in the case of a handful of deputies unable to do so. In any case the language regulations were a dead letter in the courts because German lawyers refused to use Danish. What kept the tension high in the 1840s was a quite different issue: the so-called 'succession question'.

King Christian had no male heirs, and neither had Crown Prince Frederik or the king's brother, Prince Frederik Ferdinand. After their death, according to the *lex regia* (*Kongelov*) of 1665, cognates would inherit the Danish crown. In all probability the crown would pass to King Christian's younger sister, Louise Charlotte, who was married to Vilhelm, Landgraf of Electoral Hesse, a serving Danish officer, and on to her children. The difficulty was that this could lead to the break-up of the Helstat because of the different succession in the duchies. Majority legal opinion both Danish and German believed that the female succession applied to Schleswig because in 1720 at least the Gottorp parts of Schleswig had been annexed to Denmark. But it was generally admitted that only male heirs could succeed in Holstein in accordance with the 1460 Charter. That would mean that Holstein would revert to Duke Christian August of Schleswig-Holstein-Sonderburg-Augustenburg, head of a cadet branch of the Danish royal house and brother-in-law of King Christian, and an active politician of conservative persuasions who exerted much influence in the duchies. In October 1844 the Jylland estates – one of the two Danish estates – concerned by speculation about the succession, petitioned the king to declare that the female succession applied to all parts of the Helstat and urged him to take action against all who disputed this interpretation.

When the Holstein estates met later that year conservative and liberal members alike united in support of what became known as Schleswig-Holsteinism. The duchies, it was alleged, formed the independent state of Schleswig-Holstein. This state could be inherited only by the male line of the royal house. Once this line was extinct the link with Denmark would be terminated and the duchies would go their own way under the Augustenburgs. The direction they wished to move in was made plain in 1846 when the German members of the Schleswig estates demanded that the king negotiate with the Federal Diet to secure the admission of Schleswig to the German Confederation. Dynastic claims and national animosities reinforced each other. The ambitions of the Augustenburgs – who were, incidentally, ready to settle for the duchies only if they could not attain their real objective, the crown of the Helstat – coincided with the rising tide of national feeling among the Germans who now looked forward with satisfaction to the end of the association with Denmark. However, the broad support the political élite in Schleswig-Holstein enjoyed in the late 1840s probably owed just as much if not more to mounting social misery among landless labourers accentuated by drought and rising prices.

The rift between Germans and Danes deepened in 1846 when King Christian issued a public statement on the succession issue: the Open Letter (*Aabene Bref*). While confident that the female succession applied to Schleswig, the king conceded that it was unclear whether it applied to certain parts of Holstein. Reassuring the duchies that he had no intention of encroaching on their established rights or altering the traditional ties between them, he declared his firm resolve of preserving the Helstat. The Holstein estates then in session not only rejected the claims Christian was making but protested to the Federal Diet that the Danish king was acting *ultra vires* in attempting to interfere with the relationship between the duchies. The response from Germany surpassed all expectations. Declarations of support poured in from German Landtage, universities, learned societies and mass meetings in the towns calling on the Diet to defend the 'German' nationality of Schleswig-Holstein. Conservatives as well as middle-class liberals joined in the cries of protest. For, like Metternich, they saw in the defence of the 'rights' of the duchies a bulwark against the forces of revolution in the shape of the 'democratic' Eiderdanes.

The mounting tension between Germans and Danes came to a head in 1848. In December 1847 King Christian died on the eve of announcing the introduction of a new constitution for the Helstat – a final attempt to preserve the state by giving it a liberal face-lift. King Frederik continued with these plans. At first there were signs that the offer of full financial and legislative powers for joint estates meeting alternately in Copenhagen and Gottorp, with provincial estates dealing with local matters, would set radicals against moderates in Schleswig-Holstein. But news of events in Paris, Berlin and Vienna in the spring of 1848 radicalized the situation. The Schleswig-Holsteiner insisted on separate constitutional arrangements for Schleswig-Holstein, the entry of Schleswig into the German Confederation and the restoration of freedom of the press and of public meetings, both drastically curtailed by the late king in the aftermath of the Open Letter.

In Copenhagen the National Liberals were now in the ascendancy. The Eiderdanes, as they are often called after the river separating Schleswig from Holstein, believed that if Denmark was to meet the challenge of a new era Schleswig must become an integral part of the Danish kingdom. German Holstein would be allowed to go its own way. The Eiderdanes forced King Frederik to issue a proclamation declaring that Schleswig, as part of Denmark, would have a common constitution with Denmark. When news reached

Kiel that the king had appointed a new ministry including prominent National Liberals – among them the fiery Orla Lehmann – the Germans rebelled. They set up a provisional government for Schleswig-Holstein, preserving a threadbare semblance of legality by declaring the king – duke to be 'unfree' in his own capital and appealing to the Diet for protection.

At first all went well for the Schleswig-Holsteiner. The king of Prussia espoused the cause of the duke of Augustenburg, while the Federal Diet recognized the Kiel government and asked Prussia to secure the king of Denmark's consent to the inclusion of Schleswig in the Confederation. King Frederick William responded to the Diet's call for military action. Prussian troops crossed the Eider and by the end of April had driven the Danes out of Schleswig and were commencing the invasion of Jylland. In May elected representatives from Schleswig-Holstein were received with enthusiasm by the Frankfurt Parliament.

It soon dawned on the king that he might have to pay dearly for his romantic gesture. At home the radicals were most likely to be the main beneficiaries of continued warfare, as the French Jacobins had been half a century earlier. Abroad, Prussia was brought up sharply against the realities of international politics. Russia expressed alarm at the prospect of the Helstat's collapse and strongly disapproved of the king's flirtation with 'revolution'. Though Russia would scarcely have fought over the Elbe duchies, the strictures of a brother monarch were deeply disturbing to Frederick William. Russian diplomats with British and French support exerted further pressure on Berlin and Frankfurt. The prospect of isolation frightened the king who, without consulting the Frankfurt Parliament, signed an armistice with Denmark at Malmø in July 1848. The Frankfurt Liberals at first rejected the armistice but in September acquiesced reluctantly in the *fait accompli*.

Not until July 1850 did the First Slesvig War officially end. Under heavy pressure from the Great Powers King Frederick abandoned the Schleswig-Holsteiner under the terms of the Treaty of Berlin. The Danish king then asked the newly restored Diet to help him re-establish his authority in Holstein. Left to their own devices the Schleswig-Holsteiner were decisively defeated at the battle of Idstedt. In November Austria and Prussia patched up their quarrel (analysed in the next chapter) and at the Diet's request occupied Holstein. What was left of the insurrectionary government handed over its power to them and the rebel army was disbanded.

The Great Powers were anxious to see the status quo restored in the Baltic. In July 1850 Britain, Russia, France, Austria, Prussia and Denmark placed on record in the London Protocol their conviction that the Helstat must be restored and the vexed succession question finally resolved. It proved far from easy to achieve these objectives. The National Liberals, still influential in Copenhagen, were reluctant to abandon all hope of annexing Schleswig, while Austria and Prussia were equally determined not to tolerate such a disturbance of the status quo. Eiderdanism and Schleswig-Holsteinism both had radical connotations obnoxious to the conservatives controlling Austrian and Prussian policy. They refused to hand over Holstein to Denmark until the balance of power shifted back to conservative forces. Hence their insistence that estates with local powers be re-established in Schleswig as well as in Holstein to ensure that the landed nobility in the duchies could act as an effective brake on the democratic Eiderdanes. In the end the Danes, conscious of their diplomatic isolation, abandoned Eiderdanism. With the appointment of the conservative Count Christian Bluhme as foreign minister in October 1851, negotiations with Austria and Prussia made rapid progress.

The outcome was incorporated in a royal proclamation in January 1852 in which the king undertook to return to the *status quo ante bellum* and create 'an organic and homogeneous union of all parts of the monarchy'. While traditional ties between the duchies would be respected, their demand for administrative autonomy – a major tenet of Schleswig-Holsteinism – was explicitly repudiated. The Schleswig-Holstein chancellery set up in 1834 would not be re-created. Denmark would keep the democratic constitution of 1849 while Schleswig, Holstein and Lauenburg would each have its own constitution, separate ministries and estates with deliberative powers over local matters. These estates together with the Danish Rigsdag would be consulted about a new constitution to handle common areas, i.e. foreign policy, military affairs and in part finance. The local constitution for Schleswig would include guarantees for equality of treatment for the German and Danish nationalities. A note to Berlin and Vienna accompanying copies of the proclamation reaffirmed the king's intention not to incorporate Schleswig or take any steps in that direction. In July the Federal Diet, which had not been formally involved in the negotiations with Denmark, recorded its approval of the proclamation.

In return for these promises Austria and Prussia withdrew from Holstein and accepted a settlement of the succession question favourable to Denmark. After further protracted negotiation involving the Great Powers it was agreed that on the death of King Frederik, Prince Christian of Schleswig-Holstein-Sonderburg-Glücksburg, head of another cadet branch of the royal house, would inherit the crown. The rival contender, Duke Christian August of Augustenburg, while not renouncing his claims, nevertheless surrendered his estates in the duchies for a cash payment. He agreed to live outside Schleswig-Holstein and promised not to indulge in activities likely to undermine the new succession.

Five Great Powers together with Denmark and Sweden–Norway approved these dynastic arrangements in the Treaty of London signed in May 1852. The powers, it should be noted, did not actually guarantee the integrity of the Helstat or assume any collective responsibility towards it; each power exchanged the treaty separately with Denmark so that each was bound separately to her and not to the other powers.

The ascendancy of conservative forces in Denmark and the duchies, together with a measure of economic prosperity in the 1850s from which all parts of the monarchy benefited, could not save the Helstat. On the contrary: Schleswig-Holsteinism was given a new lease of life by Danish treatment of Schleswig. In a determined effort to restore their authority and stamp out the Schleswig-Holstein party in that duchy, many German officials, pastors and judges were replaced by Danes and extremely onerous restrictions were placed on the freedom of the press, on public meetings and on associations. Even greater resentment was caused by the language ordinances.

In the spring of 1851 August Regenburg, the newly appointed Danish official responsible for churches and schools, with the support of King Frederik and of Count Carl Moltke, minister for Schleswig, announced that Danish would be used in the schools as the medium of instruction in the mixed districts of Central Schleswig. It would alternate with German in the churches and be of equal standing with German in all official transactions and in civil proceedings. It was Regenburg's passionate belief – to which he clung despite evidence to the contrary – that as the inhabitants spoke both low Danish and low German they would assuredly opt for the former once the 'German yoke' was removed.

The Schleswig-Holsteiner did not object to the use of Danish in North Schleswig, recognizing somewhat belatedly the justice of the Danish case. But they bitterly opposed its use in the mixed districts, regarding it as a crude device for driving German out of Schleswig. So determined was their resistance that, far from retarding the Germanization of the mixed districts especially in Angeln, Danish policy greatly accelerated the process. These ill-considered measures heightened the animosity between Germans and Danes and played right into the hands of the Schleswig-Holstein party. Furthermore, the Danes damaged their international standing by a stubborn refusal to consult the inhabitants – this through a well-founded fear that until the influence of German officials had been neutralized, a completely free vote would not be possible. Only most reluctantly did they modify the ordinance slightly in 1861 to appease foreign opinion.

Secondly, the constitutional arrangements inside the Helstat met with German disapproval and kept the affairs of the duchies on the agenda in Berlin and Vienna for years to come. The disagreement concerned both the position of the local estates and the common constitution. The king had submitted separate constitutions for Schleswig and Holstein to the respective estates. Although the Schleswig estates accepted only with reservations and the Holstein estates rejected their constitution, both were imposed on them in 1854. The common constitution of 1855 was an even more contentious issue. The Danish king proposed to establish a Rigsraad of eighty members meeting biannually to discuss foreign policy, defence, commerce and finance. Twenty members would be nominated by the king (twelve from Denmark and eight from the duchies) and thirty elected (seventeen in Denmark and thirteen in the duchies). In all, Denmark would have fifty-seven members to thirty-three for the duchies. As some Danish members were sure to be elected in North Schleswig, the balance would be tilted even more decisively towards Denmark. From the very beginning the leaders of the German minority were not prepared to tolerate subordination to the Danes and pounced upon every legal loophole to obstruct Danish plans. Nor did the Holstein nobility care for the democratic franchise on which some Danish members would be elected.[1] Thus, at the first session of the Rigsraad in 1856 eleven German members maintained that while the Danish Rigsdag had been allowed to approve the constitution, the estates of Holstein, Schleswig and Lauenburg had not been consulted. This, they alleged, was a breach of the promises of 1851–2, an argument which the Rigsraad rejected.[2]

However, the German minority was not without friends south of the Elbe, in part, no doubt, because of the strenuous efforts prominent exiled Schleswig-Holsteiner made at various German courts to keep the issue alive. Prussia soon took a hand in the game and an exchange of notes took place between Copenhagen, Berlin and Vienna in the winter of 1856–7. At issue was the common constitution and also the subordinate matter of the Rigsraad's right to dispose of domain lands in the duchies hitherto administered locally. It was indicative of mounting anti-Danish feeling that the Germans were soon alleging that the domain issue was the thin end of the wedge proving that the Danes planned to incorporate the duchies in Denmark. Finally, at the end of October 1857 Austria and Prussia referred the contentious issues to the Federal Diet. In February 1858 that body refused to recognize the common constitution or the Holstein constitution on the grounds that it had not been submitted to the estates as they claimed federal law required. They therefore asked the Danish king to confer on Holstein and Lauenburg the independent and equal status promised in 1851–2.

In July 1858 the Diet threatened Denmark with federal execution unless she complied promptly with this request. Carl Christian Hall, the newly appointed president of the council of ministers, being by temperament a procrastinator, was anxious to de-escalate the crisis, having no wish to be at war with Germany. Consequently he persuaded his colleagues to agree to suspend the common constitution in respect of Holstein and Lauenburg and summon the Holstein estates to discuss the new situation. This step, implemented in November, did at least remove all pretext for intervention by the Diet. An optimist as well as a procrastinator, Hall may even have hoped that the Germans might at last begin to make constructive proposals for a common constitution.

If he had really expected such a stroke of good fortune, he was quickly disappointed when the Holstein estates met in January 1859 to discuss both the common constitution and a new constitution for Holstein drawn up by the Danes. Emboldened by signs of popular support south of the Elbe, the Schleswig-Holstein party threw down the gauntlet. While paying lip-service to the concept of a reorganized monarchy, the estates stated their own preference in unmistakeable language: restoration of the administrative and legislative union of the duchies as it had existed before 1848. They flatly rejected the Rigsraad set up in 1855 on the grounds of distance from the duchies and the inability of most Germans to speak Danish. In its place they proposed that the four constituent parts of the kingdom be given equal representation in deciding matters of common concern. Legislative power would be vested in separate ministries for the duchies and in the four local assemblies. Legislation would require the consent of all four bodies: the Danish Rigsdag, the estates of Schleswig and Holstein and the assembly of the nobility in Lauenburg. In practice this meant that no progress would ever be made. A proposition which gave the 50,000 inhabitants of Lauenburg an equal voice with 1,500,000 Danes, so that the German minority in the Helstat (approximately 900,000) had a veto power over legislation, was an absurd suggestion totally unacceptable to the Danes, now well advanced on the road to constitutional government.

For good measure the Holstein estates forthrightly denounced the 'oppression' of fellow Germans in Schleswig – a duchy over which they had, of course, no jurisdiction. An ominous precedent. When the Schleswig estates met in January 1860 the German majority bitterly attacked the absence of political liberty in the duchy and declared that by suspending the common constitution for Holstein and Lauenburg only, the Danes had in effect incorporated Schleswig in the Danish kingdom. Schleswig, like Holstein, demanded the restoration of the old links between the duchies and appealed to the Diet and to Austria and Prussia for assistance. Prussia did not reply officially to Hall's protest. But the National Society organized several protest meetings about conditions in Schleswig, while the lower house of the Prussian Landtag petitioned the king to do all he could to help the duchies secure their 'rights'. However much Hall protested at foreign interference in Denmark's domestic affairs, Schleswig was now firmly on the agenda in Germany.

Whether Hall really believed in the possibility of reaching agreement with all parties on a common constitution seems doubtful. In September 1859 he persuaded the Rigsraad to agree an interim constitution for Holstein. As one Hamburg newspaper remarked, no German state had ever been offered such a liberal constitution of the prince's own free will. The estates were offered decision-making powers in local matters and a reduction in their contribution to common finances. Although Denmark assured the Diet in November that matters of common concern would be discussed with the Holstein estates, it is quite possible that Hall was taking the first step towards the separation of Holstein from the Helstat.

For the time being the Diet postponed federal execution. Then in July 1860 when the Danes published the common budget for the Helstat requiring a contribution from Holstein (as provided for in the interim constitution), there were fresh protests in Frankfurt. In February 1861 the Diet declared that the interim constitution would be legally binding only with the Holstein estates' consent. Under renewed threat of federal execution the king was ordered to submit both budget and constitution to the estates. Under pressure from Britain, France, Russia and Sweden–Norway, Hall summoned the estates. It was the old story. They simply repeated their demand for the restoration of the old ties between the duchies and, significantly, called on Germany to defend their 'established rights'. In April 1861 the Diet again referred the affairs of the duchies to committee for consideration of further action.

As the prospect of armed confrontation between Denmark and the Confederation suddenly loomed up, the Great Powers grew alarmed. For the next eighteen months one after the other they thought up schemes (including the partition of Schleswig) to reconcile the irreconcilable. Hall bent with the wind, reduced the financial contribution expected of Holstein for the current fiscal year and showed willingness to recommence negotiations with Austria and Prussia. On this basis the Diet suspended federal execution in July 1861. In the winter of 1861–2 Austria, Prussia and Denmark once again negotiated about the duchies. Neither side would budge from entrenched positions. Denmark persisted in offering Holstein a special status while stoutly maintaining that the future of Schleswig was no concern of foreign powers – to which Austria and Prussia retorted that Schleswig was indeed their concern because of Denmark's failure to keep the promises of 1851–2. They demanded that the common constitution be suspended for Schleswig as well as for Holstein as it had never been submitted to the estates. The Danes must prepare a new constitution guaranteeing absolute equality of status to the duchies and also withdraw the language ordinance in Middle Schleswig.

Controversy still rages over Hall's policy. It has been generally assumed that from his appointment in 1857 his policy was essentially Eiderdane in character and that he gladly yielded ground to the Confederation over Holstein in order to weaken the ties with Schleswig, while at the same time resisting foreign attempts to interfere in that duchy. More recently it has been argued that he genuinely believed in preserving the Helstat and changed gear to Eiderdanism only when it became clear that Danish political development was being retarded by the German connection. Whatever the truth may be – and much ambiguity surrounds the actions of this accomplished procrastinator – by June 1861 he had certainly concluded that it was impossible to reach any reasonable agreement with the Holstein estates. Domestic pressures were also of importance in pushing Hall into Eiderdanism by the back door. The National Liberals were engaged in a power struggle with more radical liberals – the *bondevennerne* – who had since 1858 held a slender majority in the Landsting (one of the two houses of the Rigsdag). The Danish National Liberals, like their German counterparts, wanted to preserve a monopoly of power for the upper classes and realized that, with elections due in 1861, they were likely to lose their shaky majority in the Folksting (the other house). The government's opponents formed a new association to attack Hall's equivocal foreign policy with the significant name Dannevirke Society (*Foreningen Dannevirke*), that being a reference to the Danish fortifications in South Schleswig constructed in medieval times to hold back the Germans. In May an address signed by almost all the members of the Rigsdag and carrying 71,000 signatures was presented to Hall. It demanded the union of Schleswig with Denmark. Hall seized this opportunity of enhancing National Liberal electoral prospects by declaring that government policy in recent months had been broadly in line with this demand and that the only solution was to give Holstein a special status in the Helstat. The appointment of the prominent National Liberal Orla Lehmann to a cabinet post in September 1861 confirmed that a new phase in Danish policy was beginning.

The moment for action arrived in the spring of 1863. In January the Rigsraad – from which Holstein and Lauenburg members were now excluded and from which many Schleswig members also absented themselves – petitioned the king to give a definitive constitution to Denmark and Schleswig. On 30 March 1863 a royal patent offered Holstein a liberal constitution with increased powers for the estates. No legislation on common matters would apply to Holstein without its consent. But Holstein's opposition would not prevent a law agreed by the Rigsraad from applying to Denmark and Schleswig. In April, opening the new Rigsraad, King Frederik reaffirmed that legislation approved by crown and Rigsraad would in future be binding on Schleswig. Strictly speaking the March Charter was an attempt to buy off Holstein, not to annex Schleswig which still retained its local institutions. But contemporaries could hardly be blamed for assuming that annexation was the government's objective after the huge popular gathering in Copenhagen's Casino theatre on 28 March had rejected all but dynastic links with German Holstein.

It is fair to say that Hall had been driven to this momentous step by the sheer logic of the situation as well as by mounting political pressure. Having retreated steadily before the insistence of the Diet that common legislation was invalid without the consent of the Holstein estates, he was left with a clear choice: either to continue the fruitless attempts to reach agreement with the Germans or to treat Holstein as a separate entity bound only by dynastic ties with Denmark. Forced by circumstances to adopt a firm policy, Hall may possibly have hoped to make the Great Powers realize that they must bring pressure to bear on Germany to prevent war breaking out.

There is no doubt that the Danes had high hopes that the Great Powers would support them in their stand. The French foreign minister, Edouard Drouyn de Lhuys, had assured them that France would do all she could to prevent a conflict between Denmark and Germany. The Danes were encouraged, too, by signs that English public opinion was on their side. Lord John Russell's proposal in September 1862 that Schleswig be given autonomous status had been roundly condemned in the House of Commons in February 1863. And the marriage of Princess Alexandra, eldest daughter of Prince Christian of Schleswig-Holstein-Sonderburg-Glücksburg, to the Prince of Wales in March sparked off popular demonstrations in Britain in favour of Denmark. Most important of all, Hall and his colleagues had strong reasons for supposing Sweden–Norway would give active support in the event of complications.

Furthermore, there was much less to fear from Germany despite angry protests in the duchies, for both Austria and Prussia were distracted by the repercussions of the Polish Crisis which rumbled on into the high summer. In addition, the serious constitutional crisis in Prussia was moving inexorably to a crisis and absorbing the attentions of German liberals. Not until July did the Diet find time to condemn the March Charter as a violation of the Danish promises of 1851–2. In August Denmark peremptorily rejected a demand for the repeal of the royal patent on the grounds that the Diet had overstepped its powers in referring to Schleswig. The Danish note went on to state bluntly that if the Diet persisted in threatening federal execution, Denmark reserved the right to consider this a *casus belli*. Nevertheless, Hall, a cautious man by nature, was still willing to negotiate if only for the sake of appearances about Holstein's new position in the Helstat. Optimistic about the outcome of the dispute, he assured the king that war was unlikely. Once the Diet realized that the Great Powers would condemn any interference in Schleswig it would surely draw in its horns and confine itself to verbal protests. At the end of September the Rigsraad began discussion of the common constitution for Denmark–Schleswig. But on 1 October the Diet, brushing aside British proposals for further negotiation, decided to proceed with federal execution against King Frederik in his capacity as duke of Holstein and Lauenburg. Hanover and Saxony were instructed to take the necessary military action on behalf of the Confederation, while Austria and Prussia were to hold forces in reserve if called upon.

On 13 November the Rigsraad finally approved the new constitution by forty votes to sixteen. Hall hurried off to obtain the royal signature, only to find King Frederik dangerously ill. In his lucid moments he expressed unwillingness to sign, preferring to leave that momentous decision to his successor. Two days later Frederik was dead. As Prince Ferdinand had died in July, the agnate succession had ended. In accordance with the Treaty of London, Christian of Glücksburg, the 'Protocol Prince' as the Germans called him, ascended the throne as Christian IX. On 18 November the new king, a retiring man not well known to the Danish public, was exposed to heavy pressure from his National Liberal ministers and from crowds demonstrating outside the palace; he was even warned by the Copenhagen chief of police that law and order could not be guaranteed unless he signed the cons-titution. Unable to find any politician to form an alternative government and much against his better judgement, King Christian gave way. His signature set in motion a chain of dramatic events which did not end until Denmark, beaten on the field of battle, was obliged to surrender the duchies to Prussia and Austria.

The day the news of King Frederik's death reached him, Duke Christian August of Augustenburg, who had promised in 1852 not to make use of his succession rights, formally renounced them in favour of his son Prince Friedrich. On 17 November Duke Ernst of Saxe-Coburg-Gotha received the thirty-four-year-old prince and recognized him as duke of Schleswig-Holstein. In his proclamation to his new 'subjects' published in Holstein on 18 November, the duke asserted the prior claims of the Augustenburgs over all international obligations. The Treaty of London notwithstanding, the agnate succession had ended. Schleswig-Holstein was an independent state of which he was the lawful ruler. When the German members of the Schleswig and Holstein estates met together in Kiel they favoured immediate recognition of the duke and refused to send a deputation to Copenhagen to swear allegiance to King Christian. Instead they appealed to the Diet to give immediate recognition to Duke Friedrich VIII of Schleswig-Holstein.

The German reaction was overwhelming in its intensity and enthusiasm. A tidal wave of national sentiment engulfed towns principally in South-West Germany in the winter of 1863–4. Addresses poured into the Diet from Landtage and from popular meetings, all demanding immediate recognition of the duke, the separation of the duchies from Denmark and their entry into the Confederation. As euphoric nationalists saw it, the right of the German duchies to join the German fatherland took absolute precedence over the paper claims of a treaty imposed on an impotent Germany by foreign powers a decade earlier. It was 1848 all over again, with the Augustenburg pretender turned overnight into a popular hero because his dynastic claims coincided with the national aspirations of the German people – or at least with the demands of its literate and vocal citizens. On 28 November, by fourteen votes to two, the Diet refused to recognize King Christian's envoy and temporarily suspended the vote of Holstein and Lauenburg.[3]

Would history repeat itself, with the Prussian king intervening on behalf of the Augustenburg duke? On the answer to that question might depend the future of the German national liberal movement. That brings us to Prussia, whose affairs since 1862 had been under the direction of the forty-eight-year-old Junker and ex-diplomat Otto Eduard Leopold von Bismarck-Schönhausen.

THE PRUSSIAN CONSTITUTIONAL CRISIS

At the beginning of the 1860s Prussia was in the grip of a serious political crisis which at one point led King William I to threaten abdication; if he was in earnest, this was a rare moment in Hohenzollern history. The crisis was the immediate cause of Bismarck's appointment as minister–president, a post for which in the normal course of events he would have been a most unlikely choice. The circumstances of his appointment had some bearing on his subsequent conduct of foreign affairs. What the precise relationship was is open to considerable argument; but certainly it is far too simplistic an explanation of Bismarck's dynamic foreign policy to attribute it to a conscious attempt to escape the implications of the domestic crisis.

Historians have argued passionately about the rival merits of Leopold von Ranke's Primacy of Foreign Policy and Eckart Kehr's Primacy of Domestic Policy, at times almost as if these were mutually exclusive explanations: either the domestic dog wags the foreign policy tail or the foreign policy tail bears no resemblance to the rest of the animal. In fact, Bismarck's contemporaries were acutely aware of the mutual interdependence of domestic and foreign policy. Conservatives believed that to keep the floodgates of revolution firmly closed, the Great Powers must make a conscious effort to uphold the status quo abroad; peace abroad implied peace at home. Liberals, on the other hand, believed that a foreign policy aimed at the destruction of the international equilibrium must lead to political change at home: disorder abroad, disorder at home. Bismarck was almost alone in perceiving other permutations, in particular that a radical foreign policy need not upset the status quo in Prussia: disorder abroad, order at home. Certainly conservatives and liberals were keenly aware of the ever-shifting relationship between foreign policy and domestic affairs. And no doubt the army crisis did sharpen Bismarck's perceptions of the mounting liberal 'threat' to the stability of the monarchy and give added urgency to his search for foreign-policy success.

The crisis arose out of the attempt to reform the Prussian army. In October 1858 sixty-one-year-old Crown Prince William became regent in place of his ailing brother. A quite different personality from the king, William had been trained as a soldier with no expectation of ever becoming king until it became apparent that Frederick William would have no children. William was a typical Hohenzollern in his belief that the growth of Prussia historically was due to a combination of strong government and army and that the maintenance of this combination was a *sine qua non* for the survival of the monarchy. An unimaginative man of rather indecisive character, lacking the brilliance of his brother, he was a natural conservative but not a reactionary of the old school. In the 1850s he consorted with the so-called *Wochenblattpartei*, the name given to a small group of high officials, diplomats and academics led by Moritz August von Bethmann Hollweg who expressed their views in the *Preussisches Wochenblatt* founded in 1857. These moderate conservatives wanted Prussia to take the lead in reviving the Erfurt Union, a view not displeasing to William who bitterly resented Prussia's humiliation in 1850. And while the *Wochenblattpartei* believed in a strong monarchy, they also believed that royal absolutism was the road to revolution and that kings could stay on their thrones in troubled times only by working within a constitutional framework and promoting the modernization of the state.

One of William's first acts as regent was to appoint Prince Anton of Hohenzollern-Sigmaringen minister–president in place of Baron Otto von Manteuffel, whose very name was a byword for political reaction. Supporters of the *Wochenblattpartei* filled the ministries of foreign affairs, finance, the interior and education. The tone of the 'New Era' was set by the first sentences in the regent's address to his cabinet:

> Prussia must make moral conquests in Germany by wise legislation of its own by emphasizing ethical values and by actively promoting elements favouring unification such as the Customs Union, which is in need of reform. The world must know that Prussia is ready to protect right

everywhere. Through a firm, logical and, if need be, energetic stance in
political matters, combined with wisdom and sober judgement, Prussia
must acquire political prestige and that authority which it cannot attain by
material power alone.[4]

Liberals enthused about these vague platitudes and averted their
gaze from other passages in the declaration which indicated that
William was no less determined than his predecessors to maintain his
royal power to the full. And despite the new ministry, the king was
surrounded at court by reactionary advisers who denounced all liberals
as dangerous revolutionaries.

Even before he became regent William was concerned about the
state of the army. Events in 1859 stiffened his resolve to set reforms in
motion. The outbreak of war in Northern Italy precipitated an
international crisis. The effect of this on Prussian policy will be
discussed later. Suffice to say here that Prussian mobilization revealed
serious weaknesses in the army, making reform even more urgent. And
when General Eduard von Bonin, the minister of war, resigned in
December 1859 – forced out by the intrigues of General Edwin von
Manteuffel, chief of the military cabinet, and General Gustav von
Alvensleben – William appointed General Albrecht von Roon, a bitter
opponent of constitutional government, as minister of war to
mastermind the reforms.

The case for a major overhaul was overwhelming. The population
had grown to eighteen million but to save money only 40,000 – about
25 per cent of those liable for compulsory service – were called up
annually so that the army had fallen behind in size compared with
those of the Austrians and French. From a professional soldier's
standpoint the Prussian army left much to be desired. Hitherto recruits
had spent three years in line regiments (though on financial grounds
they were usually released after two and a half years), two years with
the front-line reserves, and fourteen with the Landwehr – for the first
seven years soldiers were in the first levy (*erstes Angebot*) and in
wartime would fight in the front line alongside the regular army. As the
Landwehr under its part-time officers was poorly trained, such an
arrangement was scarcely a formula for victory. William and Roon
were determined to create a truly professional army. Roon proposed to
increase the annual intake to 63,000. The recruits would be kept a full
three years with line regiments and five years in the line reserves.
During this time they would be subjected to intensive training. After
that would come eleven years in the Landwehr, now completely
separated from front-line service and relegated to garrison and rear-
echelon duties. The net result would be the creation of a professional
army doubled in size from 50,000 to 110,000 with greatly augmented
reserves. To accommodate these vastly increased numbers, Roon
proposed to expand the officer corps and create thirty-nine new

infantry and ten cavalry regiments. Under the Prussian constitution of 1850 Landtag approval was required for all expenditure; so in February 1860 Roon introduced his army bill.

Reform of the army was never a purely technical matter. Behind the army's modernization programme lay mounting anxiety in the exclusive Prussian officer corps about political development since 1850. The military leaders Edwin von Manteuffel, Alvensleben and Roon chafed at criticism of military expenditure in the Landtag and resented the (not very successful) attempts of successive ministers of war to exercise more control over the army. And, as liberalism revived at the close of the 1860s, the military cabinet feared fresh revolutionary outbursts. The balance of power must be swung back towards the crown, the only bulwark of 'law and order' against 'mob rule'. To do this they must eliminate unreliable civilian elements from the army and turn it into an utterly reliable instrument over which the king had supreme command. For many officers that would be a first step on the road to counter-revolution and the abolition of the constitution. As the political crisis deepened in the winter of 1861–2, the military cabinet drew up plans for a *coup d'état* which the king endorsed in January 1862.

The so-called Old Liberals who had controlled the Landtag since 1858 had not the slightest intention of engaging in revolutionary activity. They, too, favoured army expansion but were critical of Roon's bill basically for two reasons. First, the sharp increase in expenditure of 9,500,000 talers was likely to increase taxation by 25 per cent and would retard the modernization of Prussia. Second, demotion of the Landwehr coupled with the increase in length of service and the expansion of the officer corps convinced some liberals that the Junker camarilla wanted to eliminate all traces of liberalism from the army and turn it even more into a bastion of reaction. Attempts to interfere with the Landwehr rang the alarm bells in liberal circles, for on its establishment in 1814–5 the Reformers had hoped to introduce a patriotic bourgeois spirit into line regiments as an antidote to the unthinking obedience (*Kadavergehorsamkeit*) of the Frederician army which had not prevented it going down to defeat at Jena. Both the king and his minister of war were implacably opposed to the Landwehr on political and military grounds alike and had deliberately run it down; 'civilians in uniform' had no place in a highly professional army, especially one likely to be employed by its officers in counter-revolutionary activities.

Though the military committee of the Landtag approved army expansion, it also recommended a reduction in the number of regiments, the retention of two-year service and the preservation of the Landwehr. Whereupon Roon – who showed more tactical skill than colleagues in the military cabinet – withdrew the bill. Worse followed.

The constitutional position of the army was shrouded in ambiguity. The minister of war was supposed to countersign royal ordinances, which implied some measure of Landtag control; but the army was also under the king's personal command. Pouncing on this ambiguity Roon decided to rely on the royal prerogative to implement the reforms; all the Landtag had to do was provide the necessary finance. Carefully concealing his intentions from the Landtag, Roon requested a provisional appropriation for army expansion. The Landtag agreed foolishly relying on Roon's verbal assurances that the changes they objected to would not be implemented.

Predictably the government broke its word. In the course of the summer thirty-six Landwehr regiments were replaced by an equivalent number of line regiments. To add insult to injury, in January 1861 King William dedicated the flags over the tomb of Frederick the Great in the Potsdam Garrison Church. Outraged though liberals were by such provocative behaviour, they sought desperately to avoid confrontation. In June 1861 they approved a second provisional appropriation, though still insisting that the period of service remain at two years.

Many liberals outside the lower house of the Landtag were by now thoroughly disillusioned with the meagre achievements of the 'New Era' and strongly critical of the timid and conciliatory behaviour of the official opposition. Nothing had been done to break the power of the upper house which had effectively blocked liberal measures such as the bill to abolish patrimonial jurisdiction. Yet the government still expected the Landtag to accept unpopular military measures. Accordingly a number of break-away liberals founded the Progressive Party (*Deutsche Fortschrittspartei*) with more pronounced liberal views. At the elections in December 1861 the new party emerged as the largest in the new Landtag.

Unlike the Old Liberals who were deeply disturbed to find themselves at loggerheads with the government, the Progressives were determined to press more vigorously for reforms such as greater representation in the upper house and in local administration. While as opposed as the Old Liberals to any extension of the franchise, the Progressives were especially anxious to establish the principle of ministerial responsibility. In March 1862 they demanded itemization of the budget to prevent funds being diverted from other heads of account for military purposes, and reaffirmed their rejection of the three-year service period. An angry king retaliated at once. The Landtag was dissolved and those ministers of liberal persuasions still remaining in office were replaced by conservatives. The 'New Era' was manifestly over. The elections in May resulted in a dramatic defeat for the conservatives despite heavy government pressure on the electorate. The conservatives retained only eleven seats and the Old Liberals forty-seven, while the Progressives held 133. With the support of the left-centre opposition liberals they completely dominated the lower chamber. The election result threw the court camarilla into a panic. The military braced itself for revolutionary outbreaks while the king approved plans to reconquer Berlin in the event of an uprising; cannon would be placed at all crossroads and mortars on the castle roof.

The fear of 'red revolution' was utterly groundless. Having won a famous victory, the Progressives did not know what to do with it. They, too, favoured army expansion so that Prussia could play the role an increasing number of liberals expected of her in German affairs. And as the Progressives wanted only a fairly limited degree of political change within the existing constitution, they were unwilling to call on the unenfranchised masses to support a tax boycott. They had no wish to endanger their own privileged position in society by consorting with the masses. However, in fairness to German liberals it should be remembered that they believed genuinely in the power of ideas. True followers of Kant, they pinned their hopes on the emergence of an irresistible steamhead of moral pressure powerful enough to sweep away all opposition. Until that happened they were prepared to compromise and accept the reforms, provided that the government conceded a two-year service period. This was a not unreasonable demand; most generals thought it perfectly adequate for training purposes. Even the conservative cabinet including Roon recommended that the king settle for that. But William, influenced by the diehards Manteuffel and Alvensleben, refused to budge on what he had elevated into a matter of principle with a sudden burst of obstinacy characteristic of a fundamentally weak man. On 17 September he summoned the crown prince, thereby confirming rumours that he was prepared to abdicate rather than capitulate. As the royal attitude hardened, so did the Landtag's opposition. On 23 September by 308 votes to 11 the Landtag deleted from the 1862 budget the funds already spent by the government on army reorganization. Trapped between a cabinet which refused to govern without a budget and a Landtag unwilling to give way, the king agreed to receive in audience Otto von Bismarck who had been alerted by his friend Roon to come to Berlin.

During the famous audience at Schloss Babelsberg, the king's summer residence near Berlin, Bismarck suppressed his considerable doubts about the wisdom of William's principled stand and promised to force reforms through in the teeth of the lower house's opposition. He could not deny the constitutional right of the Landtag to approve the budget but advanced the ingenious (although not original) argument that when king, upper house and lower house failed to agree a budget, the old one remain in force. The king finally overcame his reservations about his able but eccentric servant and appointed him minister–president and foreign minister, posts he held for the next twenty-eight years.

BISMARCK: THE MAN AND THE PHILOSOPHY

Bismarck's appointment did not signify any dramatic departure in Prussian foreign policy. It would have been surprising had that been the case. The broad thrust of a country's external relations is determined in large measure by a combination of factors: past history and tradition, strategic necessity, geographical location and economic power. Within these parameters individuals or groups of individuals in the corridors of power make their decisions and choose the methods they consider appropriate to advance the national or imperial 'interests' of the state they serve – or more accurately the perception they have of what these 'interests' are. In other words, the freedom of manoeuvre of policy-makers is necessarily limited and conditioned by the broad determinants of policy, whatever their particular philosophy of life may be. Nevertheless, it is a real freedom. Prussia would in any event have played a significant role in German affairs in the third quarter of the nineteenth century by virtue of her power and position. How she chose to exercise that power was the crucial question: would she be content to work with Austria and the smaller states in the hope of defending her interests in a revitalized Confederation where she would enjoy at least parity of esteem with Austria? Or would she advance the interests of Prussia at the expense of the other states and impose her will, by force if necessary, on the rest of Germany? What distinguished Bismarck from his predecessors was not so much the broad objective – the aggrandisement of Prussia – as his methods; his whole-hearted commitment to *Machtpolitik*; the cynical realism with which he assessed men and situations; the ruthless energy and sheer animal power he displayed in the pursuit of his policies; the inclination to go *va banque* at moments of crisis combined with extraordinary tactical skill and the ability to see several moves ahead in the diplomatic game and keep his options open to the very end. Such were the qualities the new minister – president brought to his task.

Prussia in 1862 was already a well-established German power and a European Great Power. Her rise to pre-eminence against the odds is a remarkable story owing something to good fortune and a great deal to the energy, determination and lack of scruple of a number of her rulers. The broad outlines of the story are worth recalling to make this point clear. The core of the Prussian state, the Margravate of Brandenburg, lying between the Elbe and Oder rivers, was created in 1157 out of the old Nordmark founded in 928 by Henry the Fowler as a frontier post during the first wave of German colonization in Eastern Europe. In 1351 the growing importance of Brandenburg was recognized when its ruler became one of the seven electors of the imperial throne. After a troubled interlude the emperor gave the electorate to Frederick of Hohenzollern, burgrave of Nuremberg. For the next two centuries

Brandenburg's history was relatively uneventful. Lacking material resources and surrounded by powerful neighbours – Sweden and Poland – she struggled to survive.

At the beginning of the seventeenth century Brandenburg acquired through inheritance territories in the west and east which were to shape the future of the small electorate. In 1614 she acquired three small territories in West Germany: the counties of Mark and Ravensberg on the Weser, the duchy of Cleves on the Rhine and the principality of Ravenstein, giving Brandenburg an interest in the rich trade of the lower Rhine. In 1618 the duchy of East Prussia, founded by the Teutonic Knights in the thirteenth century and secularized during the Reformation, passed to the Hohenzollerns on the extinction of the male line. This gave Brandenburg a substantial foothold in Slav territory. Then, after suffering appalling devastation during the Thirty Years' War, Brandenburg's fortunes began to change under her new ruler, Elector Frederick William, who succeeded in 1640. For the next forty-eight years the Great Elector, a ruler of outstanding ability, worked to turn his weak and divided dominions against all the odds into a strong state, the master of Northern Europe. He established his control over all his possessions, made the most of Brandenburg's limited resources and built up a standing army – the first in Germany – which was soon respected for its fighting qualities. At the Peace of Westphalia in 1648 Frederick William, benefiting from the decline of Poland and Sweden, acquired Eastern Pomerania, giving him a foothold on the Baltic, control of the mouth of the Oder and the port of Stettin.

This policy was continued, though not very effectively, by Frederick I – who acquired the royal title of king of Prussia in 1701 – and more effectively by Frederick William I. If Prussia acquired a reputation for being a huge barracks, this was due in large measure to the Soldier King who completed the centralization of the state and greatly expanded the army. With this superb fighting machine and with a well-filled treasury his son Frederick the Great attacked Silesia in 1740 and after fighting two costly wars retained the wealthy province. By the victory over Austria Frederick had more than doubled the population of his kingdom from 2,400,000 to 5,400,000, turned Prussia into a European Great Power and acquired for her a lasting reputation for cynical and ruthless diplomacy. Basically Frederick was more interested in eastward expansion than in the Rhineland; he would gladly have exchanged the Rhineland possessions for Saxony had that been on offer. What was on offer was the partition of Poland; Frederick joined forces with the rulers of Russia and Austria on three occasions, gained in all 2,500,000 new subjects and was able to round off the kingdom in the east, linking up East Prussia and Brandenburg.

The settlement of 1815 gave a decisive twist to the direction in which Prussian policy moved in the nineteenth century. Since 1740 the centre of gravity of the kingdom had moved steadily eastwards. The

Polish – Saxon dispute altered that. During the Congress of Vienna, Prussia, Austria and Russia quarrelled. Tsar Alexander I resolved to create an 'independent' Polish kingdom under Russian control. To achieve this, he persuaded King Frederick William III to surrender his Polish territories and take compensation at the expense of Saxony, one of Napoleon's staunchest allies. Greatly alarmed by the threat posed by these arrangements to the balance of power in the east, Britain, Austria and France threatened war unless the eastern monarchs gave way. In the end the tsar won; Congress Poland was created under Russian rule simply because no one wanted to try to force Russian armies out of Poland. As Prussia had regained only part of her former Polish possessions – West Prussia, Posen and Danzig – she had to be compensated elsewhere in accordance with the prevailing philosophy of the age. Accordingly she was given two-fifths of Saxony, Swedish Pomerania and the kingdom of Westphalia. It suited Britain and Austria to see Prussia established as the guardian of the Rhine with a corresponding obligation to resist France by force in the event of future aggression. This had the most profound strategic implications for Prussia. Consolidation of her territories in the east – hitherto a major objective of Prussian policy – soon took second place to a new objective: the extension of Prussian influence over the territories separating the Rhineland from Brandenburg-Prussia to give her uninterrupted control of a solid mass of territory stretching across North Germany.

It is true that up to 1848 cooperation with Austria within the framework of the German Confederation had established a balance of power in Europe sufficiently strong to deter France from challenging Prussia in the west. But after the Revolution of 1848–9 when Prussia and Austria confronted each other as enemies, and after the accession to power of Napoleon III had considerably increased German fears of French intentions, Prussia faced a new and far more serious strategic situation. She no longer attached any military significance to the Confederation but sought instead to create a strong power base in North and Central Germany from which to repel attacks from either France or Austria.

Her growing economic and military power in the 1860s gave a fresh impetus to Prussia's expansionist policy. To be assured of complete security against France, Austria and Russia as well, Prussia sought to establish a broader power base south of the river Main so that she could control the entire geographical area bounded in the north by the Baltic and North seas, the Rhine in the west, the Alps and Bodensee in the south, the Bohemian Forest in the south-east and the river Vistula in the east.[5] Bismarck recognized these as the 'natural frontiers' of Prussia. Writing to Foreign Minister Baron Alexander von Schleinitz in 1859 he offered the (unsolicited) advice that '. . . the present situation had put the winning card in our hands again provided that we allow Austria to become deeply involved in the war with France and then march southwards with our entire army carrying frontier posts in our big packs. We can plant them either on the Bodensee or as far south as Protestantism is the dominant faith.'[6]

It had long been obvious to the Prussian ruling élite that the main obstacle to the realization of these wider ambitions was Austria, a power unlikely to allow herself to be thrust unceremoniously out of Germany. Bismarck was well aware of this early in the 1850s. 'Because of our geographical ramifications,' he wrote to Leopold von Gerlach in 1853, 'Prussia has no other parade ground than Germany. But it is precisely this area that Austria believes she has desperate need of. There is no room for both of us in view of the claims Austria is making and we cannot trust each other in the long run. We are taking the breath from each other's mouth; either one of us gives way or the other is forced to give way.'[7] That war would be the inevitable result of their rivalry he did not hesitate to admit frankly to Otto von Manteuffel in 1856. 'German dualism,' he wrote, '. . . has regularly adjusted relationships [between the two powers] in a radical fashion by warfare and there is no other means in this present century by which the clock of development can be made to show the correct time.'[8]

The Bismarck of 1862 was a very different man from the brash young Junker who first entered political life in 1847 as a substitute delegate to the Prussian United Diet. In that assembly he quickly established a reputation as an extreme conservative, a bitter and outspoken opponent of liberalism and a tenacious defender of the class interests of the Junkers. Looking back it is apparent that even in those early days his conservatism was punctuated with bursts of pragmatic *Realpolitik*. While inclined on the whole to agree with orthodox conservatives of the Gerlach school who believed that 'red revolution' could be held at bay only if all the conservative powers stood together, at times Bismarck spoke out like a Prussian particularist, a man deeply loyal to the Hohenzollerns who would always put Prussia first. More than once he expressed deep admiration for the singlemindedness of the Great Elector and Frederick the Great in advancing Prussian interests. Writing to Prince Heinrich Reuss in 1853 he declared that 'Prussia has not become great through liberalism and freedom of the mind but through a series of strong, determined and wise rulers who carefully cultivated and husbanded the military and financial resources of the state. They held these in their autocratic hands to throw them with ruthless courage into the scales of European politics whenever a favourable opportunity arose.'[9] Already in December 1850 in defending the Olmütz agreement he revealed how far he disagreed with orthodox conservatives. He praised the agreement not so much because it brought the conservative powers back from the brink of war but because the 'liberal' connotations of the Erfurt Union would have so reduced Prussian power that it was not worth fighting for. 'Why do large states go to war nowadays?' he asked with a rhetorical flourish. His whole philosophy was encapsulated in the answer: 'The only sound basis for a large state is egoism and not romanticism; that is what distinguishes a large state necessarily from a small one. It is not worthy of a large state to fight for a thing which is not in its own interest.'[10]

The conflict between conservative romanticism and *Realpolitik* was finally resolved in favour of the latter in the course of the 1850s when he served as ambassador to the Federal Diet. He quickly made his mark as an outspoken opponent of Austrian policy, clashing frequently with Count Friedrich von Thun, the Austrian president of the Diet. True, Bismarck had little success in his attempts to weaken Austrian influence (with one exception in 1853), because Austria could always rely on the hostility of the smaller states to Prussia, a Johnny-come-lately to the ranks of the Great Powers whose history had been a story of expansion and disregard for established rights. Though Bismarck's opposition to liberalism and his defence of Junker class interest never wavered, he soon jettisoned the doctrine of conservative solidarity. By 1853 he concluded that there was no mileage for Prussia in continuing the triangular relationship with Austria and Russia. What Prussia needed was an ally outside the Confederation to help her further her ambitions. The ally he had in mind was France, a proposition which shocked orthodox conservatives to the foundations. The upstart dictator Napoleon III was in their eyes the very embodiment of the Revolution, a standing threat to peace in Europe and therefore to social order at home. Brushing aside such objections, Bismarck commented coolly that 'one cannot play chess if from the outset sixteen of the sixty-four squares are out of bounds'.[11]

His unideological approach to international affairs was in tune with the spirit of mid-nineteenth-century *Realpolitik*. Certainly there was a touch of the autocratic style of the eighteenth-century ruler in his dismissive comment that his diplomacy was not dependent upon the actions of parliamentary bodies or press barons but was concerned '. . . only with the politics of Great Powers carried on by force of arms'.[12] But he was very much of his century in his acute awareness of the political potential of the economic and social changes occurring in Germany. Already in December 1862 he was assuring King William that the Customs Union was 'the most effectual basis for the common handling of the economic and eventually of the political interests of the German states'.[13] Not, of course, that he was alone in this; Austrian leaders were equally conscious of their significance. Most Prussian conservatives, on the other hand, looked askance at the process of modernization, lamenting the growth of huge urban aggregations of population – 'hotbeds of revolutionary activity' – and the decline of rural society, the repository of 'sound' moral values and the only foundation of a 'healthy' society. Bismarck sympathized with that attitude in 1848. But by the end of the 1850s he had realized that

National Liberalism might be manipulated in the interests of Prussia. He began to contrast the 'false position' of the Federal Diet – where 'non-German' states (i.e. Austria) were determining German policy – with 'true' German patriotism which , so he claimed, coincided with Prussian interests. That is what he meant as early as 1858 when he wrote that 'there is nothing more German than the particularist interests of Prussia rightly interpreted'.[14] Already in 1859 when the liberals were discussing the formation of the National Society, Bismarck, bumping into one of their leaders, Hans Viktor von Unruh, in the hotel lobby, staggered him with the comment that the 'German people' were the only possible ally for Prussia. In fact Bismarck, who went far beyond the bounds of propriety in badgering the New Era government he was supposed to be serving, failed to persuade it to maintain contacts with the Society founded that summer.

Another indication of Bismarck's understanding of the changing nature of politics was his interest in the press, which he attempted to manipulate in Prussian interests. An inveterate newspaper reader, already in 1848 when still an orthodox conservative he persuaded colleagues to found the *Neue Preussische Zeitung* to propagate their views. His sojourn in Frankfurt convinced him that efforts must be made to counter the Austrian press. In fact, the Prussian government was well aware of the use to which public opinion could be put. Since 1841 a press section had existed in the Foreign Office. Called the 'Literary Büro' after 1860, it subsidized newspapers and journalists. Bismarck made extensive use of this apparatus. At his instigation the *Neue Allgemeine Zeitung* was founded in 1863 to replace existing government organs. He intervened personally in editing the new journal, correcting leading articles, feeding in material via the Foreign Office and attempting to influence the foreign press through his contact men. But the effect was largely wasted, simply because of his draconian measures against the free press in Prussia.

What shocked dyed-in-the-wool conservatives to the foundations was Bismarck's advocacy of representative institutions, an idea he began to toy with in the late 1850s. In 1861 in the celebrated Baden-Baden memorandum he bluntly informed his monarch that a national parliament was 'the only unifying force which can supply an adequate counterweight to the tendency of the dynasties to adopt separate and divergent policies'.[15] In other words, such institutions would act as a focal point, rallying public opinion around the Hohenzollern monarchy. If Austrian opposition at Frankfurt proved insurmountable, Prussia might consider creating a Customs Union Parliament with extended powers – for he was very well aware of the coercive power which Prussian control of the Union gave her. At this stage Bismarck was thinking in terms of an assembly of members from state legislatures. Later he proposed an assembly directly elected by universal male suffrage, having with his customary perception appreciated the truth of Pierre Proudhon's famous dictum that universal suffrage is counter-revolution. There was no need to fear manhood suffrage. On the contrary: as long as elections were conducted on the basis of open ballots, landowners would be able to exert a decisive influence on rural voters and guarantee the return of a conservative body as a prop for monarchy.

The net result of Bismarck's unorthodox thinking was to ensure that on the eve of his appointment he was thoroughly mistrusted by conservatives and liberals alike and excoriated as an irresponsible adventurer, a man without principle whose sole object in life was the aggrandisement of Prussia by any means, fair or foul, that came to hand.

AUSTRIAN POLICY

The Landtag's action in deleting military expenditure from the budget transformed the army issue into a constitutional crisis, raising in an acute form the question whether king or Landtag should control military expenditure. This turn of events was highly unwelcome to the new minister–president, whose major interest was in foreign affairs. Precisely because he believed that national liberalism could be harnessed to the chariot wheels of the Prussian war machine, he made a determined effort to de-escalate the crisis. He withdrew the 1863 budget and promised to introduce a new bill on military service. To the leaders of the Old Liberals he held out the prospect of cabinet posts and indicated a willingness to accept a two-year service period – with which Roon also agreed. But the king adamantly refused to compromise. Speaking to the budget committee at the end of September Bismarck made one more attempt to win over the liberals by restating his political strategy in the clearest possible terms: 'Prussia,' he said, 'must build up and preserve her strength for the favourable moment which has already come and gone many times. Her borders under the treaties of Vienna are not favourable for the healthy existence of the state. The great questions of the day will not be settled by speeches and majority decisions – that was the great mistake of 1848 and 1849 – but by blood and iron.'[16] Significantly enough, some Progressives were already in agreement with much of what he said.[17] But for others his speech was further proof that the leopard had not changed his spots. Heinrich von Treitschke, later one of Bismarck's greatest admirers, thought that 'its vulgarity was surpassed only by its absurdity'.[18] That was still the view of most liberals outside Prussia when the Schleswig-Holstein Question erupted once more on the German scene at the end of 1863.

Without the cooperation of Austria in the winter of 1863–4 Prussia would have been hard pressed to wrest Schleswig-Holstein from Danish hands. This is, therefore, an appropriate point at which to look briefly at the policy objectives of the second great German power: Austria.

It is unnecessary to recount the story of the rise of the house of Habsburg, a dynasty which had by extraordinarily fortunate marriage alliances built up a huge polyglot empire in Central Europe. By virtue of this vast accumulation of territory and of the title of Holy Roman Emperor – held by the Habsburgs continuously (with one exception) since the fifteenth century[19] – Austria had been the dominant power in Germany, the champion of Catholicism and defender of South-Eastern Europe against the Turk. Despite the loss of the imperial title in 1806 and twofold defeat by the French, after Napoleon's fall Austria remained a prestigious power equalled on the continent only by tsarist Russia. Thanks to the skilful diplomacy of Metternich, who controlled her foreign policy from 1809 to 1848, Austria regained her former possessions in Italy and Dalmatia. And her representative presided over the Federal Diet, a position which gave Austria more effective power in Germany than any Holy Roman Emperor had ever possessed.

Austria in the nineteenth century was a classic example of what has been recently described as 'imperial overstretch'. Her economic and social development lagged well behind her considerable military achievements. Significant reforms of the administrative structure, educational system and army in the late eighteenth century under Empress Maria Theresa and Emperor Joseph II put Austria ahead of other states for a brief period. But the French Revolution did not have as great an impact on her as it did on Prussia and some other German states. After a second defeat in 1809 – when for the first time a fleeting attempt was made to rally national feeling against the French – Austria stagnated. Emperor Francis I was a deeply conservative ruler, pathologically afraid of liberalism, who, after Kotzebue's murder, tightened up the repressive police machinery in Austria. Although Metternich was the dominant figure in European diplomacy for forty years, he was virtually powerless to influence domestic policy. That was in the hands of Count Franz von Kolowrat-Liebsteinsky, who faithfully carried out the emperor's wishes. However, Metternich's remark that he had often governed Europe but never Austria did not mean that he was a liberal *manqué*. On the contrary, he constantly assured the emperor that reform was unnecessary.

Economically Austria lagged behind Prussia in the nineteenth century, despite some advances. Most of all, Austrian finances, in a parlous state in the eighteenth century, deteriorated steadily through constant involvement in war. Austria fell into the bad habit of spending more than she collected in revenue and bridging the gap with paper money. When attempts were made to bring expenditure into line with revenue, as in 1811, the partial recovery was soon reversed by some fresh crisis requiring a display of Austrian military strength.

The simple truth is that whereas the realization by Prussia of her ambitions depended on the disruption of the status quo, Austria's very survival depended upon the maintenance of the existing order of things. The burden of trying to be strong enough to act as a barrier to the French in Northern Italy, a foil to Russia in Eastern Europe and a counterpoise to Prussian ambitions in Germany was too much for her underdeveloped economy to bear. Secondly, the multinational structure of her empire rendered her peculiarly vulnerable to the nationalist ideology. Once the genie was released from the bottle, the empire was doomed in the long run. All that Austrian statesmen could hope to do was retard the development of these forces in Germany and Italy by a negative policy of repression. This policy could succeed – as it did under Metternich – only provided that the other Great Powers agreed that the suppression of liberalism and nationalism was more important than the relentless pursuit of their own ambitions.

When this ceased to be the case, as it did following the disruption of the international status quo after the Crimean War, Austria's position became untenable. Russia, deeply resentful of Austria's equivocal, not to say anti-Russian, policy, could no longer be relied upon to come automatically to Austria's aid in the event of complications in Germany or Italy. The conservative coalition on which Austria had relied in the past was now fatally flawed. Secondly, after 1851 France was ruled by a man whose ambitions could be realized only by the disruption of the status quo. War was now a much more likely eventuality. When it broke out in Italy in 1859 it was soon apparent that Austria could no longer underwrite her imperial commitments. She suffered defeats at the hands of the French and Piedmontese and lost Lombardy, while at home her finances deteriorated almost to the point of state bankruptcy. The neo-despotic system which had held the empire together after 1849 was weakened and constitutional reform forced upon Emperor Francis Joseph. Thirdly, Austria faced a new challenge to her authority in Central Europe from Prussia. Rivalry with Prussia was of long standing, but in the past Prussian rulers had been anxious to avoid war. In the age of *Realpolitik* with Bismarck in charge of Prussia's external affairs, Austria could no longer rely upon a peaceful outcome of disagreements. To have avoided disaster in this situation would have called for diplomatic skill of a very high order and the adoption of bold alternative policies which the men of average ability who ran Austrian affairs proved incapable of adopting.

DANISH POLICY

Finally, we must look briefly at the policies pursued by Denmark which led to the crisis of 1863–4.

In the mid nineteenth century Denmark was still a significant Baltic power though her great days were long past. For most of her existence as an independent kingdom, Danish history has been surprisingly turbulent. Throughout the medieval period she was the strongest and most aggressive of the three Scandinavian kingdoms. Her influence reached its zenith in 1397 with the union of Kalmar when Norway and Sweden accepted Erik of Pomerania as heir to the three thrones. This dynastic arrangement brought under one crown not only Denmark, Norway and Sweden but also the old Norse lands of Greenland, Iceland and the Faroe Islands. This union lasted little more than a century.

In the course of the sixteenth and seventeenth centuries Denmark's relative position in Northern Europe steadily declined, although she went to war repeatedly in a desperate effort to resist the inevitable. Sweden broke away from Danish tutelage and began her spectacular rise to supremacy in the Baltic. But by the time of the peace settlement of 1720 which ended the Great Northern War, the balance of power in the Baltic had changed yet again. Sweden now ceased to be a major Baltic power, being forced to surrender territory to Prussia and Hanover. Russia, with the acquisition of Livonia, Ingria and South-West Karelia, rose to a position of pre-eminence in the Eastern Baltic. Denmark was forced to abandon all (nominal) claims to Swedish territory, thus bringing to an end two hundred years of bloody struggle between the two Scandinavian kingdoms.

For the rest of the eighteenth century Denmark enjoyed an unaccustomed period of peace. Those who conducted her foreign policy pursued two main objectives: first, the recovery by peaceful means of the Holstein-Gottorp parts of Schleswig which Denmark had been obliged to surrender in the seventeenth century; and secondly, the avoidance of entanglements in the conflicts between the Great Powers. In the first objective Denmark was completely successful, as indicated earlier. The Gottorp parts of Schleswig were incorporated in the Danish kingdom in 1721 while the Holstein portions were recovered by arrangement with Russia in 1773.

Denmark was successful for many years in her second objective. Through skilful diplomacy, as at the time of the Seven Years' War, she avoided being drawn into hostilities. However, her commercial prosperity was her undoing in the end. During the French Revolutionary and Napoleonic Wars the demand of the belligerents for corn and nautical supplies greatly increased. Copenhagen became a port of world rank and Danish–Norwegian shipping had a virtual monopoly of the carrying trade in the Mediterranean and with the Far

East. Inevitably this led to friction with Britain, who insisted on her 'right' to search all neutral vessels. Already during the American War of Independence, Denmark had banded together with Russia and Sweden in the First Armed Neutrality in 1780 to protect her shipping. But once Britain was at war with France Denmark's situation became precarious. Clashes between British men-of-war and Danish convoy vessels led to the formation of the Second Armed Neutrality in 1800; whereupon a British squadron promptly attacked the Danish fleet anchored off Copenhagen in April 1801 and forced Denmark to recognize the British right of search. Just as Napoleonic oppression produced the first sparks of popular national feeling in Germany, the battle of Copenhagen was accompanied by the first stirrings of Danish national feeling. Subsequent Danish attempts to remain neutral foundered when the British government learned that France and Russia had secretly agreed to force Denmark and Sweden to close their ports to English shipping. When the Danish Crown Prince Frederik refused to comply with a British demand for the surrender of the fleet (to be returned after the war), a British squadron bombarded Copenhagen from 2 to 5 September 1807. The Danes were forced to capitulate and surrender their fleet. Under French pressure Denmark allied with Napoleon and declared war on Britain.

The war ended disastrously for Denmark. Her foreign trade suffered heavy blows over the next seven years; she lost half her merchant fleet, the British blockade restricted her flourishing export trade, and Denmark experienced price rises, currency depreciation and eventually state bankruptcy in 1813. In that year King Frederik VI tried to change sides but was unwilling to pay the price demanded – the surrender of Norway. Finally in January 1814 Denmark was forced to make peace with her enemies. This had the most profound effects on Denmark. The four-hundred-year-old connection with Norway was terminated when that country was united with Sweden. But, as Denmark had unreservedly joined the coalition against Napoleon during the Hundred Days, she was allowed to keep the old Norse settlements – Iceland, Greenland and the Faroe Islands – together with the forts on the Guinea coast and the Danish West Indian islands. And in return for the loss of Norway she was given Swedish Pomerania which was then transferred by previous arrangement to Prussia, who then ceded to Denmark the small duchy of Lauenburg together with a payment of three million rix dollars.

The settlement of 1815 marked a watershed in Danish history. For the next century she eschewed all alliances and pursued a policy of complete neutrality which ended only in 1949 when in a vastly changed Europe she became a founder member of NATO. Economically Denmark recovered in the late 1820s from the effects of the war. As the population explosion in Europe stimulated a demand for food, especially in the industrializing countries, Denmark found a new role for the next fifty years as the exporter of corn, cattle and dairy produce, especially to Britain after the repeal of the Corn Laws in 1846. Politically the first half of the century was a period of advance for Denmark. The virile liberal movement which grew up in the 1830s combined with the peasant movement (*bondevennerne*) to overthrow absolutism during the 1848 Revolution and established constitutional government in Denmark with the passage of the Basic Law (*Junigrundlov*) in June 1849.

The growth of liberalism was accompanied by the growth of Danish nationalism referred to earlier in this chapter. Whereas the definition of the proper frontiers for a German national state posed immense political problems which plagued the Germans for the next two centuries, Danish nationalists were quickly agreed about their objective: the creation of a nation state including the whole of Schleswig but excluding German Holstein. Danish nationalism, like the German variety, was a compound of various ingredients: language, historical tradition and strategic necessity. Thus, the Danish National Liberals claimed the river Eider separating Schleswig from Holstein as Denmark's natural frontier on the grounds that it had historical significance. It also guaranteed the Danes a defensible frontier in the Dannevirke fortifications. These factors outweighed the undeni–able fact that South Schleswig was solidly German-speaking. Similarly, the German nationalists claimed the river Kongeaa (Königsau), separating Schleswig from Sonderjylland, as a historic frontier despite the presence of a Danish-speaking population in North Schleswig.

Eiderdanism gained ground in Denmark basically for three reasons, not necessarily in this order of importance: growing anxiety about the Holstein connection; the conviction that if it came to war with Germany Denmark would be supported by fellow Scandinavians; and the failure of attempts to work out the details of a common constitution for the Helstat.

In 1840 and again in 1859 when the prospect of war between France and the German Confederation loomed on the horizon, the king of Denmark was obliged in his capacity as duke of Holstein to provide a levy for the federal army. In the event of war Holstein soldiers led by Danish officers would be fighting an external foe – in all probability France, the friend of Denmark – while Schleswig and Denmark remained neutral. This intolerable situation was very likely to end up with the whole of the Helstat being dragged into war – or so it was feared in Copenhagen. The implications of the Holstein connection were revealed only too clearly between 1848 and 1852 when Denmark had been at war with Germany. To Eiderdanes it made good sense to be rid of this dangerous foreign complication as soon as possible so that they could create a homogeneous national state down to the Eider.

Secondly, the Scandinavian movement encouraged Danish nationalists to feel that they were part of a wider unity. Scandinavianism originated as a literary movement in the 1830s arousing interest in the cultural and linguistic homogeneity of the northern kingdoms. In the 1840s it assumed a political form with the foundation of the Scandinavian Society (*Scandinavsk Selskab*) in 1843, widely supported by academics, students and liberals in the towns. It was pledged to work for the political and military union of the three kingdoms in a modern populist version of the Kalmar Union. At popular festivals held in Copenhagen and Uppsala speakers enthused about the common Scandinavian fatherland which, it was claimed, had a special mission to uphold freedom in the modern world. Seen in this broader context, defence of the Danish-speaking people of Schleswig was not a narrowly Danish concern but part of the defence of the Scandinavian way of life. And during the First Slesvig War hundreds of volunteers from Sweden–Norway fought alongside Danish soldiers while the Swedish Riksdag voted two million dalers for additional armaments. Scandinavianism revived in the mid 1850s. There was a flurry of activity among students in Scandinavian universities, while the crowned heads King Oscar of Sweden, King Frederik of Denmark and Prince Carl Viceroy of Norway all evinced interest in a closer association between their realms. Above all the accession of Prince Carl, an enthusiastic Scandinavian, to the Swedish throne as Carl XV in 1859 encouraged Eiderdanes to feel that material help would be forthcoming if it came to war.

Thirdly, the failure of the attempts to agree a common constitution, described earlier in this chapter, together with the favourable international situation convinced leading National Liberals at the beginning of the 1860s that the time had come to take the initiative. Significantly Hall, Ditlev Monrad, minister for cultural affairs, and Orla Lehmann, minister of the interior, kept Swedish Foreign Minister Count Ludwig Manderström fully informed of their plans. In January 1863 they discussed the establishment of a Scandinavian union with the Swedish ambassador Count Henning Hamilton. The unification of Italy in 1860–1 greatly encouraged them to believe a dynastic union could be achieved in the near future under King Carl as ruler of the three kingdoms. In February Manderström warmly approved the decision to separate Holstein from Schleswig as a first step towards a Northern Union, though being a cautious and experienced diplomat he suggested that Hall inform the Great Powers in advance, advice which the president of the council ignored. In July when the Federal Diet demanded the withdrawal of the March Patent, Hall, well aware that a refusal would probably lead to conflict, proposed a formal alliance with Sweden. Later in July when King Carl met King Frederik at Skodsborg palace the former advised Hall to reject the Diet's demand and assured him that if Germany tried to enforce federal execution, Sweden would send 20,000 troops to defend Schleswig. Negotiations for a formal alliance were conducted through Hamilton in August. But when the Swedish ministers discussed the draft treaty early in September 1863 only King Carl, Minister–President Louis de Geer, Manderström and Hamilton were whole-heartedly in support. Their more cautious colleagues decided to delay matters until British and French reactions were known. While King Carl continued to persuade himself that the alliance was a certainty, his ministerial critics realized that, as neither Britain nor France was likely to underwrite Danish resistance, the project was a dead letter. Unfortunately the equivocal attitude of the Swedish cabinet was never made fully clear to Denmark. Nor did Denmark's political leaders seek to clarify it, hoping that the impression conveyed by continued negotiations would be sufficient to deter the Germans. On 28 September 1863 Hall introduced a revised Denmark–Schleswig constitution in the Rigsraad. Throughout October Manderström continued to encourage Danish resistance with optimistic reports of imminent assistance. As late as 16 November he assured the Danish ambassador in Stockholm that King Frederik's death would not alter Sweden's attitude to an alliance. Only on 2 December after ostentatious demonstrations of support for the duke of Augustenburg in Germany did Manderström in effect shelve the negotiations. He now argued that as the Germans were threatening to separate the duchies from Denmark, the signatories of the London Treaty would surely intervene rendering a Swedish alliance superfluous for the time being. Even on 14 December the impulsive Swedish monarch informed a Danish visitor that he would defend Schleswig, alliance or no alliance. Danish National Liberals can hardly be blamed for suppressing their growing doubts and persuading themselves that Sweden would stand by them if the crisis led to war.

At the same time that Denmark was deluding herself about Swedish assistance she was also underestimating the threat presented by Bismarck. Up to mid November it was confidently assumed in Copenhagen that the reactionary Junker, enemy of German nationalism, was well disposed towards Denmark. He had, after all, assured the Danish and British ambassadors in Berlin that Schleswig was not the concern of the Diet. Furthermore, if the Rigsraad approved the common constitution currently before it, then provided that Denmark withdrew the March Patent and offered to negotiate with the Diet about Holstein, Prussia would no longer support federal execution. Only when the November constitution was on the point of ratification did Bismarck suddenly abandon the pretence and warn Denmark that the constitution violated the promises of 1851–2 and rendered a peaceful outcome unlikely.

THE 1863 CRISIS

The Schleswig-Holstein Question rescued the Prussian liberals (or so they thought) from a hopeless situation – hopeless because once Bismarck started to raise taxes without the Landtag's consent their bluff was called. Not only were they faction-ridden and found it difficult to remain united for long, but they were utterly opposed to a tax boycott, a sanction likely to embarrass the government seriously and perhaps even force it to surrender. The re-emergence of interest in the Elbe duchies, however, infused them with new hope. Would not the pressure of national sentiment force Prussia willy-nilly to take the initiative in bringing about national unification, which in its turn must lead to significant political change, sweeping away in the process blind reactionaries like Bismarck? As a friend wrote to the prominent liberal Rudolf von Bennigsen: 'Upon the outcome [of the Schleswig-Holstein affair] depends not only the rescue of the duchies for Germany and her entire position abroad but also the course of our inner development for many years to come.'[20]

The liberal conviction that national unity and political liberalism were interdependent was not one which commended itself to Bismarck. He never wavered in his belief that the victory of liberalism would sound the death-knell of the monarchical order which he was pledged to preserve, and must, therefore, be opposed to the bitter end. As he remarked to Count Robert von der Goltz, the Prussian ambassador to Paris who was displaying alarming signs of wishing to swim with the liberal tide:

> If we now turn our backs on the Great Powers in order to throw ourselves into the arms of the small states whose policy is dictated by the democrats in the National Society, that would be the most miserable situation into which we could bring the monarchy both at home and abroad. We would be pushed instead of pushing; we would be relying on elements we could not control and which are in essence hostile to us but to which we should have to surrender unconditionally. You believe that there is something in 'German public opinion', legislative assemblies, newspapers, etc. which could be of use to us for the purpose of union or hegemony politics. I consider that to be a fundamental error and a complete fantasy. Our growth in power cannot issue forth from legislative chambers or from the press but from Great Power politics carried on by force of arms; we do not have the strength to waste it by taking up false positions or for the sake of mere phrases or for the Augustenburgs.

But he went on to reassure Goltz that he was not 'in any way frightened of war . . . you will be convinced perhaps very soon that war is also part of my programme'.[21]

As early as 1856 Bismarck had made no secret of his conviction that the interests of Prussia and nothing else must be the sole determinant of government policy towards the duchies. Unless Prussia could extract tangible benefits out of the Danish–German dispute she must leave well alone. The entry of an independent Schleswig-Holstein into the German Confederation could not conceivably benefit Prussia. Hemmed in by Prussian territory, the new duchy would be exposed to outside pressures, especially those of Austria, and become a centre of intrigue for Vienna on Prussia's doorstep. Although the preservation of the status quo did not greatly interest him either – for clearly only if the Helstat disintegrated would Prussia have room for manoeuvre – that would be preferable to the creation of a truly independent Schleswig-Holstein ruled by the duke of Augustenburg.[22]

It is often suggested that the annexation of the duchies must have been his objective throughout the crisis of 1863–4 in order to round off Prussian territory in North Germany. While the strategic importance of Schleswig-Holstein for Prussia certainly did not escape Bismarck, it is doubtful whether annexation was his primary objective. Only in February 1864 did he finally opt for that solution.[23] It has been suggested that a primary consideration was the use he could make of the crisis to benefit Prussia in the struggle with Austria.[24] The Germans could not call themselves masters in their own house as long as the Great Power signatories of the Vienna settlement – of which the German Confederation was part – could still claim a certain moral responsibility for the future of Germany. That might well preclude Prussian expansion by force of arms. Therefore an overriding priority for Prussia was to try to persuade the Great Powers to disengage themselves from German affairs. If Bismarck could shunt them on to a side track, the main line would be clear for Prussia to force Austria out of Germany. 'Seeing things from the Schleswig-Holstein angle,' as he remarked to Goltz, 'must never cloud for us the European angle.'[25]

It seems much more likely that a supreme pragmatist like Bismarck was unclear at first what use he could make of the Schleswig–Holstein affair. Certainly he was not daunted by international crises. Long ago he had commented that 'great crises represent the weather which is conducive to Prussia's growth when we use them without fear and perhaps very ruthlessly . . .'.[26] But just how to steer the ship of state through squally weather depended on circumstances. All he could do was block solutions of the Schleswig-Holstein Question inimical to Prussian interests. Two immediate problems faced him. First, contemptuous though he was of the Diet, it had become the focal point of a mounting national liberal campaign to detach the duchies from Denmark. If that cam-

70

paign succeeded it would give an immense fillip to expectations of political change throughout Germany. To combat this threat and ensure that the balance of power remained tilted firmly in favour of conservatism called for careful manoeuvring at Frankfurt. Secondly, Prussia had to prevent Austria exploiting the situation in her own interests.

His success in making sure that Austria was on Prussia's side is often regarded as one of Bismarck's great diplomatic achievements. In reality agreement with Austria was not difficult to obtain. Basically Austria faced the same problem as Prussia. Now that public opinion was beginning to count for something, she dare not seem to be lacking in enthusiasm for the national cause. On the other hand, she was frightened that if public opinion swept the Diet into precipitate action, serious international complications would arise which would draw in Austria. War cost too much and might endanger the stability of the monarchy, especially a war fought in defence of the nationality principle. And, like his predecessors, the emperor's chief minister, Count Johann von Rechberg, believed in dualism. With Napoleon on the prowl, feeling confident enough to declare in November 1863 that the treaties of 1815 were 'null and void', solidarity with Prussia was mandatory. As the Austrian council of ministers saw it, if the National Liberals swung Bismarck on to a democratic course over the duchies, the conservative order of things would be endangered and France would be the main beneficiary. Austria without Prussian or Russian support feared that she would be at the mercy of Napoleon – and it cannot be emphasized too strongly that the French emperor, not the Prussian minister–president, was regarded as the bogey-man of Europe in 1863.

Bismarck quickly reassured Rechberg that Prussia would uphold the London Treaty and would not be swept into support for the duke of Augustenburg as she had been in 1848. Nevertheless, maintenance of the status quo at all costs was certainly not Bismarck's objective. The means of disrupting it lay in the promises Denmark made in 1851–2 to the two major German powers to respect the position of the duchies. In order to keep Austria in play, Bismarck assured Rechberg that Prussia would adhere to the London Treaty. But, in order to have at his disposal a pretext for intervening in the duchies, he made this commitment conditional upon Denmark keeping her promises to Austria and Prussia. In other words, if Denmark refused to withdraw the November constitution – which conflicted with the promises of 1851–2 – Austria and Prussia would no longer feel bound to uphold the London Treaty.[27] This conditional relationship between two separate but related agreements enabled Bismarck to run with the hares and hunt with the hounds. Up to a point he could mollify the Diet by arguing that the two German powers sympathized with the nationalist cause and were certainly not unreservedly on Denmark's side, while simultaneously they were able to reassure conservative opinion in Germany and abroad by their refusal to commit themselves to the cause of the duke of Augustenburg. Behind this adroit balancing act lay the gnawing fear which Bismarck shared with many conservatives that unless Austria and Prussia could control the volatile situation the nationalist agitation would unleash the forces of revolution in Germany.[28] No doubt Bismarck did play up this anxiety in his dealings with Britain and Russia, but that does not mean he was not genuinely concerned about the domestic implications of the crisis.

In Frankfurt Austria and Prussia were already hard at work applying the brake to the nationalist movement. When Robert von Mohl, the Baden representative, attempted on 21 November to proclaim Duke Friedrich lawful ruler of the duchies and protested at the continued presence of the Danish plenipotentiary, Austria and Prussia succeeded in getting the motion referred to committee. On 28 November Baden returned to the fray to demand on behalf of the committee the suspension of the vote of Holstein-Lauenburg until the succession question had been resolved. Austria and Prussia immediately objected that the Danish plenipotentiary was fully entitled to exercise his rights in respect of Lauenburg where the succession was not in dispute. In the case of Holstein suspension was justified, not because of the succession question but simply and solely because Denmark had failed to implement the 1851–2 promises. Brushing these objections aside, the Diet carried the Baden motion.

The situation deteriorated still further when, on the same day, some middle states attempted to change the conditions upon which federal execution was to be carried out. Bavaria, supported by Baden, Württemberg and Nassau, argued that after King Frederik's death the succession question had entered a new phase. Federal execution (i.e. the occupation of Holstein-Lauenburg by federal troops) should no longer be based on the October resolution but should take account of the 28 November resolution – this represented a step away from the status quo for, as well as suspending the vote of Holstein-Lauenburg, it had declared that the Confederation must defend its rights in the light of 'changed circumstances'. The question now to be answered was whether King Christian IX had any claim to Schleswig, Holstein and Lauenburg. Only when that issue had been resolved – so the middle states argued – would it be clear whose 'rights' the Confederation was supposed to defend and what steps it must then take to enforce these rights. Anxious to keep the initiative in their own hands,

Austria and Prussia moved a counter-motion that federal execution be implemented at once but on the terms laid down by the October resolution, i.e. against King Christian as duke of Holstein. With reference to the succession question, they restricted themselves to a bare acknowledgement of the undoubted rights of the Confederation under federal law.[29] In the end the Austro-Prussian motion was carried by eight votes to seven, but only because the two major German powers made it clear that they would not give military support to any other motion and would themselves occupy Holstein if need be to stop the Diet.

The Augustenburg movement was now reaching mammoth proportions in Germany. On 18 November the executive of the National Society pledged full support to him. As the rival Reform Society was fully at one on this issue, both combined to launch an appeal to all German Landtage to dispatch colleagues to Frankfurt for an extraordinary meeting on 21 December. Five hundred attended and expressed whole-hearted support for Duke Friedrich. A permanent committee of thirty-six was appointed to organize popular meetings to express the widespread support enjoyed by the Schleswig-Holsteiner. On 30 December 'Duke' Friedrich arrived in Kiel and set up his court, an illegal act from which the federal commissioners averted their gaze.

Meanwhile important developments were taking place in Copenhagen. King Christian signed the November constitution with extreme reluctance and only because he believed that to have been his predecessor's wish. As the crisis deepened, he grew increasingly alarmed at the prospect of what he believed would be a disastrous war. On 20 December the British, French and Russian ambassadors in presenting their credentials to the new monarch told Hall bluntly that their countries would not help Denmark in the event of war. They advised him to withdraw the constitution and negotiate his way out of a *cul-de-sac*. Hall rejected this advice out of hand. This because on 16 December the council of ministers had finally decided not to yield an inch to foreign powers. Withdrawal of the constitution would not, in their view, impress the Germans but would certainly lead to a domestic crisis, so strongly was public opinion committed to Eiderdanism. Nor would such a gesture guarantee immunity from fresh demands – they had withdrawn the March Patent on 5 December but it had not mollified the Germans. Deep down they still hoped that, whatever the Great Powers might say, when the crunch came they would not allow Germany to impose her will on Denmark.

Psychologically they had come to the end of the road. Tired of endless and fruitless negotiation and uncertain about Denmark's future, they decided to go *va banque*. One of the ministers wrote later of ' . . . a courage born of desperation that sometimes conquers but more often succumbs. Such courage inspired the ministry.'[30] On receiving the advice of his ministers that a peaceful outcome was now unlikely, an alarmed king asked Hall to hold the Rigsraad in session to discuss withdrawal of the constitution. Hall and his colleagues refused and dissolved that body on 21 December. On 23 December, after further consultation with the British ambassador, John Wodehouse, the king returned to the attack, demanding the recall of the Rigsraad to discuss the issue. The ministers decided on 23 December – the day before Saxon and Hanoverian troops advanced into Holstein and Lauenburg – to resign *en bloc* rather than agree to this demand. Their calculation was that the king, after a fruitless round of conversations with various politicians, would be obliged to turn to them again. Then he would have to choose between acceptance of Eiderdanism and abdication. They were correct in supposing he would not find a conservative politician willing to form a ministry. Then suddenly Monrad broke ranks and offered his services to the king, which enabled Christian to form a new ministry on 31 December. Whether Monrad volunteered because he felt the king's abdication would seriously weaken Denmark's position or because he was offended by Hall's insistence on collective cabinet responsibility which excluded the dismissal of Lehmann to mollify the Germans, or simply because he wanted to be at the head of affairs, is an open question. A complex character who seems to have had no very clear political objectives, Monrad headed a cabinet of professional administrators who were unknown to the general public. Consequently he was much more dependent on the king who still strove desperately to avoid war. It will be seen presently that, as Monrad lived in hopes of finding a way out of the toughest corners, he was much more responsive to foreign pressure for a de-escalation of the crisis than Hall had been.[31] But by now it was too late for Denmark to avoid catastrophe.

Mounting pressure in Germany for immediate action, especially the demands being made by some states for the occupation of Schleswig and the recognition of Duke Friedrich, forced Bismarck's hand. On 28 December, in an attempt to take the wind out of the nationalists' sails, Austria and Prussia moved that the Confederation now occupy Schleswig for the express purpose of compelling Denmark to withdraw the common constitution. This motion clearly implied that King Christian was still duke of Schleswig-Holstein. On the same day Hesse-Darmstadt moved a counter-motion also calling for the occupation of Schleswig by federal forces but adding the significant phrase: 'until the current pending issues [i.e. the succession question as well as the constitutional issue] are resolved' . Both motions were referred to the appropriate committee for deliberation. However, under pressure from Prussia and

Austria, who insisted that action was an urgent necessity, the Diet agreed to take the vote before the committee – which was also examining the succession question – had made its recommendations. On 14 January 1864 the Austro-Prussian motion was defeated by eleven votes to five.

The two major German powers had now reached the parting of the ways. On 16 January they issued a joint statement in which they declared that they still hoped the Diet would have second thoughts and support their motion so that they could all work together. However, if the Diet still rejected the motion or passed a resolution on the succession question – which was outside the competence of the Confederation so far as Schleswig was concerned – then Austria and Prussia would act independently 'to make effective the rights of Germany' by demanding the withdrawal of the constitution within forty-eight hours and the submission of proposals by the Danes indicating how they intended to implement the promises of 1851–2. If Denmark rejected this ultimatum, they would occupy Schleswig. To emphasize their continued commitment to the conservative cause, they added that once in occupation they would not permit demonstrations in support of Duke Friedrich.

The Austrians suspected that they might be about to embark on a ride on a tiger. Fearing that Bismarck was planning to seize the duchies, they tried their best to commit Prussia to the proposition that they would depart from the succession laid down in the London Treaty only by mutual agreement. Bismarck avoided the attempt to pin him down, assuring the Austrians that he personally would be only too willing to oblige them but that, regrettably, his partner Mr Jaggers – the Prussian monarch – would not agree, being frankly more inclined to tear up the treaty. As it was, Bismarck pretended he was having a hard time keeping in check anti-Austrian sentiments in court circles. So, feeling they had at least a supporter of the treaty in Bismarck, Austria settled in the declaration of 16 January for a promise that in the event of war the two powers reserved the right to determine the future status of the duchies and the succession question by mutual agreement. In effect Bismarck had wriggled out of the commitment to the London Treaty. So although the Austrians persuaded themselves that Bismarck's hands were tied, as he remarked to the Italian ambassador, Austria was 'working for the king of Prussia'.[32] And paying a heavy price for her association into the bargain; Austrian diplomats in South Germany reported a sharp decline in Austrian prestige caused by this unpopular policy which was denounced in scathing terms by the central committee of German deputies in an appeal to the German people on 24 January 1864. In a statement bristling with inflammatory language the London Treaty was dismissed as nothing other than a 'pseudonym for [Germany's] earlier shame'. The cautious policy of Austria and Prussia was deplorable. The German people had right on their side and were fighting 'for the highest prizes: freedom from Austrian and Prussian servitude and for the salvation of its very existence'. Their opponents '. . . boast much but their superiority is more appearance than reality; they are only strong if the rest of Germany backs away without counsel and without courage'.[33]

Had federal forces occupied Schleswig on the basis of the Hessian motion as the central committee would have wished, international complications would have been distinctly possible. More important still, the adoption of the Hessian motion against the wishes of Austria and Prussia would have given an important fillip to the Augustenburg cause and might well have led subsequently to significant political change in Germany. By acting in their own name on the basis of promises made to them by Denmark and resolutely avoiding all reference to the inflammatory succession question Austria and Prussia could not only occupy Schleswig and minimize international repercussions but also hold at bay the 'forces of revolution' which undoubtedly worried both Bismarck and Rechberg.

Bismarck would not have been content with the withdrawal of the November constitution, which he was confident the Danes would never abandon in any case. Even that unlikely event would not have deterred him. He would still have occupied Schleswig as a pledge to ensure that Denmark fulfilled the promises of 1851–2. That would have opened up infinite possibilities for delaying tactics until Prussia was quite 'satisfied' with the new arrangements. What he wanted, quite simply, was an excuse for military intervention. As he remarked apropos of federal execution: 'Once German troops are in the duchy [i.e. Holstein] things will take their own course and the situation can alter very rapidly.'[34] Similarly, once Schleswig was in Prussian hands it would be difficult to restore the status quo.

Then at the twelfth hour Denmark nearly upset Bismarck's calculations. On 16 January Austria and Prussia delivered their ultimatum: the constitution must be withdrawn within forty-eight hours or else they would occupy Schleswig. The time-scale militated against Danish compliance short of a *coup d'état* which the king would not entertain or public opinion have tolerated. On 18 January Denmark had no alternative but to reject the ultimatum. However, on 21 January, under strong British and Russian pressure, Monrad indicated willingness to rescind the constitution and reorganize the Helstat in accordance with the promises of 1851–2. To this end he requested a six-week delay to enable elections to be held to the Rigsraad. No doubt Monrad was playing for time, as Bismarck rightly assumed when he rejected the request on the grounds that

Denmark had already had twelve years to resolve the constitutional issue. Nevertheless, the pretext for war suddenly appeared threadbare. British pleas on behalf of Denmark were curtly rejected in Berlin. But to reassure the Great Powers of his bona fides, Bismarck organized a joint declaration explaining that Austria and Prussia had recognized the integrity of the Danish monarchy in 1852 on the basis of promises made to them by the Danes. The occupation of Schleswig did not signify a departure from that principle. However, if complications arose (i.e. if Denmark resisted them) or if other powers intervened in a conflict with Denmark, Austria and Prussia gave notice that they would renounce these obligations. Even so, final arrangements would be arrived at in agreement with the Great Powers. At the same time he made much of the fears in Berlin and Vienna that a revolutionary war destructive of monarchical institutions everywhere in Europe would break out unless Austria and Prussia were firmly in the saddle in Schleswig.

There was no formal declaration of war on Denmark. On 24 December when 6,000 Saxon and 6,000 Hanoverian troops entered Holstein to carry out federal execution, the Danes at once withdrew their forces into Schleswig. Meanwhile an Austrian and Prussian force under the command of Field Marshal Count Friedrich von Wrangel stayed on the Holstein frontier at their bases in Hamburg and Lübeck. On 20 January Wrangel assumed command over all the federal forces involved in the execution. On 21 January the Austro-Prussian forces entered Holstein. Though the Saxons and Hanoverians refused to take orders from Wrangel, they were in no position to offer resistance. On 31 January Wrangel requested his Danish opposite number, General Christian de Meza, to withdraw from Schleswig. When he declined to do so, Wrangel's forces crossed the Eider at several points on 1 February and the Second Slesvig War commenced.

THE REACTION OF THE GREAT POWERS

So far the focus has been on the internal roots of the 1864 War: the tangled relationships between Germans and Danes, the clash of rival nationalisms in a frontier area, the involvement of the German Confederation and the ambitions of Prussia. That does not exhaust an inquiry into the origins of the war. Had the international situation not been reasonably favourable, Austria and Prussia would scarcely have gone to war. The changing pattern of international affairs is, therefore, part of the explanation, and to this aspect we now turn.

Reference was made earlier to the Crimean War, a conflict which had profound and lasting effects upon international relations for at least two decades. In the first half of the nineteenth century the five Great Powers – Austria, Prussia, Britain, France and Russia – despite conflicting power interests, had acted in concert to settle disputes likely to escalate into conflagrations destabilizing the existing order in Europe. After 1856 the Concert of Europe ceased to function. The war permanently soured relations between Austria and Russia, fatally weakening the unofficial alliance of the conservative powers against revolution. A further destabilizing factor was the revisionist policy being pursued by Napoleon III. When the Schleswig-Holstein crisis was at its height in the winter of 1863–4 foreign offices all over Europe believed that the real threat to peace came not from Bismarck but from Napoleon, who was thought to be planning war in the spring to bolster up his regime. The general consequence of the changing balance of power was that Prussia was able to wage a local war against Denmark without having to fear the emergence of a united front between Britain, France and Russia.

Let us look first at Britain, a power with a significant interest in the survival of the Helstat. The Baltic, like the Black Sea, had been strategically important ever since the first clash with Russia in the late eighteenth century. Secondly, Britain's Baltic trade was still of considerable value despite the fact that the steam age had made her less dependent on timber for her ships; one quarter of all British tonnage still passed through the Sound between 1860 and 1862. Thirdly, British opinion instinctively took the side of Denmark, threatened by her larger neighbour, much as it supported Belgium in 1914. For all these reasons Britain was interested in the outcome of the Schleswig-Holstein affair.

In the 1850s and early 1860s Britain made several attempts to mediate the dispute out of existence. Immediately after the 1848 Revolution Palmerston advocated the partition of Schleswig. After that was abandoned Britain canvassed the idea of autonomous status for the duchy. But when the crisis broke in 1863 the policy-makers in London were in disarray. The prime minister, Lord Palmerston, strongly supported by public opinion, was robustly pro-Danish. He and many of his cabinet colleagues insisted on the absolute validity of the London Treaty, indignantly rejecting German attempts to make its implementation dependent on fulfilment of the promises of 1851–2. Prussia he regarded with jaundiced eyes as an aggressor state manoeuvring to secure a naval base at Kiel. Queen Victoria, on the other hand, was just as firmly pro-Augustenburg and sympathetic to Prussia, while the foreign secretary, Earl (formerly Lord John) Russell, blamed both Germans and Danes for the deteriorating situation.

At first Palmerston made the running. On 23 July 1863 he nailed his colours firmly to the mast, declaring in the House of Commons that if any attempt was made to disturb the status quo in the Baltic the power responsible 'would find, in the result, that it would not be Denmark alone with which they would have to contend'.[35] As the crisis deepened, he remained firmly anti-Prussian, no doubt strengthened in this by Bismarck's off-the-cuff remark to the British ambassador on 22 December that 'a few cannon shots would settle the affair'.[36] On 2 January the cabinet took the momentous decision to aid Denmark if the Augustenburg pretender was established as duke of Schleswig-Holstein.

But even at his most belligerent Palmerston recognized the parameters within which British policy had to operate. The cabinet decision was qualified by the observation that without French, Russian and Swedish support Britain would not give military assistance to Denmark. For whatever degree of concern there might be in Whitehall about continental developments, Europe was of minor significance in the totality of things.[37] Like Russia, Britain was a world power. As the leading industrial nation her attentions were focused primarily on the defence of markets spread across the globe and on the mounting problems she faced in her colonial possessions. In India, for example, after the Mutiny of 1857–8 strenuous efforts were being made to overhaul the administration of the sub-continent. During the American Civil War she was concerned about the possibility of Fenian-inspired invasions of Canada. In addition, Britain kept an anxious eye on Russian advances towards Afghanistan and on the machinations of Napoleon III in the Mediterranean, especially in Egypt. The upshot was that over half Britain's forces were stationed abroad, chiefly in India and Canada, so that Britain could not risk war in Europe without a continental ally.

Neither France nor Russia was prepared to underwrite Britain. Furthermore, whatever reservations there were about Prussia's eagerness to start a war, the two German powers were, in fact, pursuing a moderate policy compared with that favoured by the Diet. And it was universally felt that Denmark had violated the promises of 1851–2. So when Palmerston and Russell, alarmed by the prospect of the German invasion of Jylland, informed France and Russia that a squadron of the fleet was being sent to Copenhagen, the cabinet revolted. On 24 February it vetoed this move and ordered Russell to undo the damage. Thus there remained only the option of a negotiated settlement through the calling of an international conference. That proposal Russell first put to the Danes in February 1864.

Secondly, France. She had no significant strategic or commercial interests at stake in the Baltic, but her restless new ruler saw in the dispute an opportunity to advance his general aims of upsetting the Vienna settlement at the expense of his uncle's great enemy, Austria, and of reconstructing Europe along national lines. Partly because of his belief in the nationality principle and partly because he saw in Prussia a potential ally against Austria, he favoured Prussian acquisition of Schleswig-Holstein. Denmark united with Danish North Schleswig would, he thought, be better off in a Scandinavian union which would have a role to play as a barrier to Russian expansion in the north in a Europe reconstructed along grandiose Napoleonic lines. Hence he was not interested in British overtures for joint action in support of Denmark. Relations between Britain and France had reached their nadir in the autumn of 1863. Palmerston and his colleagues were filled with anxiety about French designs on Holland, Belgium and the Rhineland. They had opposed French intervention in Italy; denounced the annexation of Nice and Savoy; left France in the lurch over Mexico; and had just rejected Napoleon's ambitious proposal for a European Congress to discuss the Polish question. Without doubt the break-down of the old Anglo-French entente greatly assisted Bismarck in his complex diplomatic game in the winter of 1863–4.

Thirdly, Russia. The tsar did not approve of the democratic tendencies at work in Denmark and considered the November constitution a violation of the promises of 1851–2. On the other hand, the maintenance of the Helstat was very much in Russian interests in view of the strategic importance of the Baltic. Most certainly the Helstat was preferable to a Scandinavian union which would leave a fairly strong power in control of the Sound. But fear of revolution in Europe and of Napoleon's restless policy – particularly his advocacy of an autonomous Poland – worried her much more. Beset by economic problems at home and continuing unrest in Poland, Russia had no wish to be involved in war over Schleswig-Holstein. The British ambassador, Lord Francis Napier, succinctly summarized her position: 'The interest of Russia on behalf of Denmark is sincere but is secondary. The interest of Russia in maintaining an alliance with Austria and Prussia on account of Poland is capital and predominant.'[38] That alliance was also essential for Russia in a global perspective. Since the Crimean War she had turned increasingly eastwards, becoming absorbed in the affairs of Turkestan and Afghanistan. She needed the support of the German powers to protect her flank in Europe while she pursued these new interests and was not willing to endanger that support for the sake of Denmark. Consequently British proposals for joint action on behalf of Denmark fell on deaf ears in St Petersburg, whereas proposals for a peaceful settlement were seized upon with alacrity.

In other words, the diplomatic configuration in the winter of 1863–4 was such that Prussia could risk war without fearing armed intervention from the major powers. This is not to deny Bismarck's skill in manoeuvring with dexterity from the autumn of 1863 to the summer of 1864, playing off one power against another to ensure that Prussia remained *tertius gaudens*. Handling Napoleon III was the most difficult task, for if the mercurial emperor formed an alliance with the tsar, Prussian attempts to gain the ascendancy in Germany would be seriously impeded. To avert this danger and at the same time to use France as a stick with which to beat Austria when the time came, he showed willingness to enter into an agreement with France. But to avoid giving offence to Britain, Austria and Russia – all of whom suspected Napoleon of planning war for the spring of 1864 – he carefully avoided binding commitments, especially, the *'entente franche et vigoureuse'* Napoleon was looking for after his disenchantment with Britain and Austria.

Between 20 April and 25 June 1864 the signatory powers of the London Treaty together with Count Friedrich von Beust, the representative of the Confederation, met in London to try to regulate the Schleswig-Holstein Question by international agreement. This was the last thing Bismarck wanted. Several factors conspired together to avert this danger. First, Bismarck managed to delay the opening session of the conference until Prussian troops had driven the Danes out of Schleswig after the storming of the Dybbøl fortifications on 18 April. Acting on the old well-tried maxim *'beati possidentes'* Bismarck calculated that the conference could not talk Prussia out of the duchies. Second, by staying in Berlin Bismarck enjoyed maximum room for manoeuvre, obliging the Prussian representative in London to await his instructions at every twist and turn of the road. Third, while outwardly professing interest in an agreed solution, Bismarck worked hard to ensure that the divergent interests of the powers sabotaged the conference.

Bismarck's task was greatly facilitated by the unfortunate tactics pursued by the Danes. Instead of accepting the British conference proposal in February – for only at the conference table could Denmark expect Great Power support – they procrastinated, hoping to hold on to Dybbøl. Their refusal was due in part to the pressure of public opinion which was oblivious to the plain fact that Denmark could not win on the field of battle. Inevitably military victory eluded them, so that when the time came to go to London their position was much weaker than it need have been. At the conference itself their failure was due not so much to intransigence in the pursuit of a clearly defined policy, as is often alleged, but rather to a combination of divided counsels and chronic inability to decide on a realistic policy. This was for several reasons. First,

King Christian, unlike his ministers, cherished the illusion that the Helstat could still be preserved. Secondly, Monrad lacked experience of foreign affairs; he presided over a cabinet of equally inexperienced nonentities; and he instructed the Danish delegation in London to pursue a negative policy. They were to fall back from one position to another and thereby forfeited the tactical advantage of having a clear goal from the start. To conciliate the king, the delegation was to support the lost cause of the Helstat in which the council of ministers did not believe. As it was extremely unlikely that a common constitution could be worked out for the Helstat at this late stage, the Danish delegates were authorized to agree to the separation of Holstein from Schleswig provided that Schleswig and Denmark could have a common constitution. Finally – but only when other powers raised it – they could support partition, the only realistic hope for Denmark. The third reason for failure was that Andreas Krieger, a convinced Eiderdane and the strongest personality in the three-man delegation, was not interested in reaching a settlement. He spent most of his time manipulating British public opinion in the expectation of either forcing Palmerston to promise military aid to Denmark or bringing to power the Tory opposition which he supposed (quite erroneously) would be ready to fight for Denmark.

Step by step Bismarck succeeded in demolishing the London Treaty and persuading the Great Powers to disengage themselves from German affairs. On 12 May Count Albrecht von Bernstorff with Austrian support announced that Prussia was no longer bound by the treaty. Five days later Bernstorff, again with Austrian approval, demanded political independence for the duchies united by their common institutions and with only the dynastic link holding them to Denmark; this, he argued, was the only way to protect them from 'the recurrence of any foreign oppression'. To confuse the issue – for Bismarck did not want the conference to settle for Personal Union – Bernstorff was told to add the rider that a decision on the succession question would be postponed for the time being. The Danish government, however, rejected Personal Union out of hand because if Schleswig had only a monarch in common with Denmark, this was tantamount to abandoning the Danish-speaking population to Germanization, a crass betrayal of the national cause and totally unacceptable to Eiderdanes.

Rejection of Personal Union opened up the way for Austria and Prussia to propose on 28 May the establishment of an independent Schleswig-Holstein under the duke of Augustenburg. This proposal, greeted with a mixture of astonishment and jubilation in liberal circles in Germany, originated with Rechberg. Suspecting rightly that Prussia was now bent on annexation, and conscious that Austrian public opinion was demanding a change of policy,

Rechberg opted for a daring solution which, if it succeeded, would restore Austrian prestige with the smaller German states at a stroke. Greatly annoyed but unable to dissuade the Austrians from raising the succession question, Bismarck went along with it for appearances' sake. But in private negotiations with the duke he made it plain that the duchies would become a Prussian satellite, a demand which the duke found unacceptable. Bismarck commented cynically that: 'At the London Conference he had [*verba ipsissima*] hitched the duke of Augustenburg as an ox before the plough to bring it ahead. As soon as the plough was in motion, he had again unhitched the ox.'[39] This solution died a natural death because of Danish opposition and Bernstorff's half-hearted support.

Proposals for the partition of Schleswig along national lines – first mooted in 1848 – made little progress. On 28 May Britain proposed the Schlei-Dannevirke line, which Denmark accepted. But Austria and Prussia, unwilling to allow the mixed districts of Central Schleswig to remain in Danish hands, proposed a line from Abenraa to Tønder. This was unacceptable to Denmark for not only did she regard the Schlei estuary as a military necessity but she still clung stubbornly to her belief that the inhabitants of Central Schleswig could be won back to their Danish cultural heritage given time.

Finally Britain proposed that the frontier line be decided by a neutral power and offered to aid the Danes if the Germans rejected an arbitration award. Austria and Prussia agreed, but only on condition that the award not be binding on them. But at the Statsraad on 20 June Monrad made a fatal mistake; lacking confidence in his own judgement, he left the decision to King Christian. Predictably the monarch turned down arbitration and opted for the maintenance of the Schlei-Dannevirke line at all costs. This was not because he wanted partition. On the contrary. He was buying time. A few days earlier he had been encouraged by the Danish ambassador in St Petersburg to believe that Personal Union was still a viable alternative if Denmark as well as the duchies entered the German Confederation. In fact, there was no basis for this belief. The Danish government now wanted to end the conference quickly before the House of Commons rose for the summer recess, hoping that its collapse would be seen as a defeat for Palmerston and Russell and would topple the government. The incoming Tory administration would surely come to the aid of Denmark. When she formally rejected arbitration on 22 June, thus effectively ending the conference, Denmark may have lost a golden opportunity of obtaining a frontier farther south than that of 1920. At the very least an award by a neutral power would have made it much more difficult for Bismarck to obtain the whole of Schleswig and would have shifted the onus for failure fairly and squarely on his shoulders. Three days later the armistice expired and the war was resumed. Things had worked out exceedingly well for Prussia. As Lord George Clarendon remarked to Bernstorff: '*Vous êtes entrés dans la conférence maîtres de la situation et vous en sortez maîtres de la conférence.*'[40]

THE WAR AND THE TREATY OF VIENNA

The Second Slesvig War commenced on 1 February 1864 and fighting finally ceased on 20 July. On 1 February 57,000 Prussian and Austrian troops commanded by Wrangel crossed the Eider. After an initial passage of arms at Missunde where the Danes stood their ground, the Danish commander evacuated the Dannevirke on the night of 5–6 February, withdrawing the bulk of his 44,000 men to the fortified positions at Dybbøl and to the island of Als. There were angry protests in Copenhagen because of the emotional connotations of the Dannevirke and the firm belief that it was an impregnable fortification. De Meza was recalled, disgraced and replaced by General Johann Gerlach. In fact, the Dannevirke defences were too weak to withstand a frontal onslaught, as de Meza was well aware, and could in any case be easily endangered by an enemy turning-movement across the Schlei. De Meza simply did not have large enough forces to cover a seventy-five kilometre front. The sad truth was that Denmark had taken up a position in 1863 which she lacked the military strength to sustain. Defence expenditure had been curtailed by the Rigsraad in the 1850s. And although the Danish fleet gave a good account of itself by blockading Prussian harbours and defeating the Austrian fleet at the battle of Heligoland on 9 May, the Danish army faced superior numbers and artillery equipped with rifled breech-loading cannon.

After the evacuation of the Dannevirke forces to Dybbøl and Als the remainder of the Danish army retired into Jylland. On 18 February a Prussian detachment crossed the Kongeaa and occupied the border town of Kolding. This unauthorized local initiative – which annoyed Bismarck – aroused the concern of some Great Powers. Britain considered dispatching a squadron of the fleet to Copenhagen, while the French suddenly grew alarmed at the forward thrust of Prussian policy.[41] As the Austrians had supposed that the occupation of Schleswig was the objective of the military operations, King William sent General Erwin von Manteuffel to Vienna to persuade them otherwise. On 6 March agreement was reached.

The conquest of Dybbøl and Als were confirmed as the main military objectives but the invasion of Jylland was now deemed necessary to protect the forces in Schleswig besieging Dybbøl. It was also agreed in the Austro-Prussian Convention that, as hostilities had broken out, they were no longer bound by the promises of 1851–2. At a peace conference they would propose the creation of a Schleswig-Holstein state bound only by dynastic ties to Denmark. The king was anxious that Prussian soldiers prove their mettle in action, while Bismarck wanted a spectacular victory to place Prussia in an unassailable position at the impending conference. The final attack on Dybbøl, the major operation of the war, began on 2 April with heavy bombardment of the fortifications by twenty-eight batteries of artillery – a proleptic hint of what modern war would be like. That was followed on 18 April by the successful storming of the fortifications by Austrian and Prussian soldiers after six hours of intense bombardment. The Danes, outnumbered six to one, fought bravely but were forced to capitulate. An armistice came into force for the duration of the London Conference.

On 26 June the war resumed. A contingent of 24,000 Prussian soldiers crossing the Sound by boat at dead of night took Als on 29 June. In July the Austrian and Prussian fleets, aided by expeditionary forces from the mainland, occupied the islands off the west coast of Schleswig-Holstein. Other forces had pushed as far ahead as Frederikshavn on the tip of the Danish peninsula. Bowing to the inevitable, King Christian asked Monrad to resign. He was replaced by a conservative, Count Bluhme, who the king hoped would be able to pull Personal Union out of the hat. This was an impossible dream, as was the government's hope that partition would still be on the cards. On 20 July a new armistice was signed and on 25 July the peace conference opened in Vienna. No concessions were forthcoming and the preliminary peace was signed on 1 August. Finally on 30 October in the Treaty of Vienna, the king of Denmark handed over to the king of Prussia and the emperor of Austria Holstein, Schleswig and Lauenburg and agreed to 'recognize the dispositions they made' for these territories.

NOTES AND REFERENCES

1.   German landowners and officials, the backbone of the Schleswig-Holstein movement, dominated the Schleswig as well as the Holstein

and Lauenburg estates through the introduction of a highly restricted franchise favouring the better off in town and country.

2. Under the Danish constitution the Rigsdag had decision-making powers. The Danes maintained that the estates in the duchies were intended to have only consultative powers in respect of constitutional changes – a dubious claim which the Germans strenuously denied. It was clearly a political blunder of the first order not to have submitted the common constitution to the German estates, if only as a face-saving exercise. Cf. Lawrence D. Steefel, *The Schleswig-Holstein Question* (Cambridge, Mass., 1932), p. 17; N. Neergaard, *Under Junigrundloven. En Fremstilling af de danske Folks Politiske Historie fra 1848 til 1866* (Copenhagen, 1916), pp. 105–6.

3. The term 'Federal Diet' is somewhat inaccurate. An *engerer Rat* conducted the day-to-day business of the Confederation, reaching decisions by majority vote as opposed to the unanimity vote at plenary sessions. There were seventeen votes in the *engerer Rat*: Austria, Prussia, Bavaria, Saxony, Hanover, Württemberg, Baden, Electoral Hesse, Hesse-Darmstadt, Holstein/Lauenburg (Curia 10) and Luxemburg/Limburg (Curia 11) had one each; the five Saxon principalities (Curia 12) had one vote; Braunschweig and Nassau (Curia 13) one; the two Mecklenburgs (Curia 14) one; Oldenburg, the Anhalt and the Schwarzenburg territories (Curia 15) one; the Reuss territories one; the Lippe territories, Liechtenstein, Waldeck and Hesse-Homburg one; and Bremen, Hamburg, Lübeck and Frankfurt one.

4. *APP* 1 no. 2, address of the Prince Regent to the Staatsministerium.

5. Not until the Bismarckian Reich was on the point of collapse in 1917 did expansion to the east – a revival of the old *Drang nach Osten* – appear as a serious theme in German history.

6. *GW* 14 no. 724, Bismarck to Gustav von Alvensleben, 23 April/5 May 1859.

7. *GW* 14/1 no. 480, Bismarck to Leopold von Gerlach 19/20 December 1853.

8. *GW* 2 no. 152, Bismarck to Otto von Manteuffel, 26 April 1856.

9. *GW* 1 no. 416, *Denkschrift* for the Prince of Prussia, September 1853.

10. Quoted in O. Pflanze, *Bismarck and the Development of Germany* (Princeton, 1963), p. 79.

11. *GW* 14 no. 789, Bismarck to Leopold von Gerlach, 2/4 May 1860.

12. *GW* 14/2 no. 999, Bismarck to Robert von der Goltz, 24 December 1863.

13. *APP* no. 86, Promemoria by Bismarck, 25 December 1862.

14. *GW* 2 no. 343, *Einige Bemerkungen über Preussens Stellung im Bunde*, March 1858.

15. *GW* 3 no. 234, *Denkschrift über die deutsche Frage*, mid-July 1861.

16. *GW* 10 no. 94, session of the budget commission.

17. Cf. Carl Twesten's comment in 1862: 'If some time or other a Prussian minister–president should come forward and say: I have moved frontier posts, violated international law and torn up treaties as Count Cavour has done – gentlemen, I believe we would not then

condemn him . . . we would erect a monument to him as Italian history will raise one to Cavour.' Quoted in Michel Gugel, *Industrieller Aufstieg und bürgerliche Herrschaft: Sozioökonomische Interessen und politische Ziele des liberalen Bürgertums in Preussen zur Zeit des Verfassungskonflikts 1857–1867* (Köln, 1975), p. 69.

18. Karl Martin Schiller, *Treitschke: Aufsätze Reden und Briefe* (Meersburg, 1929), vol. 5, p. 530; Treitschke to W. Nokk, 29 September 1863.

19. Charles VII, a Wittelsbach who was emperor from 1740 to 1745.

20. Hermann Oncken, *Rudolf von Bennigsen, Ein deutscher liberaler Politiker nach seinen Briefen und hinterlassenen Papieren* (Stuttgart, 1910), vol. 1, p. 621.

21. *GW* 14/2 no. 999, Bismarck to Robert von Goltz, 24 December 1863.

22. A year before his letter to Goltz Bismarck was brutally frank about his policy: 'I am certain of this, that the whole Danish business can be settled for us only by war. The occasion for such a war can be found at any moment that we find favourable for waging it . . . the disadvantage of having signed the London Protocol we share with Austria and cannot free ourselves from the consequences of that signature without war. If war comes, however, the future territorial status of Denmark will depend upon its results.' *GW* 4 no. 17, Bismarck to Count von Fleming, 22 December 1862.

23. That he was thinking along these lines at the close of 1863 is suggested by remarks made to relatives on New Year's Eve: 'The Always United [a reference to the popular slogan in use by the Schleswig-Holsteiner to describe the close association between the two duchies] must now become Prussians. That is the goal I am steering towards; whether I achieve it is in God's hands. But I could not accept responsibility for allowing Prussian blood to be spilt to create a new middle state which would vote with the others in the Diet against us.' Klaus Malettke, *Die Schleswig-Holsteinische Frage 1862–1866* (Göttingen, 1969), no. 10.

24. E.g. P. von Linstow, 'Bismarck Europa og Slesvig-Holsten 1862–1866', HT (78) 1978, pp. 389–435. Also A. Hillgruber, *Bismarcks Aussenpolitik* (Freiburg, 1972), pp. 56–7.

25. *GW* 14/2 no. 999.

26. *GW* 1 no. 473, Bismarck to Baron von Manteuffel, 15 February 1854.

27. The link was contained in article 3 of the London Treaty which referred specifically to 'the rights and obligations of the duchies established by the federal act of 1815 and by the existing federal law [which] shall not be altered by this treaty'.

28. The British ambassador in Berlin thought Bismarck was genuinely anxious to activate federal execution to 'prevent revolutionary movements in Germany'. *APP* no. 213, Buchanan to Russell, 12 December 1863.

29. Under the federal constitution the Diet had the right to decide a disputed succession in member states, i.e. in Holstein but not in Schleswig.

30. D.G. Monrad, *Deltagelse i Begivenhederne 1864: En Efterladt Redegørelse* (Copenhagen, 1914), p. 49.

31. The news of a change of ministry alarmed Berlin. 'Goodbye to the fine hopes of getting rid of the treaty,' exclaimed King William, while Bismarck was highly embarrassed by the possibility of Denmark returning to the path of legality. *APP* 4 no. 252, Nicolay to Oubril, 25 December 1863. Some days earlier Bismarck had admitted frankly that the promises of 1851–2 were 'not very practical to implement and that we are almost demanding that the cabinet in Copenhagen square the circle'. Talleyrand to Drouyn de Lhuys, 11 December 1863; Quoted in Lawrence D. Steefel, op. cit., p. 139.

32. *OD* 1 no. 152, Talleyrand to Drouyn de Lhuys.

33. Klaus Malettke, op. cit. no. 13.

34. *APP* 4 no. 151, Bismarck to Sydow, 29 November 1863.

35. *Parliamentary Debates*, 3rd series, CLXXII, p. 1252.

36. Quoted in Johannes H. Voigt, 'Englands Aussenpolitik während des deutsch-dänischen Konflikts 1862–1864', *ZGSHG* 90 (1965), p. 91; cf. *APP* 4 no. 381, Oubril to Gortschakov, 19/31 January 1864.

37. Bismarck visiting London in 1862 commented to his wife that ' . . . English ministers know less about Prussia than about Japan and Mongolia . . . .'. *GW* 14/2 no. 599, 5 July 1862.

38. Quoted in W.E. Mosse, *The European Powers and the German Question 1848–71* (CUP, 1958), p. 195 FN 1.

39. Quoted in Lawrence D. Steefel, op. cit. p. 256.

40. *APP* 4 no. 179. Writing to the queen on 22 June Clarendon went much further: 'M. de Bismarck is completely master of the situation – he does exactly what he pleases with the whole of Germany . . . in the pursuit of his own ends he is restrained by no principle and if no check is to be put on his bold bad policy there is nothing to prevent him dictating at Copenhagen a peace that might annihilate the political independence of Denmark.' Quoted in Johannes H. Voigt, op. cit., p. 497 FN 152.

41. Drouyn de Lhuys commented sharply to Goltz on 21 February; 'First we had seized Holstein on the pretext of Federal Execution, then although this security should have been enough for Schleswig too, we had occupied the duchy as a "material guarantee"; we had declared, though in not very clear terms, that we only wanted to enforce the stipulations of 1851–52; now we advance into Jutland and are going on to "exterminate" the Danes; for what else can we intend in ruining Denmark financially, taking one province after another from them, and finally getting on to Copenhagen?' Quoted in Lawrence D. Steefel, op. cit., pp. 189–90.

Chapter 3

THE WAR OF 1866

THE RIVALRY BETWEEN AUSTRIA AND PRUSSIA, 1848–59

Historical perceptions of the significance of the Austro-Prussian conflict of 1866 have changed quite dramatically during the last fifty years. National Liberal historians writing in the last quarter of the nineteenth century enthused about the *annus mirabilis* of 1866, the year in which Germany took the first major step on the road to national unification which was completed four years later with the defeat of France and the proclamation of the German Reich in the Hall of Mirrors at Versailles. In Johann Droysen's words: 'The war of 1866 has made it finally possible for us to launch a truly national German policy. The German nation which has been politically dead since the fall of the Hohenstaufens has now the opportunity of making its national greatness politically effective.'[1] Little German historians saw in the destruction of the Confederation and in the expulsion from Germany of 'unGerman' Austria, the 'friend of reaction' and a power indifferent to the cause of unification, part of an inevitable and divinely inspired historical process to advance the cause of nationalism and Protestantism.

A century later, after two world wars for which the Reich of Bismarck, William II and Hitler bore a large share of responsibility and which radically changed the map of Europe, the confident assertions of Droysen and Treitschke have a hollow ring to them. The war of 1866 was not just a clash of arms between two sovereign states but a civil war in which Germans fought Germans. And the outcome of the war was the exclusion of German Austria from the rest of Germany. 'You think you have given birth to a Reich,' exclaimed the Austrian poet Franz Grillparzer, 'but all you have done is destroy a people.' The separation was permanent apart from the unhappy interlude between 1938 and 1945. Furthermore, whatever the defects, many Germans regretted the passing of an institution which had preserved peace for fifty years. A contemporary described it as 'the last statesmanlike concept of European diplomacy . . . not only did Germany live at peace with its neighbours; it acted as a brake on any other European state which desired to breach the peace of the world. The only error but an unavoidable one in its organization was that it assumed all the members possessed moral stature . . . . Prussia had made it clear for a long time that she would not bow to majority decisions. On the day she said that openly the Confederation was smothered to death.'[2] Other distinguished contemporaries were filled with foreboding from the start. The liberal publicist Georg Gervinus declared that the destruction of the Confederation 'had transformed two-thirds of Germany into a warlike state capable of aggression at all times and which one suspects is a permanent threat to the peace of this part of the world and to the security of its neighbours . . . a permanently warlike power of such fearful superiority has arisen the like of which was never known even remotely during the last few centuries among militaristic states bent on conquest and expansion'.[3] Seventy-four years later Bismarck's creation went down to total defeat at the end of the Second World War. As a result of post-war developments three sovereign states came into existence: the Federal Republic of Germany, the German Democratic Republic and the Republic of Austria. True, the tumultuous events in the Democratic Republic in the winter of 1989–90 have completely transformed the situation. The re-unification of the first two states is now a virtual certainty, difficult though the process of reintegrating divergent social systems and economies at different stages of development is bound to be. Nevertheless, the emergence of three separate German states where there had been only one between 1815 and 1866 and only two from 1871 to 1938 when Austria was annexed by Hitler led in recent years to the emergence of a revisionist school in Austria and in the United States. These historians are sharply critical of the one-sided treatment of the German Confederation and of the strong pro-Prussian bias encountered in the works of the Little German historians.[4] Revisionist writing is contributing towards a more objective evaluation of the rivalry between the two German powers as well as to a more sympathetic treatment of the Third Germany, the name given to a grouping of German states which attempted in the early 1860s to contain nationalism within a reformed Confederation capable of resisting the pressure exerted on them by Austria and Prussia.

The rivalry between Austria and Prussia which ended in war in 1866 had long antecedents. Ever since Frederick the Great had seized Silesia in 1740 and fought two wars with Empress Maria Theresa to hold on to the province, a degree of tension had coloured the relationship between the parvenu and the established power. Signs of tension persisted in the pre-March period when the Prussian king and the Austrian emperor shared a common interest in preventing the spread of liberal and national sentiments. In the 1860s when national liberalism became a significant force, the power struggle between Austria and Prussia assumed a new ideological dimension. Austria, shaken by the war of 1859 and conscious of the increasing demand inside her own empire for political change, attempted to reform the Confederation as a means of maintaining her power in Germany, while Prussia tried to exploit the national liberal movement to further her Great Prussian ambitions. Thus political, ideological and also economic factors combined in the middle of the nineteenth century to confer a new intensity on the old rivalry between the two major German powers.

To understand the political factors involved in the origins of the war of 1866 we must go back eighteen years to the 1848–9 Revolution. That upheaval placed the future of Central Europe and relations between Austria and Prussia squarely in the forefront of the political arena. One of the primary objectives of the Frankfurt Parliament was the creation of a strong German Reich. But to determine the frontiers of the new state proved to be an immensely complex problem because ethnic, cultural and political frontiers have never coincided in Central Europe. Both major German powers – on whose material support the Parliament was dependent – ruled over large numbers of non-Germans. Prussia had acquired large numbers of Polish subjects in the eighteenth-century partitions. In 1816 possibly 1,500,000 of the 2,200,000 subjects in the territories outside the Confederation (i.e. West and East Prussia and Posen) were Polish-speaking. Similarly the Habsburgs ruled over a huge non-German empire; of the eleven million subjects of Emperor Francis I in the territories included in the Confederation in 1840, 5,300,000 were German and 5,700,000 non-German (Czechs, Slovaks, Slovenes and Italians).

Had frontiers been determined by counting heads, Austria and Prussia would have been drastically reduced in size and influence. In fact, the liberals of 1848 applied quite different yardsticks: past history and the language of state spoken by officials and pastors were the prime determinants of frontiers. Historically the German Confederation was the heir of the Holy Roman Empire of the German Nation, a venerable institution which had existed for almost nine centuries before its abrupt dissolution in 1806. Liberals automatically assumed that Bohemia and Moravia and the Austrian archduchy would be an integral part of the new Reich. This was confirmed, as they saw it, by the language criterion; if the language spoken by the educated classes – officials, pastors and teachers – was German, then the territory was part of the German

Reich. By the same criterion and also by virtue of historic ties with Holstein, Schleswig, never part of the Holy Roman Empire or of the Confederation, could be regarded as part of the Reich. The fact that Czech and Danish were spoken in Bohemia and Schleswig respectively by a majority of the inhabitants was a secondary consideration. These languages were looked down upon as little more than dialects and certainly culturally inferior to High German. And once the Frankfurt liberals had overcome their initial enthusiasm for Polish independence Polish, too, came into this category; as the superstructure of Prussian Posen was German, that must determine its national character and justified its inclusion in the German Reich.

The future of the Austrian empire was a make-or-break issue for the Frankfurt liberals. Nothing would be more misleading than to suppose that they divided neatly into two camps from the very beginning: Greater Germans who insisted on retaining the frontiers of the old Confederation (i.e. including Austria and Bohemia but excluding the rest of the Habsburg dominions) and Little Germans who were prepared to abandon Austria and Bohemia in order to create a united Reich under Prussian leadership, having no further ties with the Habsburgs. There was, in fact, widespread sympathy for Austria at Frankfurt, admiration for her traditions and a strong desire to maintain the closest links with the Habsburgs. Austrian delegates were listened to with respect when they advocated the inclusion of the whole of the Habsburg dominions in the new Reich, partly for geopolitical reasons – to strengthen Central Europe against the French and Russians – and partly for commercial reasons – to guarantee the markets of the Danubian basin for German merchants. Most members of the Parliament, conscious of the complexity of the problem and loath to disturb the time-honoured status quo, postponed a decision as long as humanly possible. When they finally turned their attention to it in October 1848 the tide was turning against revolution in both Berlin and Vienna and soon the authority of the Parliament itself was to be called into question.

The proposals made by the constitutional committee of the Parliament represented a victory for Greater Germanism. Article 1 of the constitution declared that the Reich consisted of the territories of the old Confederation; article 2 that if a German territory had the same ruler as a non-German territory the former must have a separate constitution, government and administration; and article 3 that where German and non-German territories had the same ruler he must either reside in the German territory or establish a regency in that territory to which only Germans would be eligible for appointment – in other words, only dynastic ties would be permissible between German and non-German territories.[5] With the benefit of hindsight it is obvious that the committee acted unwisely in advancing such proposals without recognizing the necessity for negotiation with the interested party Austria. One must remember, of course, the disturbed situation in Vienna and the fact that even in October 1848 many Frankfurt deputies supposed with incredible naïveté that nationalism would triumph all over Europe and that the Austrian empire could not survive in its present form. But on 26 October, the day before the Parliament adopted the proposals by overwhelming majorities, Prince Alfred Windischgrätz had launched an attack on Vienna which forced the city to capitulate on 31 October and led to the restoration of imperial rule in the western half of the Habsburg dominions.

It was soon made crystal clear that Austria was not prepared to dismantle her empire to please the Frankfurt liberals. On 27 October when Prince Felix von Schwarzenberg, appointed chief minister a week earlier, addressed the Kremsier Constituent Assembly (a body moved from Vienna to an obscure Moravian town where it was allowed to work out a theoretically perfect solution of the nationality problems of the empire which the imperial authorities had not the slightest intention of implementing), he left no doubt that dismemberment of the empire was a complete non-starter. On the contrary; in the so-called 'Kremsier programme' Schwarzenberg declared that the bonds between the constituent parts of the empire would be strengthened – this was Schwarzenberg's riposte to Greater Germanism. Secondly, Austria intended to remain in the German Confederation – a warning shot across the bows of the Little Germans who were now growing in support once it was clear that Greater Germanism was not on offer.

Whilst the Frankfurt liberals talked in grandiose terms about the future shape of Germany, assuming that Austria and Prussia would fall in with their wishes, in the corridors of power in Vienna and Berlin dualism was still the preferred solution of the German problem. Prince Schwarzenberg is often depicted as the reactionary executant of a hard-line policy designed to humiliate Prussia and compel her to submit to Austrian plans for the domination of Germany. True, he was a cynical political operator, ruthless in his choice of means and capable of using any stick with which to beat the Prussians and force them into line. Nevertheless, at bottom he was absolutely convinced that close cooperation with Prussia had to be the sheet-anchor of Austrian policy. This basically for two reasons. Firstly, because Vienna regarded Prussia as a stout bulwark against revolution which Schwarzenberg, like all conservatives, thought threatened thrones everywhere in Europe. Secondly, cooperation with Prussia was part of Austria's overall strategy as a European Great Power. She was prepared to accord some measure of recognition to Prussian ascendancy in North Germany on condition that Prussia recognized Austria's pre-eminence at Frankfurt. If Austria was to maintain her position in Italy and in the Balkans, she could not afford to abandon her position in Germany and the influence this gave her with the smaller states there. The European role Austria was convinced she had to play is crucial to an understanding of her – apparently – obstinate refusal to be forced out of Germany by Prussia.

Similarly the king of Prussia was predisposed to be on good terms with Austria. This was due only in part to his abhorrence of revolution. Incurably romantic in some ways, he clung all his life to his adolescent dream of a strong Christian–German Reich ruled over by the time-honoured house of Habsburg with the Prussian monarch as a second-in-command in charge of the federal army. Yet at the same time he was also a member of the house of Hohenzollern and was attracted by the prospect of enhancing the status of Prussia. At first he thought it perfectly feasible to achieve both ambitions. When Prussia took the initiative on 23 January 1849 and invited the German states to discuss the creation of a federal state (*engerer Bund*) with the Prussian monarch as the hereditary head, this was to be supplemented by a looser association with the Austrian dominions (*weiterer Bund*). Beyond that King Frederick William dreamed of an imperial alliance between the Little German Reich and the whole of the Habsburg dominions (*Grosser Reichsbund*). This formula, which originated with Heinrich von Gagern, a president of the Frankfurt Parliament, had much to commend it; unlike the more doctrinaire Little German and Greater German solutions it was sufficiently flexible to permit that fuller association with the Habsburg empire which most Germans wanted.

Six weeks later on 4 March 1849 Emperor Francis Joseph dissolved the Kremsier Assembly and proclaimed a unitary constitution for the Austrian empire. Shaken by the Magyar, Czech and Italian revolts, the Habsburgs were reverting to neo-absolutism, i.e. planning to run the empire from Vienna with the help of Austrian–German bureaucrats as Joseph II had done in the late eighteenth century. This had a decisive effect on German affairs as well as on Austrian. As the eastern half of the empire would now be subjected to the same regime as the western, Schwarzenberg proposed for the sake of preserving the unitary state that the former be included in a revived German Confederation. This would bring into being a Reich of seventy million people, stretching from the Balkans to the Baltic and run by Austro-German bureaucrats, which would in time have dominated Europe and made Germany a superpower without equal. It was to be run by a directory presided over by Austria in which Austria and Prussia would have two votes, Bavaria one and the other states four between them. This executive body was to be supplemented by an assembly of seventy deputies drawn from local Landtage on the basis of one deputy for every million inhabitants. In effect Austria would have thirty-eight deputies and the rest of Germany thirty-two. As a gesture to conciliate Prussia, the office of *Reichstatthalter* was to be held alternately by the emperor and the king of Prussia.

Faced with a stark choice between multi-national Middle Europe and nationalist Little Germany, the Frankfurt liberals opted, reluctantly, for the latter. Reluctantly, because there was little desire among the members to sever the Austrian connection nor any great wish to have a Hohenzollern ruling over them. Little Germany was an interim solution to be superseded one day by that *weiterer Bund* with Austria which most Germans wanted. Only by 267 votes to 263 (with eight abstentions) did the Parliament agree on 27 March 1849 to establish a hereditary emperorship for the new Reich – and that only after much horsetrading in which the support of the left was secured only when the moderates accepted much more democratic constitutional arrangements. The next day the king of Prussia – the only candidate – obtained 290 votes with 248 abstentions and twenty-nine absentees. When the king declined the 'crown of dirt and mud' offered him on 3 April by a deputation from Frankfurt he dealt a body blow to the Parliament from which it never recovered. What the deputation overlooked was the way the king hedged his 'refusal' with qualifications. As many of the diplomats from the middle states realized, the king really wanted the crown provided that two conditions were fulfilled: that he had the approval of the German princes and that the Frankfurt constitution – which was too radical for his tastes – was drastically amended. Despite Frederick William's high-flown rhetoric about the sanctity of monarchy, the realistic streak in his make-up – which his ministers encouraged – told him not to neglect a golden opportunity of advancing Prussian interests.

Immediately after his 'refusal' the king tried to persuade the Frankfurt Parliament to modify the constitution. Confident that the small states would respect his wishes, he declared himself ready to assume on a provisional basis overall direction of German affairs. However, the Parliament was not keen enough on a Hohenzollern emperor to do his bidding. Twenty-eight states, led by Baden, declared their support for the unamended constitution. Frederick William, with ministerial encouragement, changed his tactics. His minister–president, Count Friedrich Wilhelm von Brandenburg, denounced the Frankfurt constitution and on 25 April the king appointed General Joseph von Radowitz, a Catholic nobleman of Magyar–Westphalian extraction, minister – president. The emphasis shifted from the Frankfurt Parliament to the German princes. On 28 April Radowitz invited them to Berlin to discuss a new constitution for Little Germany. This turned out to be a drastically amended version of the Frankfurt one; the king's absolute veto on legislation was re-introduced; and a college of princes would now share power with a Reichstag elected not by universal male suffrage but on the restricted franchise of the three-class system introduced into Prussia in December 1848.

The military situation favoured Prussia. At the end of April revolution broke out again in Württemberg, Saxony, Baden and the Palatinate as well as in Silesia and Westphalia. Radowitz promptly sent in Prussian soldiers who restored order in South-West Germany in the course of the summer. Initially the small states had declined to attend the Berlin conference. Frightened by these revolutionary outbursts and feeling that discretion was the better part of valour, they changed their minds and accepted the Radowitz constitution. By the end of the summer only Bavaria stood aloof from the general trend. The Austrians, who had accepted the invitation to Berlin but had thought better of it the next day, could do no more than protest in view of their own mounting internal problems. For although their position in Northern Italy improved after the defeat of the Piedmontese at the battle of Novara in March 1849, on 14 April – the day Brandenburg denounced the Frankfurt constitution – Louis Kossuth declared Hungary an independent state. Not until mid August did the Habsburgs succeed in subduing Hungary and then only with the help of the tsar's soldiers who poured over the Carpathians to encompass the defeat of Kossuth's forces.

Revisionist historians have argued that some of the middle states such as Hanover, Saxony, Württemberg and Baden took a positive interest in the Erfurt Union (as this association of states became known in 1850). This because they were genuinely interested in working out a solution of the German problem which avoided what they regarded as the centralizing and democratic tendencies of the Frankfurt Parliament while at the same time safeguarding states' rights against the attempts of Prussia to dominate the new Reich.[6] If that is so, then the Interim of September 1849 came as a great disappointment to them. Prussia was perfectly willing to negotiate with Austria provided she conceded Prussian primacy in North and Central Germany. Schwarzenberg, freed of domestic worries and anxious to hold Prussia in check, approached Bernstorff, the Prussian minister in Vienna. The latter, erroneously believing that this vital concession had been made, agreed to the Interim: a commission of four (two Prussians and two Austrians) would meet under the presidency of an Austrian to exercise the central power in Germany which Archduke Johann, head of the Frankfurt Central Government, was to hand over to them. The agreement which was to last until May 1850 had as its express purpose the maintenance of the Confederation. And for the interim period the German princes were to draft yet another constitution. The Interim – by

which Radowitz in his eagerness for agreement with Austria hope-
lessly compromised his own position – did, of course, encourage
Schwarzenberg to believe that Prussia wanted to re-establish the old
dualism which had served Austria so well before 1848.

Relations between Austria and Prussia did, in fact, deteriorate in
the summer of 1850. This because Radowitz went ahead with the
holding of elections to the Erfurt Union parliament. When this
body, which was packed with men of moderate persuasions, met at
Erfurt in April 1850 it quickly approved the Union constitution.
But as Radowitz closed the parliament without making it clear
when Prussia intended to set up the machinery of government provided for in the constitution, Schwarzenberg seized the initiative.
He announced that, as it had not been possible to extend the life of
the Interim, this would end on 1 May. Austria had no alternative
but to reactivate the old Confederation. All states were invited to
send representatives to Frankfurt on 10 May for the first session of
the reconvened Federal Diet which would have on its agenda
reform of the Confederation.

Support had been ebbing away from the Erfurt Union for some
months. In February Saxony, Hanover and Württemberg deserted it,
formed the Four Kings' Alliance with Bavaria, drafted their own
constitution and pledged support for the seventy-million Reich.
After Schwarzenberg's declaration another eight states led by Baden
left the Union. Nevertheless, for some months it looked as if
Prussia intended to fight to preserve her creation. The frontier gar-
risons in Saxony and Silesia were strengthened; in May General
Edwin von Manteuffel was dispatched to Warsaw to ascertain what
support Prussia could expect from the tsar in the event of war; in
July Prussia signed the Treaty of Berlin freeing her from the
Slesvig war; and in September the king appointed Radowitz foreign
minister, an act which infuriated the Russians who detested him.

Two issues precipitated the final crisis: the affairs of Holstein
and Electoral Hesse. In respect of the former the king of Denmark,
encouraged by Schwarzenberg, requested the restored Diet – which
Prussia refused to recognize – to order federal execution to restore
his authority in the duchy. That proposal was resisted by Prussia,
not out of love for the Schleswig-Holsteiner but out of an inability
to retire gracefully from the affair. Electoral Hesse was a much
more serious matter. The tiresome elector and his maladroit chief
minister, Hans Hassenpflug, dissolved the Landtag when it refused
to vote taxes. In retaliation many middle-class people refused to
pay taxes. In September the elector requested the Diet to use military force to restore law and order in his dominions. The electorate
occupied a vital strategic position commanding three roads between
Berlin and Cologne. Prussia had by treaty the right to use them
and was not prepared to see federal troops enter the electorate.

Early in October the Erfurt Union agreed to support Prussia in the event of war. On 11 October Austria concluded a war alliance with Bavaria and Württemberg. It was agreed that Bavarian troops occupy the electorate; if Prussia resisted, Austria would field 150,000 men, Bavaria 50,000 and Württemberg 20,000. The crisis deepened on 16 October when the Diet agreed to send military assistance to the elector.

As the prospect of war loomed large, Frederick William's resolve weakened. The sober truth was that Prussia's unreformed army would have been no match for the Austrians, as the policy-makers in Berlin realized. On 17 October Brandenburg was dispatched to Warsaw to establish precisely what the tsar intended to do in the event of war. While Nicholas made it clear that he had no wish to intervene in the quarrel between the two German powers and did not intend to force Prussia to abandon the Erfurt Union, he did regard it as Prussia's duty to disarm the rebellious Holsteiner and allow the Diet to subdue Electoral Hesse. If Prussia resisted the Diet's attempts to pacify Holstein, this he would regard as a *casus belli*. When Francis Joseph and Schwarzenberg arrived in Warsaw a few days later, Brandenburg reached agreement with them on 28 October. Austria withdrew her demand that Prussia recognize the Diet. In return Prussia agreed to postpone implementation of the Union constitution. And it was agreed that the future of Germany be discussed by all the German states. Frederick William was perfectly happy to accept these terms; for he was simply not prepared to fight conservative Austria, a bulwark against 'red revolution', for the sake of the Erfurt Union. Indeed if the Union was to be supplemented by agreements with Austria, war was a nonsense. Secretly he assured Francis Joseph that he wished to act jointly with Austria over the affairs of Electoral Hesse and that the Prussian troops – who entered the electorate on 2 November – would occupy only the roads and surrounding territory. In vain did Radowitz fight in the council of ministers for general mobilization. On 2 November he tendered his resignation.

There was a last flurry of activity on the Prussian side on 5 November when the king after all suddenly ordered mobilization because of Russian troop movements towards the Prussian frontier and the entry of federal troops into Electoral Hesse. This was not intended to be a prelude to war, which Prussia knew she could not win, but a response to pressure from extreme conservatives who wanted Prussia to rattle the sabre as a matter of honour. Reported Austrian troop movements added urgency to the situation. So for the first time since the eighteenth century, war between Austria and Prussia seemed – on the surface at any rate – a distinct possibility. On 8 November when the federal army (Bavarian troops supported by a battalion of Austrian chasseurs) approached Bronzell near

Fulda, the Prussian outposts opened fire. Six Austrians were wounded and a Prussian horse killed. Neither commander wanted war and the soldiers quickly disengaged before the skirmish escalated. Still, the crisis continued because the presence of Prussian forces in Electoral Hesse held up the progress of the federal army. Furthermore Brunswick, a state through which it would have to pass en route for Holstein, suddenly declared that she would fight if invaded. Prussia immediately declared support for Brunswick. On 21 November Frederick William delivered a bellicose speech which so infuriated the tsar that he reactivated military measures temporarily suspended a few days earlier after receiving a conciliatory response from Prussia. Schwarzenberg determined to force the issue. On 25 November he demanded that Prussia notify Austria within forty-eight hours of her willingness to allow federal forces to pass through the electorate. Frederick William, failing to obtain British support against Russia, decided to settle the quarrel at once on the basis of the agreement of 28 October. On 28 November Baron Otto von Manteuffel, now minister–president since the sudden death of Brandenburg, hurried off to meet Schwarzenberg in the hotel Zur Krone in Olmütz. Next day they signed the celebrated Olmütz Punctation. On 1 December Frederick William accepted the terms and the crisis ended.

Little German historians condemned the Olmütz Punctation as a total and unmitigated humiliation for Prussia. She had to agree to help Austria restore law and order in Holstein and Electoral Hesse. She allowed federal forces in Hesse the use of the vital military roads. And she agreed to join with Austria in demanding that the Schleswig-Holsteiner cease all hostilities, withdraw all troops north of the Eider and reduce their army by one-third. On the other hand, the fundamental issue underlying the clash between Austria and Prussia – the future of Germany – remained unresolved and was to be turned over to a conference of all the German states meeting at Dresden. And by coming to terms with Prussia without reference to the Federal Diet, Austria had contrived to offend many states who felt betrayed by her summit diplomacy and cavalier disregard of them.

In fact the confrontation between the major German powers really ended in a draw. Much depends upon the interpretation one places on Schwarzenberg's policy. Historians have too readily assumed that he was deeply committed to the seventy-million Reich; that this break with past policy heralded a more aggressive Austrian stance; and that this in turn justified Prussia's stand over the Erfurt Union. Hence Schwarzenberg's failure to persuade the Dresden Conference to opt for Middle Europe dealt a serious blow to Austrian policy. More recently it has been pointed out that Schwarzenberg, like Buol and Rechberg after him, were all disciples of Metternich. They all kept in touch with the master and, far from pursuing a more aggressive policy after 1848, simply continued his policy of cooperation with Prussia to keep the forces of revolution at bay. Although Schwarzenberg had admittedly made up his policy as he went along with cynical disregard for consistency, seizing – foolishly – on Bruck's scheme as a weapon against Prussia, at the end of the day he believed in Austro-Prussian dualism as much as Metternich had done.[7] Certainly there is little hard evidence that Schwarzenberg – a pragmatist, not a dogmatist, by inclination – considered the seventy-million Reich a make-or-break issue.[8] If this is the correct interpretation, then Olmütz was a reassuring sign that Prussia preferred negotiation to war and was ready to restore the dualistic relationship.

Here, perhaps, one perceives the basic weakness in Austrian policy between 1848 and 1866. It was not that Austrian statesmen lacked ability or did not suspect Prussia of aggressive designs, as has been sometimes suggested. The real malaise in Vienna was a propensity to believe, despite ominous signs to the contrary, that Prussia would agree in the final resort that dualism was the only salvation for conservative monarchy. The Austrians avoided facing up to the simple fact that the ruling élite in Prussia, while as determined as the Austrians to fight liberalism all the way, did not have a vested interest in the status quo. And, in an age when *Realpolitik* was superseding the old anti-revolutionary solidarity of the Great Powers, Prussia might well be tempted to use force to overturn the established order of things, confident that she could still keep the revolutionary wolf from the door. The Austrian tragedy was that any alternative policy – even if Francis Joseph had agreed to it – would have been fraught with greater perils.

At the Dresden Conference held between December 1850 and May 1851 Schwarzenberg quickly discovered that while the middle states were prepared to preserve the association with Austria, they had no wish to escape from Prussia's Erfurt Union only to be swallowed up in Middle Europe, to which Schwarzenberg was still nominally committed. Furthermore, the Great Powers were hostile to Middle Europe. Britain and France, both of whom regarded changes in the German balance of power as matters which concerned them directly as signatories of the Vienna settlement of 1815, did not care for Middle Europe. The decisive factor was Russia. From being a sympathetic supporter of this solution she changed in April 1851 to an oppositional stance, largely because France was making acceptance of it dependent upon compensation elsewhere. If the Erfurt Union had to be abandoned at Dresden, so did Middle Europe. This left a restoration of the Confederation as the only alternative. Here, too, Schwarzenberg suffered a reverse. To enable the Diet to act promptly in the event of fresh revolutionary outbursts, he wanted to strengthen the executive. To this end he proposed to replace the *engerer Rat* with a streamlined directory of seven states: Austria and Prussia with two votes each, Saxony, Hanover, Württemberg and Bavaria with one each and the two Hessian states with one between them. But Prussia, bent on parity of esteem at all costs, opposed the scheme for she shrewdly surmised that the smaller states would vote more often with Austria than with Prussia. A Prussian proposal that the presidency of the Diet alternate between the two powers was equally unacceptable to Austria. Thus the Confederation was restored in 1851 in its old unreformed state, much to Schwarzenberg's disappointment.

There were consolation prizes for Austria. Prussia cooperated fully with Austria in implementing the Olmütz Punctation in respect of Holstein and Electoral Hesse. And in May 1851, just after the end of the Dresden Conference, she concluded a three-year alliance with Austria in which she guaranteed the Austrian dominions against attack. While the alliance reflected the king's genuine belief that conservative powers must stand together against the 'radicals and the reds', it in no way signified the abandonment of Prussian territorial objectives, as some perceptive Austrians realized.[9] On this uncertain note the first major confrontation between the German powers since Frederick the Great's attack on Silesia came to an end.

The conflict between Austria and Prussia for mastery in Germany rumbled on throughout the 1850s, peaking in 1855 and again in 1859. When hostilities broke out between Russia and Turkey in October 1853 the tsar quickly discovered that he could not expect active support from Austria and Prussia in the spirit of the old Holy Alliance. And on that support he had relied to render British and French intervention on Turkey's side a hazardous business.

Austria pursued a complex policy during the Crimean War. Deeply disturbed by the prospect of the Ottoman Empire collapsing with far-reaching consequences for the stability of her own empire and for the European balance of power on which her survival depended, Foreign Minister Count Karl von Buol-Schauenstein did his best to check Russian advances and uphold the integrity of the Ottoman Empire. At the same time he was concerned to protect Austrian interests in the Danubian Principalities Wallachia and Moldavia, an area of vital strategic and economic importance to Austria which the tsar occupied in July 1853 in the hope of forcing Turkey to comply with his demands. Austrian threats of military action, which forced Russia out of the Principalities and allowed Austria to occupy them, were deeply resented in St Petersburg. Only in the 1860s did the full effects of the breakdown of the old friendship between Austria and Russia become fully apparent.

If Prussian policy wavered during the war, this was a reflection of the influence competing cliques could exert over the impressionable king. At times the pro-western, anti-Russian and anti-Austrian *Wochenblattpartei*, and at other times the pro-Russian and pro-Austrian court camarilla, was in the ascendancy. The latest research, however, suggests that the king was very much in charge of policy; policy-making was, as Leopold von Gerlach remarked, 'a state of anarchy moderated by good will'.[10] In February 1854, just before Britain and France declared war on Russia, the pro-westerners tried to make the running. As Prussian interests were not directly at stake in the Balkans, narrow self-interest dictated that she avoid involvement and extricate maximum advantage out of the situation. Accordingly – without the king's knowledge – a *Wochenblattpartei* emissary went to London where he offered Prussian assistance against Russia in return for help in promoting Prussian hegemony in North and Central Germany.

It was the king who put a stop to this intrigue which cost the war minister his post. For already Frederick William had embarked on a pro-Austrian policy. He offered Austria not only renewal of the 1851 alliance but a defensive – offensive alliance for the duration of the war. This treaty, signed in April 1854 and eventually endorsed by the Diet, provided for partial mobilization of the federal army to protect Austria and Prussia. Only if Russia attacked in the Balkans or refused to evacuate the Principalities would the offensive element in the alliance become operative, in which case Prussia would put 200,000 men into the field. There was more than a touch of self-interest in this arrangement. The treaty kept Austria away from the western powers who might otherwise drag Prussia into the war. And if that happened Napoleon would be tempted to attack in the Rhineland, the area which gave Prussia greatest cause for concern.

Having achieved her objective in the Principalities and being anxious to bring the war to an end, Austria concluded an alliance with Britain and France in December 1854. She turned to Prussia and demanded that she mobilize in an exercise designed to force the Anglo-French peace terms on Russia. Prussian policy changed abruptly. She refused the request, earning a sharp rebuke from Austria who accused her of breach of treaty. Though Buol argued that the Austrian aim was the altruistic one of trying to contain the war before it spread to Germany, most German states were alarmed by the thought of mobilization and involvement in Balkan affairs. Prussia succeeded in February 1855 in persuading the Diet to reject an Austrian motion for mobilization of the federal army against Russia. Instead the Diet opted for armed neutrality against threats 'from any direction', i.e. against both east and west. So Buol's policy was thwarted, while for once Prussia ended up on good terms with the smaller states and with Britain, France and Russia too. Shortly afterwards the tension between Austria and Prussia died away. Nicholas I died and his successor Alexander II wanted peace. During the complex negotiations leading to the Peace of Paris in 1856, Prussia veered back to the pro-Austrian line and helped her persuade Russia to accept the Anglo-French peace plan.

Three years later when war broke out in Northern Italy, the conflict of interest between Austria and Prussia surfaced once more. In the summer of 1859 many Germans feared that France was about to launch an attack in the west. Most states began to mobilize and by June the Diet had 250,000 men under arms. Austria enjoyed a burst of popularity because, while liberals conceded that Italian national aspirations were as legitimate as German, nevertheless many thought that the presence of predatory France behind Piedmont justified Austrian resistance in Northern Italy. It was widely felt that Prussia, who had mobilized three army corps, should come to the aid of Austria at once. A new wave of *Rheinlieder* swept through West Germany; Ludwig Bauer's '*O Deutschland hoch in Ehren*', a firm favourite during the First World War, was written in these months.

The new regent William was prepared to stand by Austria. But a majority of the crown council insisted on extracting a pound of flesh. So Prussia argued that, strictly speaking, the French attack on Austria had not endangered the territory of the Confederation and she would not, therefore, activate article 47 of the federal constitution which would have authorized member states to help Austria. The price of consent was Austrian agreement that Prussia command the armies on the Rhine in the event of a French attack in the west - a not unreasonable request once Austria was fully committed in Italy. To Prussia's surprise, Rechberg would not agree. So Austria fought on unaided. Only after the Austrian defeat at the battle of Magenta on 4 June did the regent decide in a fit of conscience to mobilize another three army corps, talked of 'armed mediation' and declared that Austria must not lose her Italian possessions. Foreign Minister Count Alexander von Schleinitz delayed action in the hope of involving Russia and Britain in this operation. By the time it was evident that neither would oblige Prussia, Napoleon had played upon the Prussian 'menace' to persuade Francis Joseph to agree to the Villafrancha armistice early in July. The emperor was concerned about the situation at home; the Viennese press was attacking not only the system of absolutism but the emperor himself, and his worried ministers urged him to end the war at all costs before worse befell them. Austria's reputation was badly shaken by the loss of Lombardy. But Prussia, too, had come out of it badly. By her reluctance to aid Austria the reputation she was beginning to acquire during the New Era was tarnished in the eyes

103

of many (though not all) liberals.

THE ECONOMIC DIMENSION

The conflict between Austria and Prussia for mastery in Germany had an important economic dimension, to which we now turn.

To trace the economic roots of their rivalry we must go back beyond the 1848–9 Revolution to the 1830s and the formation of the German Customs Union (*Deutscher Zollverein*). Its economic significance can easily be exaggerated. It was by no means the only or even the principal factor which eventually turned Germany from an agrarian into an industrial society. The origins of industrialization lie back in the eighteenth century and especially in the Napoleonic era. By 1815 there were already the beginnings of industrialization in the Rhineland, Westphalia, Saxony and Silesia. And before 1850 the Customs Union does not appear to have done a great deal to promote industrialization. Of course, the removal of some 1800 customs barriers criss-crossing the Confederation from end to end did stimulate trade and increase the demand for agrarian produce. But customs barriers were only one of the obstacles causing economic stagnation; poor communications, a scarcity of credit, the low purchasing power of the population and social immobility were just as important. Only when all the variables had changed could industrialization take root in Germany. In fact, the significance of the Customs Union lies less in the economic than in the political field. It was not so much what it actually achieved in economic terms during the first two decades of its existence but what German nationalists *thought* it was achieving – i.e. promoting the economic unification of Germany – which convinced them that the Customs Union represented a giant step forward on the road to political unification. It was indicative of this belief that when moderate liberals from South and West Germany met at Heppenheim in 1847 to formulate a programme they declared that political unification would most easily be promoted by establishing a customs parliament to regulate tariff policy.

As the Federal Diet made little progress towards the rationalization of the customs systems, the larger states took their own initiatives. For some time in the 1830s three regional customs unions competed with each other: a Prussian, a South German and a Central Customs Union. The primary motive behind them all was not, however, a desire to stimulate economic growth but simply to obtain new sources of revenue to pay for the expensive wars

Napoleon involved them in, as well as for the extensive reforms some states had embarked upon.

Prussia was first in the field in 1818. She abolished all internal duties and introduced a uniform low tariff for the whole of the kingdom. Her pressing need was to raise revenue to meet the substantial state deficit as well as to unify her scattered possessions. At first she had no thought of creating a united Germany. All the same, the history of the German Customs Union illustrates the impossibility of disentangling economic from political strands in any historical situation. When the forceful Friedrich von Motz became Prussian finance minister in 1825 he embarked upon a determined campaign to extend the Prussian Union. As he remarked in 1829:

> If it is true as every statesman knows that import export and transit
> duties are only the consequence of the political division between
> various states . . . then the contrary is also true that the unification
> of these states in a customs or commercial union will lead to one
> and the same political system. And the more natural the attachment
> to a customs and commercial system is . . . the more intimate and
> deep will be the attachment of these states to one political system.'[11]

Count Christian von Bernstorff, the foreign minister, entirely agreed. When Prussia concluded her first major extra-territorial treaty with Hesse-Darmstadt in 1828 he commented that, however one-sided the agreement (which favoured that state much more than Prussia), it was well worthwhile for it would 'place Prussia in a position to exert its influence over the [smaller states] in the most equitable manner'.[12]

Metternich, with his usual short-range perception, recognized in the forward policies of Motz and Bernstorff a new threat to Austrian influence in Germany. Accordingly he encouraged the formation of the Central Customs Union headed by Saxony and Hanover. In vain. The Prussian Union swallowed up its rivals and founded the German Customs Union in 1834. Actually, after Motz's death in 1830 and Bernstorff's resignation in 1832 their conservative successors eschewed power politics and treated the Customs Union as a purely commercial undertaking – which probably helped to reassure other states about Prussian intentions at a crucial stage in the union's history. However, in the 1840s middle-ranging officials in the ministry of commerce resurrected the aggressive power-oriented tactics of Motz and Bernstorff. As the Customs Union blossomed in this decade, Prussian power increased correspondingly. Prussia controlled vital lines of communication between north and south; she had become the mediator in all commercial disputes between members; and she constituted a large and attractive market for other states. All the same, it was still the assurance of financial independence from their local estates rather than commercial advantage which attracted many rulers to the Customs Union.

Metternich did attempt to persuade Emperor Francis Joseph to pursue a more aggressive commercial policy in Germany. But having little say in domestic affairs, he had no success either in the early 1830s or between 1841 and 1843 (at the time of the renewal of the Customs Union treaties) when he proposed a lowering of Austrian tariffs. The hard fact was that Austrian economic interests pointed her away from Germany. Trade between Austria and Hungary in the first half of the nineteenth century was twice as large as that with Germany, and growing faster. Austrian industrialists had established markets in the eastern half of the empire and a particularly lucrative one in Lombardy and Venetia. Nor had they any wish to be exposed to foreign competition, which they feared changes in the prohibitive (i.e. 100 per cent) tariff system would lead to. In the last resort foreign policy mattered more than economics to Metternich; if he had to, he was prepared to avert his gaze from the growing threat of the Customs Union and rely on dualism to see Austria through troubled times.

In the autumn of 1849 Austria's attitude changed quite abruptly. This was due as much if not more to political rather than economic considerations. Just before the emperor's soldiers restored order in Vienna, an article in the semi-official *Wiener Zeitung* outlined the shape of things to come. The article proposed the creation in easy stages of a new customs union but one embracing the whole of the Habsburg monarchy as well as the Confederation. This would bring into being a potential market of seventy million certain to dominate the economic life of Central Europe. It would be surrounded by high though not prohibitive tariffs on manufactured goods, but foodstuffs and raw materials would enter free. The article, intended to test the water temperature, reflected the views of Karl Ludwig von Bruck, one-time director of the Trieste chamber of commerce and a former member of the economic committee of the Frankfurt Parliament. In November he became minister of commerce.

This grandiose scheme was not without considerable attraction for the smaller states, who felt that Middle Europe might be a means of protecting themselves against the vaulting ambitions of Prussia. Schwarzenberg, a power politician of the old school, was not greatly interested in its economic possibilities but pounced on the scheme as a stick to use in the campaign to make Prussia see reason and return to the old dualistic policy. Bruck met his match in Rudolf von Delbrück, a leading official in the Prussian ministry of commerce. He took the scheme seriously (as did Bruck), seeing in it a threat to the German Customs Union. While readily conceding that cooperation with Austria might be possible on a whole range of issues such as monetary reform and railway development, he threw cold water on the main proposal. The economic needs of the Customs Union and those of the Habsburg dominions were so incompatible that a common tariff was beyond the bounds of possibility. Secondly, he sharply rejected Bruck's proposal for one central authority with extensive powers to regulate tariffs and negotiate commercial treaties. Delbrück preferred a federation between the Habsburg dominions, the German Customs Union, the Tax Union and North German coastal towns.[13]

Despite the interest shown by some South German states, nothing came of Middle Europe. At loggerheads with colleagues over financial matters and disheartened by the lack of progress towards an Austro-German customs union, Bruck resigned in May 1851. Delbrück promptly seized the initiative and strengthened Prussia's position enormously through the conclusion of a commercial treaty with Hanover in September – Bismarck, incidentally, playing a major role at the negotiating table. In exchange for extremely favourable terms Prussia gained control of the finances of a key state controlling the north-west coastline of Germany and linking up Prussia's western provinces with her eastern possessions. This treaty gave Prussia virtually complete control over the commercial life of North Germany. Many southern states protested about both the lack of consultation by Prussia and the generous concessions made to Hanover. But they were now too dependent on the Customs Union to do anything about it.

The same applies to the negotiations Bavaria, Württemberg and Saxony conducted with Austria in January 1852 and again in the spring at their Darmstadt conference. As always in economic matters, the Third Germany was impaled on the horns of a cruel dilemma. These states agreed that the entry of Austria into the Customs Union would afford them much-needed political protection against Prussia, even though there was some suspicion that Austria was using them to prop up her empire. But at bottom there was too much at stake economically for them to insist on Austrian inclusion as a pre-condition of their continued membership of the Customs Union. Public opinion in the South German states made it abundantly clear to their governments that withdrawal would be little short of disastrous for their economies and certainly for their finances.

They were rescued from their dilemma by the sudden death of Schwarzenberg. His successor Buol, after one last attempt to play off the German states against Prussia, decided on negotiation with her. Being much more preoccupied by the rising tension with Russia in South-Eastern Europe, he was only too relieved to wash his hands of the customs issue. Left in the lurch by Austria, the smaller states had no alternative to agreement with Prussia. So Delbrück was able to renew the Customs Union treaties (which lapsed in 1853) for a further twelve years, largely on Prussian terms.

Prussia did not have it all her own way. Under pressure from the other members Prussia did negotiate a commercial treaty with Austria on generous terms. No import duties would be charged on Austrian raw materials and on certain semi-manufactured goods. Preferential treatment varying from 25 to 50 per cent would be given to many manufactured goods on a reciprocal basis – an important departure from Customs Union policy which gave preferences only in exceptional circumstances. Austria also enjoyed most-favoured-nation treatment in respect of new tariff concessions given by the Customs Union to other states. Finally, Prussia promised to enter into negotiations for a Mid-European customs union no later than 1860. As Bruck was prepared to reduce Austrian duties on industrial goods, he assumed that industrialists in the German Customs Union would become more favourably disposed to a Mid-European Union. As a result of this treaty Austrian imports from the Customs Union increased from 17 per cent in 1856 to 34 per cent by 1864. But Austrian exports rose only from 29 to 32 per cent. And despite Prussia's promise, Delbrück was quite determined to sabotage future negotiations with Austria by proposing tariffs so low that her industries would be endangered by outside competition.

Economic development in the next decade favoured Prussia rather than Austria. The story has been told in detail elsewhere. Suffice to say that Prussia enjoyed several natural advantages which put her decisively ahead of Austria. By an accident of geography the major industrial areas were in Prussian territory: the Ruhr, the Saar, Saxony and Upper Silesia. Heavy industry developed rapidly in these areas because of a plentiful supply of key raw materials: coal, iron and zinc. In the area covered by the Customs Union 80 per cent of total coal and iron production was Prussian. She had an abundant reservoir of labour for the new industrial regions as the handicraft system declined and peasants drifted to the towns. The foundation of credit banks in the 1850s supplied an abundance of risk capital for industrial development. In the countryside the abolition of the remnants of feudalism facilitated the emergence in the east of efficient estates which became major grain exporters. State intervention was also a major factor through its direct involvement in the running of certain industries such as coal-mining, and also by removing restrictive legislation impeding the growth of capitalism.

It would be quite wrong to suppose that Austria stagnated in the 1850s. Very real progress was made in modernizing the Habsburg lands. Flourishing iron, woollen and cotton industries sprang up in Lower Austria, Bohemia and Lombardy. In 1850 the customs barriers between Austria and Hungary were removed. In 1851 prohibitive tariffs on foreign imports were abolished and replaced by high tariffs; and the number of tariffs was reduced from 614 to 338. In 1853 tariffs were further reduced. Trade both internally with Hungary, which supplied food and raw materials for the industrial areas, and externally was greatly increased. A significant expansion of the railway system improved north–south (but not east–west) communications. In 1859 access to trades and professions was freed of all restrictions. In the countryside the process of abolishing the robot was completed and the peasants, freed of feudal relics, provided a new labour force for industry. Also the fiscal unification of the Habsburg dominions was carried out in this decade.

But industrialization still lagged behind Prussia. In 1865–6 70 per cent of all Austrians still worked on the land compared with 45 per cent in Prussia. Whereas Prussian officials actively encouraged rapid industrial development, in Austria the top-heavy bureaucratic machine, a feature of the neo-absolutist era, impeded changes and slowed down economic expansion. The power of the guilds and the resistance offered by deep-rooted feudal traditions were further obstacles. Thus, although tariff reductions in the early 1850s gave an impetus to development, the pace of change slackened after the depression of 1857 which affected Austria severely. Coal and textile manufacturers strongly opposed to tariff reductions were able to veto further changes. It has to be remembered here that as key raw materials – iron and coal – were widely separated in Austria (unlike the situation in Prussia), costs were much higher in comparison with those of Prussia. But the greatest single handicap was chronic insolvency, which plagued Austria from 1811 onwards. Between 1848 and 1866 the national debt trebled, amounting on the eve of the Austro-Prussian war to 1,670 million florins compared with 290 million talers in Prussia. Armed mediation during the Crimean War gravely strained Austrian finances. But the war of 1859 brought them virtually to the point of complete collapse. Only through massive loans – absorbing capital which would in part at least have been attracted to industrial development – did Austria keep going financially, with over 40 per cent of total expenditure being spent on armaments.

Meanwhile in Germany at the close of the 1850s, middle-class pressure for far-reaching economic and social change was becoming increasingly vocal. The Congress of German Economists founded in 1858 articulated the exuberant laissez-faire beliefs of the business world. This body attracted the support of prominent figures in the world of economics and politics, had extensive connections with business and commerce and exerted considerable influence in government circles. It demanded the removal of all barriers to completely free trade and the destruction of state controls which restricted the development of individual entrepreneurship. One of its demands was for a drastic reduction of Customs Union tariffs, a demand which the Prussian government was very willing to take up both for economic reasons and because lower tariffs would widen the gulf between Austria and Prussia. But the unanimity rule in the general congress of the Customs Union stopped Prussia in her tracks; the protectionist-minded South German states steadfastly opposed further tariff reductions.

Frustrated by constant opposition in the general congress – which met every two years to consider tariff changes – Prussia launched out on a new forward policy in the early 1860s. The occasion was the Cobden Treaty negotiated by Britain and France in 1860. In this treaty Napoleon abandoned the traditional protectionism of the French and reduced tariffs over a wide range of British manufactured goods. Napoleon's dream of a low-tariff zone covering the whole of Western Europe gave the Prussian ministry of commerce an opening to negotiate a similar treaty and so outmanoeuvre the obstructionist middle states. In the Franco-Prussian Commercial Treaty signed in August 1862 Prussian duties were generally lowered to the same level as French duties on British goods, much to the satisfaction of German manufacturers who would otherwise have been disadvantaged by the Cobden Treaty. Both partners agreed to a most-favoured-nation clause by which concessions made to third countries were automatically extended to the other partner. Political considerations were paramount on both sides. Napoleon was paving the way for better relations with Prussia, hoping to use her as a lever against Austria, while the Prussian negotiating team led by Delbrück wanted the treaty because it would make it virtually impossible to negotiate another Austro-Prussian commercial treaty when the 1853 treaty lapsed.[14] The Prussians were 'willing to give France more than they received in order to give Austria less than they promised'.[15]

Austria was well aware of the political implications of the 1862 treaty. By the late spring of 1861 Rechberg concluded that he could not obtain an alliance with Prussia. Therefore he began to object vigorously to the Franco-Prussian commercial negotiations and did all he could to stiffen the resistance of the middle states to tariff changes. With Austrian support Bavaria, Württemberg, Hesse-Darmstadt and Nassau at first rejected the treaty and talked bravely of defying Prussia. But when Rechberg offered them a customs union with Austria the schizophrenic nature of their position was quickly apparent.

All Prussia had to do was stand firm and insist that the renewal of the Customs Union (the treaty lapsed in December 1865) would depend on acceptance of the Franco-Prussian Treaty by all members. She held all the aces. A reduction of tariff levels corresponded with the general trend in Europe towards free trade in the midnineteenth century. Secondly, middle–class opinion articulated through bodies such as the Congress of German Economists and the National Society was strongly in favour of the treaty. Thirdly, much as many middle states and small states, too, disliked Prussia, the economic life of Germany was becoming far too interdependent to permit them the luxury of repudiating the Customs Union. Fourthly, the alternative of some form of Mid-European Union was no longer practical politics and was now opposed by many Austrian manufacturers. As public opinion began to count in both states, Austria and Prussia were driven further apart. In Prussia middle–class opinion favoured more free trade; in Austria after the 1857 crisis opinion was increasingly favourable to the introduction of higher tariffs to protect the iron and textile industries. Left with no realistic alternative, all the member states had by October 1864 accepted the substantial tariff reductions incorporated in the Franco-Prussian Treaty. In May 1865 the Customs Union was formally renewed for a further twelve years commencing on 1 January 1866. However, thanks to the continued resistance of the middle states Prussia was still unable to replace the unanimity rule with a majority voting system.

Austria was unable to negotiate a renewal of the 1853 treaty. Bismarck, curiously enough, was willing to renew the promise of future negotiations for Austrian entry into the Customs Union. But the ministry of commerce refused to make this harmless gesture. All hopes of entering the Customs Union came to an abrupt end and the tariff walls round Austria took on an air of finality. The maximum concession Prussia was willing to make was a trade treaty signed in April 1865 which offered Austria only most-favoured-nation treatment so that she forfeited her privileged position in the German market. Prussia had, in effect, inflicted a serious defeat on Austria, a 'commercial Villafrancha', a year before she was expelled from Germany for ever.

Clinical separation of the political–strategic factors from the economic ones is a purely hermeneutic exercise. Their interdependence emerges clearly enough from the above. Nevertheless, it is arguable that the economic issues at stake in the confrontation between Austria and Prussia foreshadowed the Reich of 1871 much more clearly than the political development. When reform of the Confederation was being debated in the early 1860s many Germans still hoped to associate Austria in some form or other with the new Reich. On paper (though not in practice) the pro-Prussian National Society was committed to the creation of a wider association (*weit-*

erer Bund) with Austria as well as to the formation of an *engerer Bund* – Little Germany. The economic issues were much clearer cut. The German Customs Union, which coincided more or less with Little Germany, was a growing concern tied into international markets and quite capable of existing without Austria, a fact which could not but strengthen the growing conviction that a wider association with Austria was superfluous. As the most recent writer on the Customs Union has remarked: 'the growing economic ties [between the states] were in no sense destined to lead to political unification but they did at least impede any step backwards in a federalist direction'.[16] One might go further: Little Germany was, as Marx observed, essentially an expression of the development of German capitalism though, of course, the creation of this state depended on the coincidence of economic and politico–strategic factors. For Austria the economic writing was on the wall. Trade within the empire was bound to remain more important than trade with Germany, this because of the growing pressure exerted on governments by key sectors of Austrian industry whose high production costs made them uncompetitive in world markets.

THE IDEOLOGICAL CONFLICT

Finally, we turn to the ideological element in the struggle between the two German powers. National liberalism enjoyed a new lease of life after the war of 1859 and emerged as a significant ideological force attracting wide support from the articulate middle class organized in professional bodies and in the National Society. The desire for a strong Reich to defend Germany against her foes – especially the French – was shared, albeit in only a rudimentary and intermittent fashion, by an even wider cross-section of the population participating in the general revival of popular festivals in the 1860s. The resurgence of German National Liberalism was no isolated phenomenon. The national idea triumphed in Italy in 1860–1 (or perhaps more accurately, Italian nationalism was exploited by Cavour to advance Piedmontese interests). In Britain, Belgium and the Netherlands constitutional liberalism underpinned by industrialization was ushering in a period of unparalleled material progress. Even in Napoleonic France autocracy was beginning to crumble in the early 1860s. These national and international pressures forced Austria and Prussia to take account of the spirit of a new age.

Individual members of ruling classes all over Germany were as capable of being moved by genuine sympathy for the claims of the new ideology as anyone else. On the other hand, conservatives who controlled the governments of the larger states tended to regard nationalism as a force which could be exploited in the interest of the state, as the Piedmontese had done so successfully. Nor must it be forgotten – a point made earlier – that even those rulers who sympathized with the *Zeitgeist* were haunted by memories of the frightening experiences of 1848–9. Objectively speaking, it was highly unlikely that barricades would be erected in the streets in the 1860s. That did not prevent rulers seeing in the demands nationalists were making for constitutional government a serious threat to their established power which might be rendered innocuous more effectively by coming to terms with the new ideology than fighting it.

In 1858 Prussia had embarked on the New Era. And although her conduct during the Italian war had done nothing to enhance her standing with German liberals, she remained committed to the policy of 'moral conquests' in Germany; in other words, aware at last that physical force alone would not do, she knew that she had to try to win the minds and hearts of articulate Germans if she was to succeed where Radowitz had failed a decade earlier. But although the fiasco of the Italian war had – by highlighting the military weakness of the Confederation – placed reform fairly and squarely on the political agenda, neither Austria nor Prussia took the initiative. Both of them were at first engaged in negotiations for a new alliance, for when Francis Joseph met William I at Teplitz in July 1860 a French attack seemed imminent. Prussia offered to conclude a defensive alliance against French aggression on the Rhine and in Venetia provided that she was given military command of the federal armies and that the presidency of the Diet alternated with Austria. The latter power, however, was still not prepared to compromise her primacy in Germany on which she supposed the stability of the whole empire depended. But while Rechberg, a sincere believer in dualism, continued to hope for an alliance, Prussia changed course. The cabinet lost interest in an Austrian alliance and in January 1861 commenced negotiations with France for the commercial treaty which was designed to keep Austria out of the Customs Union. Only when it was clear by July 1861 that an alliance could not be concluded did the negotiations lapse, and both powers began to pay more attention to the mounting pressure for federal reform.

By this time the Third Germany was making the running on the reform issue. During the Crimean War a group of states led by

113

Baden, Württemberg, Bavaria and Saxony began to emerge as a third force in German politics. Alarmed at the prospect of being driven into war through Austrian policy, they attempted to act as an independent force for the first time. On the initiative of Count Friedrich von Beust, chief minister in Saxony, and Baron Ludwig von der Pfordten, chief minister in Bavaria, eight states met at Bamberg in 1854 to coordinate policy. When Austria and Prussia asked the Diet to endorse their new alliance the Bamberg states tried to impose conditions on them, though without success. After the war the Third Germany continued its efforts to act independently of Berlin and Vienna. When Grand Duke Friedrich I of Baden was alarmed by the possible implications of the meeting between Tsar Alexander II and Napoleon at Stuttgart in 1857 and by the failure of the Diet to reinforce the federal fortress of Rastatt in his territory, he turned not to Austria and Prussia but to King William I of Württemberg and Grand Duke Ludwig III of Hesse-Darmstadt in the hope of creating a united front against French aggression in South-West Germany. During the Italian war Beust took a more ambitious initiative, touring the major German capitals to drum up support for a meeting of the middle states which took place in Württemberg in November 1859. At this conference they discussed measures to strengthen the legislative power of the Confederation and attempted to coordinate their own policies in the hope of forcing Austria and Prussia to negotiate with them collectively in the Diet.

Schemes for reform were thick on the ground in the early 1860s. The proposals from Baden and Saxony call for special mention. In 1861 Baron Franz von Roggenbach, newly appointed foreign minister of Baden, a state whose ruler was supportive of Prussia, proposed the creation of a Little German state led by Prussia but with a liberal face; there would be ministerial responsibility, a directly elected national parliament and – to maintain the connection with Austria – a guarantee covering the Habsburg dominions. As the grand duke of Baden was the king of Prussia's son-in-law, the latter forwarded the plan to Berlin. In September the king, supported by the new foreign minister, Count Albrecht von Bernstorff, endorsed it as a basis for reform of the Confederation – but only after the grand duke had jettisoned the liberal provisions. Shortly afterwards Beust, no lover of a Little German state, proposed a far-reaching reorganization of the Confederation. The revamped Diet would have a supreme court; the executive power would be strengthened; the federal military machine would be overhauled; and legislative power would be conferred on a chamber of deputies chosen by the various states.

The hope that measures such as these would save the Confederation was certainly entertained by several rulers. To evaluate their mixed motives is not easy. Some, such as the king of Hanover, were moved by the kind of woolly Christian–German patriotism exemplified by King Frederick William IV, while others, such as the king of Württemberg, were calculating *Realpolitiker* with an eye for the main chance. All were frightened by the 'democratic' overtones of National Liberalism and hoped to contain the nationalist ferment within a conservative framework. They opposed directly elected assemblies and even where they did not forbid National Society activities – as was the case in Mecklenburg and Electoral Hesse – they imposed restrictions on them. And above all, they believed they could best preserve their sovereign independence in a reformed Confederation which, unlike a Prussian-dominated Little Germany or an Austrian-dominated Middle Europe, would enable them to play the two major states off against each other. It is only fair to add that some leading ministers, especially von der Pfordten, took a loftier view of the role a reformed Confederation might play in European politics as a bulwark against the growing power of Russia in the east and Napoleonic France in the west.

No doubt, as revisionist historians maintain, the history of Germany and of Europe would have been very different had the Confederation survived in an updated form as a moderating influence in Central Europe. Yet the hard fact remains that co-ordination of policy between the middle states, the backbone of the Third Germany, was virtually impossible because of divergent interests and rivalries. Economically Saxony, the leading industrial power among these states, was drawn irresistibly towards the Customs Union, as was Württemberg, whereas Bavaria looked much more towards the Danubian basin. Politically the pretensions of Bavaria to become the dominant power in South Germany were resented by Württemberg and Baden. And in the case of the grand duchy, further tension was caused by Bavarian claims for compensation arising out of territorial adjustments made in 1815.

At first Austria stood aloof from the agitation for reform, being perfectly satisfied with her position in the Confederation. But in December 1861 Foreign Minister Bernstorff, a man much less well-disposed towards Austria than his predecessor Schleinitz, rejected the Beust plan out of hand. In an attempt to divert attention from Prussia's internal difficulties, he took the initiative, declaring bluntly that the only acceptable solution of the German problem was a Little Germany led by Prussia though associated with Austria in a *weiterer Bund*. The bluntness of Bernstorff's language, arousing memories of Radowitz and the Erfurt Union, set the alarm bells ringing in Vienna.

By this time Austria had, in any case, become a reluctant convert to the cause of reform. The 1859 war had shaken the empire to its foundations. Not only were her finances plunged into disarray. Trouble was brewing among the Magyars and the Czechs, while the liberal middle class in Vienna – whose money was committed to state loans – was becoming restive. The neo-absolutist policy pursued since 1849 had to be abandoned. The leading exponents of this policy, Baron Alexander Bach and Baron Johann Kempen, were summarily dismissed. The emperor, still surrounded by conservative aristocrats, appointed one of them, Count Agenor Goluchowski, minister of the interior, entrusting him with the task of drawing up a new constitution. The October Diploma of 1860 did little more than modify the centralized system which had just failed the empire. The old estates were revived and given local powers of decision-making. But a Reichsrat composed in part of delegates from these estates and in part of imperial nominees would still run the empire. The Magyars, who still wanted the 1848 constitution, were dissatisfied with these minimal changes, while the Germans resented their own demotion in favour of the aristocracy. In December 1860 Goluchowski was abruptly dismissed and replaced by Baron Anton von Schmerling.

Schmerling's appointment was the price Francis Joseph had to pay to escape from the financial crisis. Schmerling, a representative of the influential Austrian middle class, had been a member of the Frankfurt Central Government and was an enthusiastic supporter of Greater Germany until Schwarzenberg's Kremsier declaration had put paid to that solution of the German problem. In the February Patent of 1861, a modified version of the Diploma, Schmerling shifted the balance of power back to Vienna. The Reichsrat became a bicameral chamber: the upper house was in the hands of the landed aristocracy while the lower house was elected by the estates. As the dissatisfied Magyars and Poles withdrew from the Reichsrat, the Germans effectively controlled that body. But by the autumn of 1861 it was apparent that the Patent was not likely to reconcile the peoples of empire to the regime, with the sole exception of the Ruthenes who welcomed an arrangement affording them protection against the Polish aristocracy. The failure of the Patent was probably another reason why Schmerling turned to Germany in the hope of making 'moral conquests'.

The situation looked very hopeful for Austria in the summer of 1862. There was widespread disillusionment with Prussia in liberal circles as the constitutional crisis mounted in intensity. Austria's image was much brighter. She had abandoned the repressive policy of the 1850s and had proved her willingness to introduce constitutional changes at home. Schmerling and Baron Ludwig von Biegeleben, secretary of state for German affairs in the foreign office, concocted a plan to reform the Confederation. Rechberg, having failed to obtain a Prussian alliance, reluctantly agreed to the alternative strategy of outbidding Prussia over the reform issue.

Austria approached the exercise with sophistication. To avoid a Prussian veto the Austrians proposed the setting up of a national chamber of deputies drawn from local estates together with an executive committee as purely ad hoc bodies to tackle matters of general concern, namely the reform of the civil and criminal codes on which agreement could be reached by majority vote. Once in being, the Austrians hoped the arrangements would become permanent. In August 1862, despite strong Prussian opposition, the Diet sent the proposals to committee. The opponents of Little Germany took heart. In October the German Reform Society (*Deutscher Reformverein*) was founded in Munich by South German radicals and at once gave enthusiastic endorsement to the Austrian proposals. However, now that Bismarck was at the helm Prussian policy hardened; massive pressure was exerted on Hanover and especially on Electoral Hesse to reject the proposals. In January 1863 the Diet rejected them formally by nine votes to seven. What shocked supporters of the motion was the bluntness of Bismarck's declaration that the only acceptable basis for reform was the creation of a directly elected assembly chosen by the people in each state according to population.

Having failed to persuade the Diet to support reform, Schmerling turned, as Radowitz had done thirteen years earlier, to the German princes. The situation was still favourable for Austria. Bismarck's intervention on the side of Russia during the Polish uprising had displeased both Britain and France, while in May he had issued draconian press ordinances virtually destroying freedom of the press in Prussia. Even the crown prince joined in the chorus of protest against Bismarck. On 3 August Francis Joseph invited King William to attend a congress of princes to be held at Frankfurt to discuss reform of the Confederation. Under pressure from Bismarck the king reluctantly gave an evasive reply, playing for time by suggesting that a conference of ministers of the leading states discuss the proposals before binding decisions were taken. On 16 August, the day before the congress met, Schmerling revealed details of the Austrian plan to create a German federal state. A congress of princes – in whom sovereignty resided – would meet periodically; a parliament of 302 delegates drawn from local estates would decide the federal budget; a directorate of five (Austria, Prussia, Bavaria and two alternates from the other twenty-two states) would act as the federal executive; and a federal court (with an eye to common legislation on commerce and tariffs) would be set up.

When the congress met on 17 August it at once dispatched King Johann of Saxony to invite King William to attend. Only after a dramatic interview with Bismarck did the monarch reluctantly refuse. Ironically enough the King's (i.e. Bismarck's) reason for refusing was that decisions about reform must be made after consultation with his ministers, not by the king acting in his capacity as a German prince – this breathtaking subterfuge from a ruler at loggerheads with his Landtag. In September Bismarck made known the only conditions on which Prussia would accept the Frankfurt proposals; Prussia and Austria must have a right of veto before war was declared (unless a confederate territory was the victim of a direct attack); Prussia must have absolute parity with Austria in running the new state; and instead of a delegate assembly there must be a directly elected parliament.

So Prussia effectively sabotaged the last attempt to solve the German problem by agreement round the conference table. By the early autumn on the eve of the Schleswig-Holstein crisis the battle lines were clearly visible. Austria, shaken by defeat in Northern Italy, could not afford to abandon her primacy in Germany without serious repercussions on her position in the rest of her empire and on her standing as a European Great Power. Prussia, in the other corner of the ring, was determined to upset the status quo whenever circumstances permitted it. Ideally, as Bismarck revealed in brutally frank conversations in December 1862 with Count Alois Károlyi, the Austrian ambassador in Berlin, Austria should abandon her pretensions to be a German power, concentrate her efforts on her dominions and allow Prussia to establish Little Germany. If Austria did so, Prussia would be prepared to underwrite Venetia and support Austria in the Balkans. Given his grasp of power realities, it is hardly likely that Bismarck intended to come to Austria's support in areas of no direct concern to Prussia. One thing was made crystal clear to Károlyi: if Austria persisted in her present policy, war could be the only outcome. The school bully, having unjustly accused the headmaster of tyrannous conduct, was offering him protection against the other boys on condition that he countenanced the bully boy's behaviour. But while Bismarck believed that the force of economic development as well as the pressure of National Liberalism made the creation of Little Germany virtually inevitable, he recognized that this might well lie in the distant future. Therefore, he constantly dangled before the Austrians a minimum programme: the recognition of Prussian predominance in North Germany. This would leave the future of Germany unresolved and South Germany would act as a useful buffer zone between the two of them. On that basis the old dualism could continue and Bismarck would refrain from manipulating Little German opinion against Austria in the battle for the minds and hearts of the Germans.

THE DEEPENING CRISIS : OCTOBER 1864–JUNE 1866

The twenty months between October 1864, when Denmark surrendered the duchies of Schleswig, Holstein and Lauenburg to Austria and Prussia, and June 1866, when the Diet mobilized its forces against Prussia, was a period of mounting tension in Germany. Crisis followed crisis over the disposal of Schleswig-Holstein, each edging the German powers nearer the brink of a war which when it came in the summer of 1866 utterly transformed the German scene.

After the conclusion of hostilities against Denmark, Austrian policy reached a crossroads. The duchies were the joint possession of the two powers. Would Austria now press for the installation of the duke of Augustenburg as she had done – albeit reluctantly and without success – during the London Conference? In the Ballplatz some officials led by Schmerling and Biegeleben favoured a forward policy in Germany. The time had come in their estimation to support the Augustenburgs, seek a close association with the middle and small states and, if an understanding with Prussia eluded them, conclude an alliance with France as a certain way of containing Prussian ambitions. Such a policy spelt conflict with Prussia. Moreover, despite considerable apprehension about the general thrust of Prussian policy, Rechberg clung to dualism to the bitter end. The alliance he had tried in vain to obtain in 1860–1 had come to pass in 1864 and must be maintained at all costs. This was not just the instinctive reaction of a conservative fearful of the effects of revolution on the empire, but a matter of sober calculation. Peace was mandatory for Austria. Her financial situation in 1864 made war unthinkable. And why look for trouble in Germany when complications in Italy were likely in the not-too-distant future? The Italians, aided and abetted by the French, would surely seize the next favourable opportunity to acquire Venetia. When that happened Austria did not relish the prospect of a repeat performance of 1859; the Prussian alliance was absolutely essential if Austria was to maintain her watch on the Adriatic. At the end of the day the decisive voice in the corridors of power in Vienna was not that of Rechberg, Schmerling or Biegeleben but that of Francis Joseph. And he came down unequivocally on the side of dualism.

In Prussia by this time opinion was strongly in favour of the annexation of the duchies. Bismarck decided on this early in 1864, defending it to the king on the grounds that every Hohenzollern worth his salt had acquired territory for the kingdom. In May the minister-president began to whip up public opinion in Prussia, persuading a friendly landowner Count Adolf von Arnim-Boitzenburg to launch a petition in favour of annexation. Towards Austria, however, he remained conciliatory and seemed anxious to play down any differences between them. Writing to the Prussian ambassador in Vienna he commented that: 'we regard the Danish war as essentially an episode in the struggle between monarchical principle and the revolution and our yardstick for handling the question of the duchies is based upon our view of how they impinge on the larger issue.'[17] The larger issue, as he put it to Austria, was to consolidate and extend the understanding between the three conservative powers so that if France started a war, probably in Italy, the lines of battle would be clearly drawn along ideological lines. This tongue-in-cheek talk greatly encouraged Francis Joseph and Rechberg to feel that they could still arrive at some broader agreement with the Prussians. Of course, this did not exclude other diplomatic manoeuvres to hold Prussia in check; Rechberg did, in fact, make strenuous efforts to improve relations with Britain, Russia and France. But the Prussian alliance offered a lifeline in Germany which the policy-makers in Vienna felt they could not dispense with.

This atmosphere of entente led to the Schönbrunn convention in August 1864. During the state visit of King William to Vienna, Bismarck and Rechberg worked out a comprehensive package deal. Rechberg agreed to Prussian annexation of the duchies and was prepared to recognize Prussian predominance in Germany down to the line of the river Main provided that Prussia support Austria not only to hold on to Venetia but to re-conquer Lombardy. This type of agreement cutting across the claims of nationality would have gladdened the heart of Metternich, who in his day had cheerfully moved peoples across the European chess board to maintain a favourable balance of power for Austria. In 1864 it was all illusion. For one thing the king of Prussia, not yet committed to annexation, rejected the convention out of hand, as did the emperor. For another Bismarck, the *Realpolitiker*, would never have fought for Austria in Italy. Come to that, neither would Russia for the days of anti-revolutionary crusades were over – at least until after the First World War. It simply suited Bismarck's book to pretend to put the clock back when all the tides of history were moving in the opposite direction.

Nor was Rechberg taken in for long about the motives behind Prussian policy. During the negotiations for the renewal of the customs treaties in the autumn of 1864 it was quickly brought home to Austria that, despite the fine promises at Schönbrunn, Prussia would make no economic concessions to Vienna. As mentioned earlier, Bismarck would have been more accommodating or at least have left the question of a future customs union with Austria shrouded in ambiguity. But the economic experts in the ministry of commerce persuaded the king that this was a make-or-break issue permitting of no dubiety. During Bismarck's absence from Berlin in October 1864 they persuaded King William against a future customs union with Austria, i.e. not to renew the promise of 1853. Even before Austria was informed of this decision at the end of October, Rechberg had lost faith in Prussia. The last straw was Bismarck's letter on 29 September. While careful to play down the significance of the commercial negotiations for their future cooperation, Bismarck declared that this depended solely on the convergence of their power–political interests. He went on to say that: '. . . we could be more certain of making progress in our common course if we both based our positions on the practical foundation of cabinet policies without allowing ourselves to be disturbed by the mist arising out of the doctrinaire and emotional policies of [some] German politicians' – a clear reference to the anti–Prussian policies of Schmerling and Biegeleben.[18] Presenting this letter to the emperor Rechberg commented bitterly: 'The conduct of business is rendered difficult to an unusual degree if one has to deal with a man who so openly confesses his political cynicism . . . such language is worthy of a Cavour. Holding on to legal rights is a misty and emotional policy! The task of restraining this gentleman and making him give up his utilitarian policy of expansion at all costs . . . surpasses all human efforts.'[19]

The resignation of Rechberg at the end of October did not signify the abandonment of dualism. On the contrary: his successor, Count Alexander von Mensdorff-Pouilly, an aristocratic soldier and ex-governor of Galicia, was just as committed to that policy. The only difference was that, being inexperienced in the world of diplomacy, Mensdorff was much more vulnerable to the openly anti-Prussian policy of Biegeleben. Consequently under Mensdorff Austrian policy oscillated uneasily between the poles of cooperation with and opposition to Prussia.

At first Mensdorff attempted to strike a bargain with Prussia over Schleswig-Holstein. The Austrian put two alternative scenarios to Bismarck. The duchies could either become an independent state under the duke of Augustenburg or they could be annexed by Prussia, in which event Austria must receive compensation elsewhere – perhaps part of Silesia? Bismarck stonewalled throughout the winter of 1864–5, partly because he was nursing along the renewal of the Customs Union on Prussian terms but perhaps also because he sensed that confrontation with Austria was more likely after Rechberg's resignation. He made it clear to Mensdorff that territorial compensation was not a possibility because no Hohenzollern ruler would agree to such a cession. Turning to the other alternative, he argued that it did not follow that the duke of Augustenburg was the legitimate heir; the claims of the grand duke of Oldenburg and even those of the king of Prussia must be seriously examined. In any event if Prussia was to forgo annexation, she must have special rights in the duchies. Only in February 1865 after constant pressure from Vienna did he reveal that these 'rights' would make Schleswig-Holstein a Prussian satellite: the army and navy of the duchies would become part of the Prussian forces; Prussia would establish a naval base at Kiel and garrison troops in the duchies; and Schleswig-Holstein would enter the Customs Union.

Incensed by the February conditions which made it perfectly plain that Prussia would neither allow the duchies to be independent nor pay any compensation to Austria, Francis Joseph changed course. First, Austria threw her weight behind the Augustenburg cause in the duchies where hitherto Prussia had been making the running drumming up support for annexation. Second, Austria persuaded Bavaria, Saxony and Hesse-Darmstadt to move in the Diet that Austria and Prussia hand over Holstein and Lauenburg to the duke of Augustenburg. They demanded a vote on this motion in seven days' time. Austria supported the motion, arguing that the Diet was not exceeding its powers but merely asking the two major German powers to reach a decision. Prussia then demanded that the motion be referred to the Holstein-Lauenburg committee (so that a vote on the issue would not be taken in the near future) because the legitimacy of the Augustenburg claims could not be taken for granted but had to be investigated alongside claims from other princely houses. But the Diet decided by nine votes to six to proceed to a vote on 6 April. On that day the motion was carried, again by nine votes to six.[20] The Austrian representative immediately declared that just after the ratification of the peace treaty with Denmark, Austria had been willing to cede her rights to the duke of Augustenburg and was still willing to negotiate with Prussia to this end. The Prussian representative, while expressing his country's willingness to negotiate, insisted that the claims of all pretenders to the ducal throne must be considered.

As the tension between the two powers mounted in April and May, the king of Prussia called a council of ministers on 29 May. Although William was now converted to annexation largely because of the sacrifices Prussian soldiers had made during the war, he was worried about the hostile attitude of Austria and the middle states and bared his conscience to his ministers. Should Prussia annex the duchies or be content with a satellite Schleswig-Holstein? Furthermore, should Prussia shrink from war if either solution led to complications? Bismarck replied that as the population of Schleswig-Holstein wanted annexation – having been subjected to a barrage of Prussian propaganda, he might have added – the only relevant question was how best to attain this objective. He sketched in three scenarios: an 'independent' Schleswig-Holstein subject to minimum conditions and loaded with a heavy war debt which would create such discontent that the inhabitants would prefer outright annexation; the duke of Augustenburg might be bought off and then Austria might agree to outright annexation; or, thirdly, Prussia might stick to the February conditions which amounted to the annexation of the duchies. If that led to war, '. . . the present moment offers more favourable chances for a warlike confrontation with Austria which, given the traditional policy of the Vienna cabinet, can scarcely be avoided sooner or later'.[21] Most of those present agreed with Bismarck that annexation was the preferred solution. Nevertheless, they wished to avoid war with Austria fearing that France and Italy would intervene on the Austrian side – a fear Bismarck discounted. The crown prince, though confident enough that once Schleswig-Holstein was under Prussian control Prussia would be able to assume the leadership in Germany, wanted to preserve the peace and denounced all talk of conflict with Austria as 'civil war'. To which Bismarck retorted that if annexation resulted in war the prize would not just be Schleswig-Holstein but 'the creation of a constitutional relationship between the middle and small states and Prussia such as His Royal Highness the Crown Prince has described as desirable'.[22] All the same, Bismarck advised the king to commence with the least provocative solution; if he wanted outright annexation then the monarch alone must make that decision. On that somewhat uncertain note the king closed the meeting. Shortly aferwards he decided to uphold the February conditions although Bismarck favoured some modifications, being prepared to drop the requirement that the Schleswig-Holstein army and navy be integrated with the Prussian forces.

The note of caution noticeable in Bismarck persisted as the war clouds gathered in June and July 1865. For example, while Bismarck was quite determined to put an end to Austrian-inspired agitation in the duchies in support of Duke Friedrich and on 11 July threatened to act independently in Schleswig-Holstein in the event of Austrian non-cooperation, nevertheless he let Mensdorff know that he was ready to negotiate about this matter.

There has been a good deal of speculation about Bismarck's motives in negotiating the Gastein Convention with Austria in August. The suggestion that he was really an old-style conservative who yearned for a lasting settlement with Austria as a bulwark against the revolution can be dismissed out of hand. Everything he said at this time indicated a firm determination to force Austria out of Germany sooner or later. But this was not the moment for war. In the first place, despite his confident assertion in the crown council that Prussia could rely on French and Italian neutrality, he may well have had last-minute doubts. Secondly, the fact that the king was taking the waters at Bad Gastein on Austrian soil did rule out war at least for the next few weeks. Thirdly, it has been suggested with some justification that financial considerations militated against war.[23] As the government was locked in conflict with the Landtag – which the king prorogued in June – war preparations had to be financed by other means. But complex plans to sell the state-owned Cologne to Minden railway, or to persuade a consortium of bankers to loan money to the Prussian merchant navy to enable it in turn to buy from the government the right to Danish war indemnities, came to nothing. An angry Bismarck blamed failure on the tender consciences of the finance and commerce ministers who had scruples about the constitutional propriety of such manoeuvres. But it did mean that Prussia would have had difficulty in financing a war in the summer of 1865.

Nor had the Austrians any desire for war. As usual their finances were in a parlous state; by now the national debt was five times Austria's annual income. Secondly, Francis Joseph's attempts to solve the constitutional problems of his dominions were entering a crucial stage. For some time it had been apparent that the February Patent had failed. Both the Germans and the Magyars were becoming restive. The former were threatening in the Reichsrat to curtail military expenditure to force the emperor to restore their traditional power monopoly in the Austrian lands. The Magyars, observing that the conservatives led by Count Moritz Esterhazy, a close friend of the emperor and a former chargé d'affaires at the papal court, were gaining the upper hand in the corridors of power in Vienna at the expense of the liberal ministers led by Schmerling, made overtures to Francis Joseph. In a series of articles in April and May 1865 Francis Deak offered to share power with the Habsburgs on condition that the Hungarian constitution of 1848 was restored. Francis Joseph grasped eagerly at this opportunity of coming to terms with the Magyars and paid a state visit to Budapest. On 30 July Schmerling resigned and a new ministry was formed under Count Richard Belcredi, a conservative prepared to rule without the Reichsrat (which remained dissolved) and do a deal with the Magyars. At such a delicate moment in the history of the monarchy, war was highly undesirable. And, as always, the international perspective could not be ignored. While Francis Joseph and his ministers had no illusions about Prussia's aggressive intentions, war without allies would be an act of imbecility and one which would play into the hands of France, a power with a vested interest in the disruption of the status quo. So the emperor dispatched Count Gustav von Blome, the Austrian ambassador in Munich, to Bad Gastein to confer with Bismarck who had arrived there to attend on his monarch.

Bismarck made not the slightest attempt to meet Blome halfway. By making ostentatious inquiries in Paris and Florence about the French and Italian attitudes should war come, he deliberately increased the pressure on Austria to give way. 'I am very friendly to him [Blome],' he wrote on 30 July. 'I reject nothing completely for at all costs we must win time.' In other words, only when the king left Bad Gastein and when Prussia had the funds for war would Bismarck be ready to fight Austria.[24] But out of his meetings with Blome emerged a compromise. While Austria dare not relinquish joint sovereignty over the duchies for fear of public reaction in Vienna, she was prepared to work out an interim agreement. She offered to allow Prussia to administer Schleswig while Austria administered Holstein. Furthermore, she was willing to sell Lauenburg to Prussia for two and a half million Danish talers. It was agreed that Schleswig-Holstein enter the Customs Union; Kiel would become a federal port and base for a future German navy (but under Prussian administration); and Rendsburg would become a federal fortress. Prussia would be allowed the use of two military roads through Holstein and postal and telegraphic communications, and agreed to build a railway from Lübeck to Kiel. Finally, Prussia would be allowed to build a canal through Holstein linking the North Sea with the Baltic. Bismarck was well satisfied with the 'papering over of the cracks in the edifice'. However provisional Austria intended the Gastein Convention to be, in practice Prussia could not now be dislodged from Schleswig. And as Austria could not bring herself to abandon Holstein, Bismarck had a convenient means of exerting pressure on her when he was ready for action. On 5 August the Austrian council of ministers accepted the package deal. Most, including Belcredi, believed this was no more than a breathing-space before the inevitable conflict. As the Viennese *Allgemeine Zeitung* mordantly observed: 'Peace and friendship – until further notice'.[25] Austria paid a heavy price in the eyes of the middle states, who denounced conservative Austria rather than predatory Prussia for this 'shameful horsetrading'. On the other hand, Austria gained valuable time in which Belcredi suspended the February Patent and restored the Hungarian constitution of 1848, shifting the balance of power to Budapest where the court took up residence.

The fragility of the convention – ratified on 20 August by king and emperor – was quickly apparent. In the autumn Bismarck began to angle for French neutrality in the event of war by informing the French ambassador that he would not object to French expansion 'wherever French was spoken in the world'.[26] In October he hurried off to Biarritz to talk face to face with Napoleon. His objective was two-fold: first, he had to reassure the emperor that the Gastein Convention, like the Schönbrunn agreement, had no permanent significance. For Napoleon's constant fear was that any agreement between the two major German powers would contain a

Prussian guarantee of Venetia which would put paid to the emperor's hopes of securing the province for the new kingdom of Italy. Once reassured on this point, Napoleon was ready to discount the idea of an alliance with Austria, a policy which was, as Bismarck knew, favoured by Edouard Drouyn de Lhuys, the French foreign minister. Secondly, Bismarck sought assurances of French neutrality when war came. At this stage he was not seeking binding commitments. Talk of compensation in return for French neutrality was, therefore, limited to generalities and hints that if Prussia became master of North Germany France might seek compensation in Belgium and Luxemburg. But that was sufficient to enable Bismarck to reassure William that Napoleon had forgiven Gastein and would 'dance the cotillon with us without knowing in advance when it will begin or what figures it will include'.[27]

Relations with Austria began to deteriorate early in October, in the first instance over Frankfurt. On 1 October that city was the venue for a meeting of delegates from several Landtage which had roundly condemned the Gastein Convention. A meeting of the National Society later in the month would very likely be equally critical. Bismarck succeeded in persuading Austria to join with Prussia in protesting to the Frankfurt senate about their tolertion of 'revolutionary' demonstrations The senate rejected interference in its internal affairs. But when Bismarck proposed that Austria and Prussia demand action by the Diet and threaten independent action against the city in the event of refusal, Austria demurred. All Mensdorff would agree to was a joint motion in the Diet asking for stricter enforcement of federal rules governing the meeting of 'revolutionary' assemblies. Austria's refusal convinced Bismarck that the usefulness of the alliance was virtually at an end.

Throughout the autumn Prussia had been hard at work suppressing the Augustenburg movement in Schleswig and consolidating her hold over the duchy. In November Bismarck launched a vitriolic campaign against the Augustenburg agitation in Holstein. The new governor of Schleswig, General Edwin von Manteuffel – whom Bismarck and Roon had successfully moved from Berlin on account of his inflexible conservatism – had begun to interfere in Holstein's administration. Much to Bismarck's annoyance, this boosted the Augustenburg movement. On 23 January 1866 a mass demonstration in Altona expressed enthusiastic support for Duke Friedrich and demanded the calling together of the Schleswig-Holstein estates. The Austrian governor, Baron Anton von Gablenz, quickly regretted his decision to allow the meeting to take place, while Francis Joseph was greatly upset by its radicalism. Bismarck pressed home his advantage, demanding joint action to repress 'revolutionary' movements in the duchies. If Austria refused, Prussia would be forced to consider the 1864 alliance at an end. Prussia would then be completely free to pursue a policy more in accordance with her interests.

Austria was now at the parting of the ways. If she could not and would not abandon Holstein – which she thought would be tantamount to surrendering her claims to primacy in Germany – she had to stand firm against Prussian encroachments. On 7 February in her reply to the Prussian note, Austria, though apologetic enough about the Altona incident, defended her right to act as she pleased in Holstein. On 21 February the council of ministers endorsed a tougher policy. No one wanted war or thought there was any cause for war. But in view of Prussia's provocative policy the ministers agreed with the emperor that precautionary military measures were in order. Orders to this effect were at once sent to the war ministry. Meanwhile, Austria would continue her diplomatic efforts to avoid war but would, if need be, 'show her teeth'.[28]

Seven days later the Prussian crown council moved on to a collision course. Though the king and some ministers paid lip service to the desirability of a peaceful outcome, all were well aware that, as Austria would not change her policy, war was the almost certain outcome. By now the king was converted to Bismarck's line: Schleswig-Holstein was not the real issue – Prussia, he said, could negotiate with Austria on that; what was at stake was the right of Prussia to a 'decisive political preponderance in North Germany'. Bismarck spelt it out with characteristic bluntness: 'the whole historical development in Germany and the hostile attitude of Austria is driving us to war. It would be a mistake to try and avoid it'. Indeed, 'it would be cleverer to bring about [a war] when the situation is favourable to us than to wait until Austria starts it in conditions advantageous to herself'. The council agreed to approach France and Italy as a matter of urgency. Moltke believed that active Italian participation in the war was of crucial importance; Austria could put 240,000 men in the field in Bohemia which Prussia could match without relying on the Landwehr, but only if Austria was obliged to station 52,000 men in South Germany to protect her southern flank against the Italians. The hope that war could deflect attention from the constitutional crisis occurred to some ministers; Count Fritz zu Eulenburg, the interior minister, thought a war fought for the honour of Prussia would result in a more amenable Landtag being elected. Significantly Bismarck rejected this as a primary reason for war: 'domestic considerations do not make war a necessity though they are indeed additional reasons to make it look opportune'. So the council resolved on 28 February to persevere with the present policy on Schleswig-Holstein and the larger German question 'without regard for the danger of a break and a war with Austria'.[29] The crown prince's strictures on conflict with Austria as 'civil war' were listened to in stony silence.

As the crisis deepened in the spring of 1866, inevitably Francis Joseph's military advisers began to get the upper hand in Vienna. Acutely aware that Prussia could mobilize her forces in four weeks compared with Austria's seven to eight weeks, they urged that further precautionary measures be taken without delay. Rumours of Prussian plans to occupy Saxony when war broke out and reports of practice mobilization in Berlin strengthened their entreaties. On 14 March on Francis Joseph's orders twenty infantry battalions and several cavalry regiments were dispatched to reinforce the Austrian army in Bohemia. Predictably King William signed orders on 27 and 29 March placing the five divisions guarding the Austrian and Saxon frontiers on a war footing and arming the frontier fortresses in Silesia. Mensdorff struggled on manfully to avoid disaster. On 31 March in an attempt to win international support he assured the Great Powers that Austrian intentions were peaceful and that troop movements in Bohemia were solely for the purpose of putting down anti-semitic outbursts, and challenged Prussia to explain her warlike measures.

Secondly, knowing – as did all Europe – that Bismarck exerted enormous influence over King William, 'winding him up every morning', Mensdorff tried to outflank the minister–president by appealing personally to court circles in Berlin who viewed the prospect of war with conservative Austria with sheer horror. The influential group included: Queen Augusta, the king's wife; the crown prince and his wife 'Vicky'; Dowager Queen Elisabeth; Grand Duchess Alexandrine of Mecklenburg-Schwerin, the king's sister; and the duke of Coburg, the king's son-in-law. The so-called 'Coburg intrigue' worked up to a point. King William was ready enough to fight Austria but had not yet overcome residual moral scruples.[30] Consequently he ordered Bismarck to moderate his belligerent language. But even so the Prussian note of 6 April was still sufficiently sharp in tone to provoke an acrimonious reply on 8 April drafted by Biegeleben which rejected the accusation of warlike intentions and demanded of Prussia that she stand down her forces.

The circle of mutual mistrust was now complete and the descent to war gathered pace. On 8 April Prussia concluded an alliance with Italy. Bismarck had persuaded the crown council on 28 February to send a mission headed by General Count Helmuth von Moltke to Florence. In fact the Italians took the initiative. Conscious of their military inferiority *vis-à-vis* Austria, they hoped that negotiations with Prussia would frighten the Austrians into surrendering Venetia. This dodge – instigated by Napoleon – did not work. But out of the conversations in Berlin emerged an alliance. In the event of Prussia declaring war on Austria within the next three months, Italy would declare war on her as well. The prize was Venetia. While this treaty left the initiative with Bismarck it should be noted that it set a July limit by which time he had to begin the war. The Prusso-Italian alliance was a flagrant violation of article eleven of the federal constitution which forbade members to enter into binding commitments directed against other member states, a moral lapse which weighed heavily on the king's conscience.

In his dealings with France Bismarck was much less successful. Quite correctly he calculated that Napoleon hoped to be *tertius gaudens* when war came and would try to keep his hands as free as possible. Nevertheless, at the crown council Bismarck emphasized the need for specific assurances of neutrality from France. At his request King William wrote to Napoleon early in March proposing an *entente plus intime* between the two countries. Napoleon replied evasively that while he would remain neutral, he would seek agreement with Prussia only if the European balance of power was disturbed, which put the ball back in the Prussian court. Hints of compensation dropped by Bismarck did not alter the French stance. In June Austria, frightened by the possibility of a Franco-Prussian alliance, came to terms with Napoleon. It was agreed that if Austria won the war she would surrender Venetia to France – this, incidentally, made a complete nonsense of the Prusso-Italian treaty for whoever won in Germany Venetia was certain to become Italian. Napoleon agreed to Habsburg expansion in Germany but carefully qualified this by stipulating that this must not upset the balance of power. Verbally Austria promised to strengthen the middle states – Bavaria, Saxony and Württemberg – at the expense of the smaller brethren and indicated her willingness to accept an independent Rhineland state. It has been quite rightly pointed out that, because Bismarck could not obtain the specific assurances from Napoleon, the war was a high-risk operation and not the inevitable victory which the German chancellor later pretended it had been .The betting odds were heavily in favour of an Austrian victory. Unless Prussia could win quickly, a long drawn-out war with Great Power intervention was a likely outcome. That would lead in all probability to a compromise settlement and the dismissal of Bismarck from office.

Another danger threatened Bismarck's war plans. Throughout April Mensdorff was working for peace. On 15 April Prussia replied to the Austrian note of 8 April. Predictably Prussia rejected the Austrian demand for unilateral disarmament. But – thanks to the tender conscience of the king – Prussia offered to stand her forces down provided Austria did so first, as she had been the first to take military measures. The council of ministers in Vienna, still favouring a peaceful solution if at all possible, authorized Mensdorff on 18 April to withdraw Austrian forces from the Bohemian frontier when Prussia acted in like manner, either on the same or even on the next day. At King William's insistence and much to Bismarck's chagrin, Prussia accepted the Austrian proposal on 21 April. Prussia was to stand down her forces when she received confirmation that Francis Joseph had issued similar orders.

Whatever slim possibility there had been of a de-escalation of the crisis at the twelfth hour vanished on the same day, much to Bismarck's relief. For on 20 April news arrived in Vienna of threatening Italian troop movements. On 21 April , on the insistence of his generals, Francis Joseph ordered the mobilization of the southern army. In retaliation King Victor Emmanuel ordered general mobilization on 26 April. The knowledge that Italy had an agreement with Prussia obliged Francis Joseph on 27 April to order mobilization against Prussia. On 1 May the emperor ordered a further strengthening of his armies in the north. When this news reached Berlin the king, though still resisting the advice of Roon and Moltke that he at once order general mobilization, did authorize them to put five army corps on a war footing on 4 May. On 7 May mobilization orders were issued for the rest of Prussia's forces.

Meanwhile the struggle to capture the support of public opinion – or at least the articulate sections of it – for the coming conflagration was well under way. Bismarck's determination to turn the dispute about the duchies into the broader issue of reform of the Confederation and the establishment of a Little German state was plain enough at the crown council in February. In fact, throughout the winter of 1865-6 he had been toying with the idea of harnessing national liberal opinion to the chariot wheels of Prussian expansionism. And in view of his failure to obtain definite assurances from France it became all the more necessary to play the national card to hold Napoleon in check should the war be long drawn–out and the emperor intervene in the struggle. The claim that Prussia was unifying Germany would, so Bismarck calculated, make it more difficult for Napoleon, the supporter of nationalism in Italy, to oppose Prussia. Prussia fired the first shot in a circular note to all German governments on 24 March. She protested that the military measures she had taken in Silesia were a necessary response to provocative Austrian moves. And as the Confederation in its present form clearly could not afford security to the members, Prussia had to rely on the goodwill of individual states. The purpose of the note was to ascertain the members' attitude *vis-à-vis* the dispute with Austria. To prove her bona fides, Prussia went on to raise the question of reform but without entering into specific detail. The response was not encouraging. The states simply drew

Prussia's attention to article eleven of the constitution which obliged disputants to submit their case to mediation and arbitration by the Diet. On 9 April Karl von Savigny, the Prussian representative at Frankfurt, rejected this procedure as far too dilatory. Neither the Frankfurt Parliament nor the Congress of Princes had succeeded in overcoming the disunity of Germany. The only way forward – and this was the sensational feature of the speech – was to call an assembly chosen by direct election on the basis of universal manhood suffrage to discuss reform of the Confederation on the basis of proposals which would be drawn up in advance by member governments.

The response was no better. Conservatives everywhere were horrified by Bismarck's readiness to resort to the revolutionary weapon of universal suffrage. Predictably the tsar and his chief minister, Prince Alexander Gortschakov, denounced the proposal as a grave violation of monarchical principle, while King William was thoroughly shocked by Bismarck's bold tactics – but nevertheless clung to the man who had kept the Landtag at bay for three years. All shades of liberal opinion dismissed the proposal as a meaningless threat, the last gasp of a desperate and isolated gambler still locked in bitter conflict with the Prussian Landtag. Liberals simply did not believe that universal suffrage – for which they had no liking – would produce majorities supportive of reactionaries such as Bismarck. And in any case his recent attempts to remove the immunity of Landtag deputies and so enable the government to prosecute their leaders for allegedly seditious remarks had thoroughly enraged liberal opinion and extinguished any hopes – which Bismarck still cherished – of diverting attention away from illiberality at home by holding out the prospect of a 'national' war against Austria.

The response to the Prussian note of 24 March made it abundantly clear that the middle and small states would not support Prussia in the coming conflict. However, while universal suffrage aroused grave misgivings among the middle states and in Vienna, to reject the Prussian proposals of 9 April when public opinion was beginning to count in German politics would have been a blunder. Accordingly they were referred to committee on 21 April in what was clearly a delaying manoeuvre. Baron Aloys von Kübeck remarked that while Austria repudiated the insinuation that her armaments presented a threat to Prussia, she was willing to discuss reform of the Confederation – provided Prussia put some concrete proposals before the Diet, which she had not done so far.[31] A few days later war loomed much nearer with Austrian and Prussian mobilization. Saxony, whose frontiers would certainly be violated in the event of war, began to take military measures at the end of April. This led to Prussian threats against Saxony. Anxious to

131

avoid a conflict if at all possible, Bavaria and Württemberg, supported by Hesse, Saxe-Weimar, Saxe-Coburg-Gotha and Nassau, moved a motion to this effect which the Diet adopted on 24 May:all states which had armed above peace-time levels were asked to inform the next session of the Diet whether and under what conditions they were prepared to stand down their forces simultaneously and on a day to be determined by the Diet.

On 1 June Austria replied to the resolution in a manner which made it clear that the days of shadow-boxing with Prussia were over. Kübeck declared that Austria's military measures were thoroughly justified by Prussia's determination to resolve the Schleswig-Holstein issue by force and by her deplorable decision to seek the assistance of the enemy of Austria (Italy). Austria could demobilise her forces only when 'law and treaty rights, not the politics of violence, reign in Germany' and when Prussia complied with the lawful decisions of the Diet. Her attempts to resolve the Schleswig-Holstein question by negotiation with Prussia had been frustrated so that she now passed the issue over to the Diet whose decisions Austria would respect. Meanwhile, the Austrian governor of Holstein had been ordered to summon the Holstein estates to express their views on the future of the duchies.

As Austria was now in breach of the Gastein Convention, Bismarck easily persuaded King William to take action ostensibly to restore joint rule over Holstein. On 8 June Manteuffel sent his forces into the duchy. The Holstein estates were prevented from meeting by posting guards with fixed bayonets at the door of the assembly hall. However, the anticipated clash did not occur. On the contrary, much to the surprise of Berlin and Vienna Gablenz withdrew his forces into Hamburg and from there to Bohemia. The chivalrous behaviour of both commanders was such that the Austrian brigade left its headquarters in Kiel to the strains of the Austrian national anthem played by the band of the Prussian marines.

On 9 June Savigny replied to Austria. She had acted illegally, he declared, in asking the Diet to resolve the question of the duchies. The exclusive rights of Austria and Prussia in this matter had been stated clearly enough in the Austro-Prussian alliance in January 1864, in the Peace of Vienna and in the Gastein Convention. In a last desperate attempt to rally liberal opinion, he concluded his speech by assuring the Diet that Prussia would welcome a settlement of the Schleswig-Holstein question in a nationally elected body which would be a counterweight to 'particularist interests' and which would guarantee that the 'whole fatherland' and not 'dynastic avariciousness' would benefit from Prussian sacrifices in the war against Denmark.

Kübeck rejected the charge of breach of treaty, pointing out that

Austria had repeatedly assured the Diet that she was seeking a resolution of the Schleswig-Holstein question which took full account
of the rights and interests of the Confederation. In sending troops
into Holstein Prussia had breached the Gastein Convention which –
Kübeck was careful to point out – was a purely provisional
arrangement which Austria had been upholding only until such
time as the Diet resolved the contentious issue. Furthermore, by
assuming powers of government in Holstein Manteuffel had violated the terms of the Peace of Vienna. Because of these misde-
meanours, and also to protect the threatened rights of member
states, Austria moved the mobilization of all non-Prussian federal
forces on 11 June. The motion was carried on 14 June by eight
votes to five. Voting with Austria were Bavaria, Saxony, Hanover,
Württemberg, Electoral Hesse, Hesse-Darmstadt and curia 16
(Liechtenstein etc.).[32] Prussia, whose representative did not vote,
was supported by the Saxon princedoms, Luxemburg/Limburg, the
Mecklenburgs, curia 15 (Oldenburg) and curia 17 (Hamburg,
Bremen and Lübeck). Baden abstained, Holstein/Lauenburg had no
vote and the votes of Brunswick and Nassau in curia 13 being
cast on opposite sides cancelled each other out.

The last scene in the drama took place immediately after the
vote was taken. Savigny stood up and declared that the resolution
clearly conflicted with the federal constitution; admittedly this guaranteed the territory of each member, but that could not possibly
apply to Prussia's position in Holstein which was regulated by the
Peace of Vienna – an agreement to which the Diet was not a party.
Furthermore, despite the steady build-up of Austrian armaments
against Prussia, all the Diet had done in response to the Prussian
appeal for assistance was to allow several members to arm themselves without good cause. Prussia regarded these military measures
as a threat depriving her of that security which article two of the
constitution guaranteed to all members. This feeling of insecurity
was deepened still further by the Diet's action in carrying the
Austrian motion despite Prussian protests. Prussia held this resolution to be in breach of the constitution and consequently Savigny
declared the Confederation dissolved in Prussian eyes. However,
that did not mean that the national foundations of the
Confederation were null and void. On the contrary, Prussia regarded it as the bounden duty of all states to give appropriate expression to the unity of the German nation. Prussia for her part was
ready to form a new confederation based on detailed proposals
which Savigny now laid before them. The new state would exclude
Austria from Germany but made provision for a *weiterer Bund* to
be negotiated later. As Savigny walked ostentatiously out of the
hall, the Württemberg delegate was speaking in support of the
Austrian president's protest that the Confederation was an indissol-

uble union from which Prussia had no right to contract out. After several members spoke in like manner the president adjourned the proceedings with the comment that responsibility for the serious situation which now arose lay solely at Prussia's door. The members loyal to the Confederation would know how to do their duty to each other and to the German nation by standing on the firm ground of federal law.

On 15 June Prussia sent ultimatums to the neighbouring states of Saxony, Hanover and Electoral Hesse demanding that they stand down their forces and join the new state Prussia intended to construct on the ruins of the old Confederation. If they agreed within twelve hours, their sovereign rights would be respected; otherwise Prussia would declare war on them. When they failed to reply Prussia carried out her threat. At midnight on 15 June Prussian troops invaded these three states. On 18 June at the request of Electoral Hesse the Diet asked all members to give military assistance to states under attack from Prussia. Prussia did not formally declare war on Austria. But when Austria declared her willingness to assist any state invaded by Prussia this was interpreted in Berlin as equivalent to a declaration of war. That this was what Austria intended was clear from the war manifesto issued by Francis Joseph on 17 June. In this roundabout way the Austro-Prussian War began. The Italians declared war on Austria on 20 June and hostilities commenced three days later.

Looking back over the century since the dramatic defeat of Austria in 1866, it is easy to fall into the trap of supposing that the three wars of 1864, 1866 and 1870–1 were inevitable steps on the road to the creation of a German Reich excluding Austria from Germany. The implication of this interpretation is that Little Germany was the only 'national' solution on offer and, therefore, historically 'inevitable'. This is said with hindsight, the great enemy of the historian. Contemporaries did not share this view. The most important German states were ranged against Prussia. Many spoke of the clash of arms as a dishonourable 'civil war', not as a struggle for national unification. Bismarck remained a thoroughly unpopular figure; the failure of an attempt on his life in May did not evoke a wave of sympathy but expressions of regret in several quarters that the assassin had missed his target. And, finally, he had failed in his bid to mobilize middle-class support because his conflict with the Prussian Landtag alienated liberal opinion from a man whose Great Prussian objectives did, in fact, coincide with the Little Germany so many North German liberals were working for. Small wonder that when Bismarck, walking in the garden of the foreign office at midnight on 15 June, informed his companion Lord Augustus Loftus, the British ambassador, that the Prussian attack had begun he added: 'If we are beaten, I shall not return here. I shall fall in the last charge. One can but die once: and if we are beaten it is better to die.'[33] It has rightly been said of Bismarck that 'when a situation reached crisis point [he had] a tendency for *va banque* play bordering on the self-destructive'.[34]

Further proof that the war was a high-risk operation in which he was perfectly prepared to use unorthodox methods can be seen in Bismarck's efforts to stir up national resentment against the Habsburgs. In the spring of 1866 reports from Count Karl Georg von Usedom, Prussian ambassador in Florence, that Hungarian émigrés in Italy with the support of King Victor Emmanuel would stage a diversion in the event of war were sufficient for Bismarck to instruct Usedom to keep in touch with these circles. Early in June Hungarian general Stefan Türr, adjutant to King Victor, and General Georg Klapka, a veteran of the 1848 uprising, were summoned to Berlin for conversations about the formation of a Magyar legion. Recruitment for this began in Prussia under Klapka's direction. Similarly, when Bismarck was informed of plans to found a Serbian legion to invade Austria he telegraphed approval and sent a Prussian envoy to Belgrade. Nothing came of these plans simply because of the decisive defeat of Austria at Königgrätz. The argument that Bismarck intended to threaten Austria only with this bogey-man and never intended to release the nationalist genie from the bottle does not convince. Had the war dragged on, the legions would have marched, and national passions would have been aroused in the Habsburg dominions and would soon have spread to Prussian Poland.

If the origins of the war of 1866 are separated out from the consequences, one must conclude that it was a power struggle for mastery in Germany, an eighteenth-century war fought with nineteenth-century weapons. Austria was seeking to maintain a particular balance of power which would enable her to continue to play a European role despite her woefully inadequate resources, while Prussia, her territorial ambitions underpinned by industrial power and the Customs Union, was equally determined to destroy the status quo and acquire control of at least North and Central Germany. Both powers had endeavoured to exploit the new forces of liberalism and nationalism with varying degrees of success. On the eve of the war public opinion favoured Austria rather than Prussia. Certainly there was an outburst of national feeling in North Germany after the defeat of Austria. But there was little sign of this in June 1866; to contemporaries it seemed much more a clash between rival particularisms than a struggle to unite Germany. Whether post-Königgrätz nationalism extended to the broad mass of the population in the countryside remains an open question. Bismarck's own comments − admittedly written twenty-five years later – are instructive.

> In practice a German needs a dynasty to which he is devoted or a
> stimulus which arouses him to anger and drives him to action. The
> last-mentioned phenomenon is not a permanent institution in the
> nature of things. He is much more ready to demonstrate his
> patriotism as a Prussian, a Hanoverian, a Württemberger, a Bavarian
> or a Hessian than as a German. And in the lower classes and in
> parliamentary parties it will be a long time before it is any different .
> . . the Germans' love of fatherland requires a prince on whom they
> can focus their devotion. If one assumes circumstances in which all
> the German dynasties were suddenly removed it is unlikely that
> German national feeling would hold all Germans together according
> to international law . . . . The Germans would fall victim to tighter-
> knit nations once the bonding agent which lies in the princely houses
> was lost.[35]

THE WAR, THE PEACE OF PRAGUE AND ITS SIGNIFICANCE

Hostilities in the Austro-Prussian War commenced on 16 June with
the invasion of Saxony, Hanover and Electoral Hesse. Apart from
the initial setback Prussian forces suffered at the hands of the
Hanoverians at the battle of Langensalza, Prussia successfully over-
ran the three states within a few days. She encountered little serious resistance from the other states which had sided with Austria.
In general they were slow off the mark in mobilizing their forces.
By mid June only the troops of Hesse-Darmstadt and Nassau – a
total of 12,000 men organized in three infantry brigades and one
cavalry brigade – were ready to march. The Bavarians, who could
have put 50,000 infantrymen and 7000 cavalry in the field, dragged
their feet partly because of the indifference of the people who were
neither pro-Austrian nor pro-Prussian. Secondly, little attempt was
made to coordinate the strategies of these states with that of
Austria. Bavaria, for example, refused point-blank to strengthen
Austrian defences in Bohemia. On 4 and 10 July the Prussians
repelled Bavarian attempts to advance into Thuringia; on 19 July
the Prussians occupied Frankfurt; and on 27 July they finally broke
the resistance of the federal army corps near Würzburg.

The battle of Königgrätz, or Sadowa as the French preferred to
call it, was the turning-point of the war. The Austrians had been

forced on to the defensive by the rapid defeat of Saxony. It was no longer possible to invade Prussian territory now that the mountain passes were under Prussian control. General Ludwig von Benedek, the Austrian commander, concentrated the army of the north around the fortress of Königgrätz. The aim of the Prussian strategy, based on the teachings of Karl von Clausewitz, was to strike an annihilating blow at the enemy. The tactics were those of Moltke, chief of the general staff. Three armies – the second commanded by the crown prince on the left flank, the first army commanded by Prince Friedrich Karl in the centre and the army of the Elbe commanded by General Herwath von Bittenfeld on the right flank – advanced separately into Bohemia. They met only on the field of battle – a tactic tried out for the first time in 1866 and sharply criticized in the war council before its adoption.

The outcome of the passage of arms on 3 July was decisive for the course of the war. Benedek, with 245,000 men and 600 guns under his command supplemented by 25,000 Saxons and sixty guns,was defeated by 280,000 Prussians with 900 guns. The Prussian victory was due to several factors. First, the role of the general staff. At that time general staffs were little more than collections of clerks and adjutants assisting the commander-in-chief. Moltke, chief of the Prussian general staff since 1857, turned it into a most efficient planning body which coordinated all aspects of mobilization and ensured that the railway and road systems were used effectively to move Prussian forces with great rapidity to key strategic points where it would be costly for the enemy to attack. Secondly, the Prussian infantry was fully equipped with the breech-loading needle gun which guaranteed more effective firepower over the Austrians who were still using muzzle-loading rifles; a Prussian infantryman at Königgrätz could loose off six shots to every Austrian one. Thirdly, Austrian planning, like that of other armies, was much less methodical than that of the Prussians. And fourthly, Benedek, appointed commander of the army of the north only in May and against his will, failed to exploit the advantages of his defensive position. The second Prussian army was advancing so slowly that had Benedek attacked the exposed lines of communication of the first army on his right flank, the outcome might have been very different, But, as always on the battlefield, the victory goes to the side making the fewest mistakes. Moltke's meticulously worked-out plan was not completely successful. The Austrians were not annihilated. Thanks to superior artillery – reorganized after the 1859 campaign – and to the cavalry, the Austrians held up the Prussian advance so that only 22,000 Austrians were taken prisoner. Though by 18 July the Prussian armies were only nineteen kilometres from Vienna, the bulk of Benedek's army had crossed the Danube where it hoped to join up with the victorious army of the south which under Archduke Albrecht had defeated the Italians at Custozza on 24 June. But lengthening lines of communication and an outbreak of cholera – which affected the Austrians too – slowed down the Prussians. More decisive, however, was Napoleon III's intervention. Although King William's belligerent instincts were now fully aroused and he, like his generals, wished to march in triumph through Vienna, Bismarck was able to persuade him after arduous interviews to agree to an armistice which came into force on 22 July. On 26 July preliminary peace terms were signed at Nikolsburg. And the definitive peace settlement, the Peace of Prague, was signed on 23 August.

This peace treaty encapsulated the essence of the 'German Revolution'. This was how friends and enemies of Prussia regarded the outcome of the Seven Weeks' War. 'The present war,' wrote the moderate liberal Johann Bluntschli, 'is the German Revolution taking the form of war directed from above instead of from below in accordance with the nature of the [Prussian] monarchy.'[36] The most important consequence of the war was, of course, the exclusion of Austria from Germany; she acquiesced in the dissolution of the old Confederation and recognized the creation of a new association of states north of the river Main – the North German Confederation as it became in 1867. South of the river a new association of states would be formed which would have 'independent existence' internationally but would have 'national connections' with the North German Confederation to be arranged later by both parties. For the rest Austria surrendered Venetia to the kingdom of Italy and agreed to pay a war indemnity of forty million Prussian talers. It was also stated in the peace treaty that a plebiscite would be held in North Schleswig to allow the Danish-speaking population to decide their own future – article five was, in fact, repudiated by Prussia in 1879.

Prussia seized the opportunity to round off her territories in North and Central Germany at the expense of the defeated states – further proof that the aggrandisement of Prussia, not the unification of Germany, had been the primary objective of the war. As well as Schleswig-Holstein, Hanover, Electoral Hesse, Hesse-Homburg, Nassau and the city of Frankfurt were annexed by Prussia. This increased her population from 17.2 to 24.6 million and at last linked up her western and eastern territories. The violation of the principle of legitimacy – a king, an electoral prince and two dukes were deposed – shocked many conservatives. The conservative philosopher Ludwig von Gerlach expressed his horror in forceful language.

> That Hanover, Nassau and Frankfurt were eaten up by Bismarck quite in accordance with the laws of natural history, I do not have the least

doubt. My pain is not sentimental pain that Hanover, Nassau and Frankfurt do not exist any more but the pain that a Prussian German Christian feels that my party and my fatherland Prussia has violated the ten commandments of God in this terrible manner and through a depraved pseudo–patriotism had done damage to her soul and stained her conscience.[37]

King William, too, had moral scruples about the annexations; initially he had been willing to settle for a change of ruler in these territories and some adjustment of frontiers at their expense. But, as usual, he gave way without too much opposition before Bismarck's arguments. This was a proleptic hint of what was to come when bills for the annexation of Hanover and Electoral Hesse were debated in both houses of parliament. Gerlach's scruples were brushed aside by the overwhelming majority of conservatives who rejoiced to see Prussia dominant in North and Central Germany.

The victory over Austria led to an impassioned outburst of national feeling which gripped wide sections of the German people. As we have seen already, when war broke out it was essentially a conflict between Prussian and Austrian particularism. Government propaganda and Bismarck's determined attempts to harness national liberalism to Prussia's expansionist policy had singularly failed. But as news came in of the progress of the Prussian armies, the popular mood changed. Through conscription nearly every Prussian family had some members on active service which ensured that Prussian victories – won virtually unaided against Austria and her allies – sparked off a wave of patriotic feeling which merged into and was sustained by the solid block of middle–class opinion supporting a Little German solution of the German problem. Middle–class liberals in South Germany who also favoured Little Germany were caught up in this new mood in part because the real possibility of French intervention reawakened anti-French feelings south of the Main. The conversion experience of Rudolf von Ihering, professor of law at Göttingen University, was typical of many liberals in the summer of 1866. On the eve of war he confided to a friend that 'a war has perhaps never been advertised with such shamelessness and with such ghastly frivolity as the one Bismarck is currently seeking to launch against Austria. One's innermost being is revolted by such a crime against all moral and legal principles.' In August, writing to another friend, his attitude had changed dramatically.

I bow before the genius of Bismarck who has accomplished with great energy a master stroke of political teamwork. I have forgiven this man all that he has done in the past, yes more than that I have convinced myself that what we uninitiated thought was criminal arrogance was necessary; it has since then become evident that it was

139

an indispensable means to the goal . . . for such a man of action I would give a hundred men of liberal opinions [but of] impotent honesty. Could I have believed nine weeks ago that I would be writing a dithyramb to Bismarck?[38]

Finally, the victory over Austria had significant repercussions upon the political situation in Prussia. Even before news of Königgrätz reached Berlin, elections to the Landtag had resulted in dramatic changes. The Conservatives captured 142 seats where previously they had held 28, while the left liberals fell from 110 to 65 seats and the Progressives from 143 to 83. With the support of nine Old Liberals, the Conservatives controlled the lower house. Although liberals and conservatives alike expected that Bismarck would revise the constitution in the conservative interest, in fact he placed an indemnity bill before the Landtag. While the government refused to apologize for collecting taxes since 1862 but justified its actions on the grounds of national emergency, nevertheless the right of the Landtag to consent to future legislation was conceded. The passage of the bill by 230 votes to 75 marked a turning-point in the history of German liberalism. It is too facile an interpretation to say that most liberals preferred unification to freedom. They wanted both. As Karl Twesten, one of their leaders, put it: 'no one may be criticized for giving precedence to the issue of power at this time and maintaining that the issues of freedom can wait provided that nothing happens which can permanently prejudice them'.[39] Many moderates now left the Progressive Party and after the elections to the Reichstag of the North German Confederation joined with like-minded deputies from other states to form the National Liberal Party, a grouping whose main objective was the completion of unification.

NOTES AND REFERENCES

1. Quoted in Hans Kohn, *The Mind of Germany: The Education of a Nation* (London, 1961) p. 160.
2. Quoted in Hans-Ulrich Wehler, *Das deutsche Kaiserreich 1871–1918* (Göttingen, 1980), p. 39.
3. Ibid.
4. Leading American revisionists include Paul W. Schroeder, Roy A. Austensen and Richard Elrod. An overview of their arguments in Roy A. Austensen, 'Austria and the Struggle for Supremacy in Germany 1848–1864', *JMH* 52, 1980. Representative of Austrian revisionism is Michael Derndarsky, 'Österreich und die deutsche

Frage zwischen 1848 und 1866/71: Konzeptionelles Dilemma und situative Probleme der Donaumonarchie gegenüber Deutschland,' in Josef Becker/Andreas Hillgruber (eds), *Die deutsche Frage im 19 und 20 Jahrhundert* (München, 1983). Cf. H. Bleiber, 'Der deutsche Bund in der Geschichtsschreibung der DDR', *HZ* 248, Heft 1, 1989.

5. Article one was carried by 340 votes to 76, article three by 316 to 90.

6. The argument is advanced by two Austrians: Helmut Rumpler, *Die deutsche Politik des Freiherrn Beust 1848–1850* (Vienna, Cologne, Graz, 1972), and Hubert Glaser, 'Zwischen Grossmächte und Mittelstaaten: Über einige Konstanten der deutschen Politik Bayerns in der Ära von der Pfordten', in Heinrich Lutz and H. Rumpler, *Österreich und die deutsche Frage im 19 und 20 Jahrhundert : Probleme der politisch-staatlichen und sozial-kulturellen Differenzierung von deutschem Mitteleüropa* (Vienna, 1982). But cf. review by Eberhard Kolb, *HZ* 1973, which suggests that Rumpler greatly exaggerates the 'clash of principle' between the middle states' concern for states' rights and the power politics of Prussia – more likely the middle states, like the others, were simply protecting their interests.

7. To Prokesch-Osten he wrote on 15 November 1850: 'Therefore, I see salvation for both of us, indeed for all humanity, only in Prussia's open break with her recent past; with her self-seeking treasonous friends; and in her intimate alliance with Austria for a common struggle against the revolution, in whatever guise it appears.' Quoted in Roy A. Austensen, op. cit., p. 213. It is interesting, too, that he conducted a private correspondence with Manteuffel from February to April 1851 in the course of which he offered to share the functions of the Confederation with Prussia if she would concede the presidency to Austria: Hans Julius Schoeps, *Von Ölmutz nach Dresden 1850-1851. Ein Beitrag zur Geschichte der Reformen am deutschen Bund* (Cologne and Berlin, 1972), pp. 178-213.

8. He referred to it on one occasion as a 'bugbear' : Friedrich Walter (ed.) *Aus dem Nachlass Carl Friedrich Kübeck von Kübau: Tagebücher Briefe Aktenstücke 1841-1855, Veröffentlichungen der Kommission für neuere Geschichte Österreichs, vol. 55* (Graz, and Cologne, 1960), p. 79.

9. Writing to Metternich on 3 May 1850 Anton von Prokesch-Osten commented: 'My faith in Prussia is pretty well ended. The conservatives as well as the swindlers put Prussian vanity and expansionist interests above all else; and the struggle against revolution is at best in second place, which is as good as none at all.' Quoted in Roy A. Austensen, op. cit., p. 214.

10. Winfried Baumgarten, 'Zur Aussenpolitik Friedrich Wilhelms IV 1840–1858', in Otto Büsch and Klaus Zernack (eds), *Jahrbuch für die Geschichte Mittel und Ost-Deutschlands* (Berlin, 1987), vol. 36, p. 146.

11. Quoted in Hans-Werther Hahn, *Geschichte des deutschen Zollvereins* (Göttingen, 1984), p. 56.

12. Quoted in Lawrence J. Baack, *Christian Bernstorff and Prussia:*

Diplomacy and Reform Conservatism 1818–1832 (New Brunswick, 1980), p. 125.

13. The Tax Union formed in 1834 consisted of Hanover, Brunswick, Oldenburg, Schaumburg-Lippe. Brunswick joined the Customs Union in 1841, Hanover and Schaumburg-Lippe in 1851 and Oldenburg in 1852. Lübeck joined in 1868, Hamburg in 1881 and Bremen in 1884.

14. Delbrück admitted in his memoirs that this was his objective throughout: . . . we wanted no German–Austrian customs union; we wanted no [equalization] of the tariff schedules: we wanted, at least as far as I was concerned, only a limited development of the February treaty.' Quoted in Theodore S. Hamerow, *The Social Foundations of German Unification: Struggles and Achievements* (Princeton, 1972), pp. 129–30.

15. Ibid. p. 129.

16. Hans-Werther Hahn, op. cit., p. 187.

17. *APP* 5 no. 147, Bismarck to Karl von Werther, 14 June 1864.

18. *GW* 4 no. 149, Bismarck to Rechberg, 29 September 1864.

19. *DPO* 4 no. 1825, Rechberg to the emperor.

20. Voting with Prussia were Hanover, Electoral Hesse, Mecklenburg, curia 15 and the curia of the Hansa towns.

21. *APP* 6 no. 100, Preussischer Kronrat, 29 May 1865.

22. Ibid.

23. John C.G. Röhl, 'Kriegsgefahr und Gasteiner Konvention. Bismarck, Eulenburg und die Vertagung des preussisch–österreichischen Krieges im Sommer 1865', in I. Geiss and Bernd Jürgen Wendt (eds), *Deutschland in der Weltpolitik des 19 und 20 Jahrhunderts* (Düsseldorf, 1974); cf. Fritz Stern, *Gold and Iron : Bismarck Bleichröder and the Building of the German Empire* (London, 1977), pp. 64–5.

24. Q voted in John C.G. Röhl, op. cit., p. 101.

25. C.W.Clark, *Francis Joseph and Bismarck before the War of 1866: The Diplomacy of Austria before the War of 1866* (Cambridge, Mass., 1934), p. 294.

26. *OD* VII no. 1590, Lefebvre de Béhaine to Drouyn de Lhuys, 27 September 1865.

27. *GW* 14/2 no. 1129, Bismarck to Hermann von Thile, 23 October 1865.

28. *DPO* 5 no. 2325.

29. *APP* 6 no. 449, Crown Council minutes, 28 February 1866, and no. 500, Moltke's notes on the Crown Council. Cf. Heinrich-Otto Meisner (ed), *Kaiser Friedrich III Tagebücher von 1848–1866* (Leipzig, 1929), pp. 541–4 for a more outspoken version.

30. The British ambassador in Berlin summed up the king aptly as 'a hesitating sovereign with an intermittent conscience acting under mixed and shifting influences'. *APP* 6 no. 325, Napier to Russell, 14 October 1865.

31. Equally tongue-in-cheek Berlin informed the committee on 11 May of the changes Prussia envisaged. The powers of the Diet over members would be greatly strengthened; all restrictions on trade and

commerce must be removed; and a German navy would be founded while Germany's land forces would be made more efficient.

32. Bavaria, Saxony and Electoral Hesse, while supporting the motion, pointed out that as the condominium in Schleswig-Holstein had not been recognized by the Diet, breach of it could not be used as the reason for mobilization.

33. Lord Augustus Loftus, *Diplomatic Reminiscences* (London, 1894), vol. I, p. 60. Cf. J. von Gerlach, *Ernst Ludwig von Gerlach. Aufzeichnungen aus seinem Leben und Wirken 1795–1877* (Schwerin, 1903), vol. 2, p. 292: 'There was something disturbed and desperate in his attitude'. 18 May.

34. Hagen Schulze, *Der Weg zum Nationalstaat, Die deutsche Nationalbewegung vom 18 Jahrhundert bis zur Reichsgründung* (Munich, 1985), p. 114.

35. *GW* 15, p. 198. The whole discussion (pp. 197–203) is highly interesting.

36. Quoted in Lothar Gall, *Bismarck: Der weisse Revolutionär*, p. 381.

37. Quoted in Ernst Engelberg, *Bismarck Urpreusse und Reichsgründer*, p. 620.

38. Karl-Georg Faber, 'Realpolitik als Ideologie', in *HZ* (203), 1966, pp. 15–6.

39. Quoted in Otto Pflanze, *Bismarck and the Development of Germany: The Period of Unification 1815–1871* (Princeton, 1963), p. 330.

Chapter 4

THE WAR OF 1870–1

NATIONAL ATTITUDES IN FRANCE AND GERMANY

The War of 1870–1 which led to the collapse of the Second Empire and the proclamation of the German Reich in the Hall of Mirrors at Versailles was in one sense another chapter in the old power struggle between the French and Germans which stretched back to the sixteenth and seventeenth centuries when the French kings had intervened actively in German affairs and which culminated in two world wars in the twentieth century. But it was also the first of the modern wars when national passions were loosed in the mass of the population and thrown into battle on an unprecedented scale with lasting effects on the international scene – at least until today when nuclear weapons have rendered major conflicts between Great Powers obsolete as a means of resolving contentious power-political questions. To this aspect of the origins of the war we now turn, commencing with the changing attitude of the Germans to their Gallic neighbours.

Frequent incursions into Germany during the Thirty Years' War and the devastation caused by the wars of Louis XIV had not endeared the French to many German princes or to those Germans unlucky enough to be caught in the maelstrom of war. Still, they did not attribute this to barbarous instincts inherent in the French 'national character'. On the contrary: French cultural values were widely accepted throughout Western Europe in the eighteenth century. Despite the growth of an indigenous German cultural movement, at the *fin de siècle* French remained the language of the educated classes. Frederick the Great's preference for it and his friendship with Voltaire are well known. And the generality of German princes aped the court etiquette and the lavish architectural tastes of the Sun King.

The growth of German nationalism has been commented on

already. It is sufficient to emphasize once more that at the time of the War of Liberation nationalism was an essentially negative force directed at the foreign invader. Popular hatred of all things French died away after the Congress of Vienna. It is true that some anti-French sentiments lingered on among middle-class liberals who remained highly critical of the xenophobic nationalism of the French, rejected French constitutional models and insisted that constitutional change must grow out of indigenous German traditions. But, on the other hand, the much more virile and more radical liberal movement in the south and west of Germany was greatly influenced by French political ideas. They looked to Paris to give a lead to the rest of Europe as she had in 1830. And in the aftermath of that revolution many radical liberals of the Young Germany school, including Heinrich Heine, Ludwig Börne and Arnold Ruge, forced to leave their native land, found a welcome haven in the Paris of the Citizen King among the liberal bourgeoisie who had put him on his throne.

A second wave of anti-French feeling gripped Germany in 1840. French policy had run into difficulties in the Near East. France had supported Mehemet Ali, an ambitious subject of the sultan who was eager to expand at the sultan's expense. Britain, for whom the maintenance of the Ottoman empire as a barrier against Russia was the sheet-anchor of her Near Eastern policy, was determined to force Mehemet out of Syria, which he had seized. With the help of the other Great Powers, Palmerston successfully isolated Mehemet and brought him to heel. The government of Adolphe Thiers reacted violently to this humiliation and stirred up the Paris press to demand compensation in the Rhineland. Although surprisingly little is known about the extent of the national outburst in Germany, it seems possible that it gripped all classes of the urban population, if only temporarily. Its spontaneity suggests that, although popular anti-French feeling died away after the War of Liberation, the experience of French occupation had made an indelible impression certainly on the generation which experienced the stirring events of 1813–4, so that it surfaced again quickly at moments of crisis. Perhaps press censorship and the ban on associations in the 1830s which hampered political protest had obscured the smouldering resentment of France. Significantly Nikolaus Becker's poem *'Die sollen ihn nicht haben den freien deutschen Rhein'* ('They shall not have the free German Rhine') became a firm favourite overnight; set to music it became an unofficial national anthem sung in the streets and clubs. Around this time Max Schneckenburger wrote *'Die Wacht am Rhein'* and Hoffmann von Fallersleben *'Deutschland Deutschland über alles'*. The tide of feeling ran strongly enough to affect the two major German powers. In November they agreed a common plan of operations in the event of war, with France referring specifically to national feeling as the reason for their initiative. In 1841 the Diet agreed to build fortresses at Rastatt and Ulm.

But although the 1840 crisis gave an enormous boost to the growth of nationalist organizations in the next decade, the intense anti-French mood of that year quickly evaporated. When the 1848 Revolution broke out most German liberals happily exchanged fraternal greetings with their French counterparts whom they regarded as allies fighting the same battle against the forces of reaction. It is true that the accession to power of Napoleon III and his suppression of political liberties soon alienated liberal opinion east of the Rhine from France, but for political, not nationalist, reasons. Again, French involvement in the Crimean War did something to stimulate anti-French feeling when France and Britain attempted to pressurize the reluctant German states into joining in the war. But opinion was very divided in 1855: while some liberals were strongly anti-French, others regarded France as a potential ally against despotic Russia. Conservative circles were equally divided: Protestant Prussia, with vivid memories of 1813–14, remained anti-French but Catholic Austria applauded the new alliance with imperial France as a victory for the principle of legitimacy.

The real turning-point in Franco-German relations occurred in 1859–61. The French attack on Austria in Northern Italy in 1859 in an area where the first Napoleon had won his spurs set the alarm bells ringing in Germany. While liberals sympathized with Italy's struggle for independence, which they admitted was as legitimate as their own, many feared that if France defeated Austria, Napoleon would attempt to seize the so-called 'natural frontier' in the Rhineland. For that reason even those who were highly critical of Austrian illiberalism expected Prussia to stand by Austria in the fight against the hereditary enemy. When Prussia did not come to Austria's aid and the latter suffered defeat, the military weakness of the Confederation was thrown into sharp relief, a humiliation which only intensified the demand for a strong Reich to uphold Germany's honour abroad. The great flood of pamphlets and newspaper articles and the demonstrations at popular festivals and scientific congresses and in Landtage all over Germany testified to the intensity of anti-French feeling in 1859. The nationalist agitation reached a high point in November with the centenary celebrations of Friedrich Schiller's birth which fell on the same day as Austria formally ceded Lombardy to Italy.

This time anti-French feeling did not die away. On the contrary, it received a further impetus in the spring of 1860 when Napoleon acquired Savoy and Nice from Piedmont as the price of French intervention in Northern Italy. All shades of opinion liberal and conservative were at last united in the belief that Napoleon's 'hidden agenda' had at last been revealed and that an attack on the Rhineland was imminent. Napoleon had become a figure of obloquy to all Germans; to Protestant conservatives who denounced the friend of revolution; to Catholics who blamed him for the threat to the Church from Italian nationalism (many believed the Pope's spiritual independence rested on his temporal power in the Papal States); to democrats who hated his despotism; and to liberals who feared French domination in Europe. All were resolved to resist attempts to secure the frontiers of 1814. Significantly, demands were now being made for the annexation of Alsace-Lorraine to safeguard German frontiers against French aggression. As excitement mounted in the summer of 1860, many German states including Prussia began to prepare for war. Regent William publicly declared his readiness for war to the knife against the French. When he met Emperor Francis Joseph at Teplitz in July both rulers expressed their intention of resisting France together, although the question of command of the federal forces still prevented further agreement.

Anti-French feeling, institutionalized in the nationalist organizations which proliferated in the 1860s, remained a permanent and visible feature of Franco-German relations during the next decade, and for that matter until well into the twentieth century. At a popular level it was sustained by propaganda works such as Anton Tellkampf's *Die Franzosen in Deutschland: Historische Bilder* (*The French in Germany: Historical Pictures*), a phenomenal success first published in 1860 and in its third edition by 1864. In the preface the author made no bones about his intention of keeping the flame of hatred burning bright by enlightening the public about 'the injustice . . . which the German people . . . has suffered on their own soil from the French; how they . . . plundered, destroyed towns, devastated countries, treated the oppressed with contempt and scorn and tore whole areas away from the German Reich'. The Germans must remember, he concluded, that 'only common action . . . could safeguard them for the future against successful attack by the old enemy'. Equally successful was Johannes Janssen's *Frankreichs Rheingelüste und deutschfeindliche Politik in früheren Jahrhunderten* (*French Longing for the Rhine and their Anti-German Policy in Earlier Centuries*), a scholarly if one-sided work which, though its Greater German bias did not please Little German historians, nevertheless helped to confirm for the reading public the picture of France, 'the hereditary foe'.[1]

Turning now to the French attitude to Germany. At the close of the eighteenth century when France was still dominant politically and culturally in Europe, French intellectuals had no high opinion of the Germans. This changed dramatically after the publication in 1814 of Madame Germaine de Staël's *De l'Allemagne*. A daughter of Louis XVI's finance minister, Jacques Necker, she visited Berlin, Weimar, Munich and Vienna at the turn of the century and returned home full of enthusiasm for what she had experienced there. In her book she painted a glowing though tendentious and naïve portrait of the Germans as an idealistic, upright and high-minded people. Disturbing features such as the outburst of savage anti-French feeling during the War of Liberation were not mentioned at all. Despite the lacunae the book introduced into French literary salons a positive image of the Germans as a *Kulturvolk* which quickly replaced the negative impression of a nation of bucolic bumblers. The Rhineland crisis of 1840 notwithstanding, this remained the dominant image for many educated Frenchmen until well into the 1860s. Of course, not all Frenchmen were whole-hearted admirers of things Teutonic. Conservatives, while admiring German culture, were not blind to latent anti-French feeling much in evidence, for example, at the Hambach Festival, while many old Bonapartists never forgot the German role in the defeat of Napoleon. But most members of the liberal-minded bourgeoisie – notably the opponents of the Napoleonic regime – were staunchly pro-German. Literary figures, dramatists, poets and historians continued to admire Germany. Austria was dismissed as clerical and absolutist by French liberals, whereas Prussia was admired as the home of the Reformation and of Kant, the laboratory of scientific advances and the driving force behind liberal trading policies. With considerable justification the French historian Hippolyte Taine wrote as late as 1867 that 'in the field of science and literature in philosophy and scholarship the Germans are the initiators, yes, perhaps the instructors in the modern spirit'.[2]

Admiration for Germany's cultural achievements was not a major determinant of French foreign policy. Power-political considerations weighed much more heavily with the conservatives in the Quai d'Orsay. After 1815 Restoration governments continued to pursue the traditional policy since the days of Cardinal Richelieu of keeping Germany (and Italy) weak and divided, playing off Prussia against Austria and the smaller states against both to maximize French security. In the 1820s they had still not given up hope of one day recovering the Rhine frontier which France had held under Napoleon, perhaps even by agreement with Prussia who might be compensated elsewhere in Germany. But as Prussian power increased with the growth of the Customs Union, suspicion of her ambitions deepened. The French foreign minister, Prince Auguste Jules de Polignac, restated traditional policy bluntly in 1829: 'It is very important for us to prevent the unification of Germany into one or two states. If it ever happened, this country which is [divided?] up today among the princes, who need our protection, would become for us a jealous rival and even a hostile force.'[3]

This was not official policy in the spring of 1848. On the contrary; during the initial euphoria which gripped revolutionaries all over Europe the French National Assembly offered fraternal greetings and a 'pact between brothers' to the German people. That theme was reiterated by the new foreign minister, the poet Alphonse de Lamartine, in a rhetorical manifesto to Europe. But by the summer the next foreign minister, the conservative-minded Jules Bastide, was expressing grave concern about the 'aggressive nationalism' of the Germans in Posen and Schleswig-Holstein and their disregard for treaty rights. With a sigh of relief the Quai d'Orsay resumed normal business and returned to the traditional line. In August Bastide commented that 'German unification as it is now emerging would turn a people of 40 millions into a very different power than Germany is today – and one to be feared. Therefore I do not believe that it is in our interests to desire unification let alone to press for it.'[4]

With the establishment of the Second Empire in 1852 the personal rule of Napoleon III became a factor of major importance in the formulation of French foreign policy. It has rightly been said of this enigmatic ruler's policy that it 'is no less puzzling and confusing to historians as it was to contemporaries: a confused mixture of fantasy and calculation, idealism and Machiavellianism, tenacity and indecision, which confuses every judgement and which by general consensus has been described as that of the sphinx'.[5] Several strands can, nevertheless, be detected in his policy. First, like any dictator he was interested in maintaining his own power base and perpetuating his dynasty. Secondly, he was determined to avenge the defeat of 1815, disrupt the Vienna settlement and make France the dominant power in Europe. Thirdly, because his stated objectives were disruptive of the status quo, he had to manoeuvre carefully to avoid becoming isolated in the face of the combined opposition of the three conservative powers: Austria, Prussia and Russia. To guard against such a combination, he regarded friendship with Britain – the power Napoleon could not break – as the cornerstone of his diplomacy. And from time to time he tried to disrupt the solidarity of these powers by, for example, working for a Prussian alliance. On occasions, as in 1866, he hoped to benefit from clashes between them. Fourthly, there was an ideological infrastructure; he subscribed to some extent to the principle of nationality. Indeed, he seems to have genuinely believed in the romantic nonsense he wrote in 1839 in the *Idées Napoléoniennes*, a treatise in which he depicted his uncle not as an odious tyrant menacing the peace of Europe but as a prophetic Mazzini-like figure, 'the Messiah of the new ideology' whose life-long ambition had been the creation of a harmonious comity of nations organized in accordance with the principle of nationality. At the same time – this is a fifth strand –

he was too astute a *Realpolitiker* not to appreciate the need for a balance of power in Europe which a united Germany and Italy would threaten to upset as Polignac and Bastide had feared in their time. Partial unification around Prussia in North Germany and Piedmont in North and Central Italy would square the circle between power-political objections from conservatives and his personal predilection for nationalism. Add to this a free Poland, independent states in South Germany looking to Paris, and Austria holding back Russia in the east and France would be the dominant power in Europe. There was more than a touch of his uncle and proleptic hints of General Charles de Gaulle in his remark in 1859 that '. . . *une grande nation est comme un astre; elle ne peut pas vivre sans satellites*'.[6] And even partial solutions of the German and Italian problems would weaken his and his uncle's great enemy: Austria.

Finally, Napoleon was always anxious to ensure that his foreign policy was in tune with public opinion. Under the authoritarian system established in 1852 Napoleon had a firm grip over France. Through the mayors and prefects he controlled the administrative machine. The Senate and Corps Législatif – the latter '*un parlement anonyme*' elected by universal male suffrage – had limited powers and were packed with his supporters, while the press was completely under the thumb of the government. But precisely because a free press did not exist, Napoleon, like any authoritarian ruler, had to have reliable sources of information about the attitude of his subjects. This information he received from the *procureurs généraux* and the prefects. The former were the officials, twenty-eight in number, attached to courts of appeal and in charge of the prosecution staff. On a quarterly basis they sent in reports about economic conditions and public attitudes based on material gathered from officers down to local magistrates. The prefects in the eighty-eight departments also sent in regular reports to Paris. Digests of these were prepared for Napoleon, though how carefully he scrutinized them we do not know.

The state of public opinion in Napoleonic France is a complex area bristling with difficulties. Most scholars have concentrated on an analysis of newspaper opinion rather than popular attitudes. There seems to have been a sharp division of opinion between the *bonapartisme des notables* and *bonapartisme populaire*. The former was the attitude taken by middle-class admirers of German culture who believed that it was the special mission of France to spread the gospel of nationality far and wide and bring into being an association of nationally organized states. Many liberals and some democrats subscribed to this point of view.

On the other hand, in the working population in the towns and in the countryside anti-Prussian feeling was fairly widespread. It was very easy to drum up support in these circles for demands for 'natural frontiers' and compensation for changes elsewhere. Significantly, democratic papers such as *Le Siècle* and *L'Avenir* were the first to raise such demands, which did not meet with approval in middle-class circles. This was a complete contrast to the position in Germany where the middle class was anti-French in attitude and where, arguably, the rural population was much less affected by nationalism. For in France the impact of social and economic changes brought about by the Revolution had committed the rural population to the concept of a nation of citizens to a much greater extent than in Germany where allegiance to local dynasties remained a potent force.

The year 1859, so significant in moulding German attitudes to France, was not particularly significant for French attitudes to Germany. True, in court and military circles there was some resentment of Prussian behaviour which had forced Napoleon to make peace. And when Savoy and Nice were annexed in 1860 (Napoleon's reward for allowing Piedmont to annex the Central Italian duchies) some democrats publicly demanded the return of the Rhineland. As one paper expressed it: '. . . the least even-minded men . . . take delight in the thought that having retaken the line [of the Alps] France must one day recover the Rhine territory'.[7] But these were isolated voices. As tension between Austria and Prussia mounted in the spring of 1866, French opinion was overwhelmingly pacific and favoured non-intervention in the event of war in Germany. The spectacular victory at Königgrätz, skewing the balance of power against France, aroused some uneasiness. 'We felt,' remarked the historian Pierre de la Gorce, 'that something in the soil of old Europe had just crumbled . . . .'[8]

Still, not until the peace preliminaries were signed at Nikolsburg in July were the worst fears of the critics realized. Terms which doubled Prussia in size were universally condemned. As one *procureur* report observed: 'The territorial expansion of Prussia raising her in the space of a few days to the rank of a first-class power, as a result of forceful annexations, has not only been considered an abuse of force but a menace to France . . . the memories of the last half-century have not effaced, rather have combined, in regard to Prussia animosities and mistrusts strongly revived in the circumstances we have just traversed . . . .'[9] This was the turning-point in French attitudes to Germany. Not only were the anti-Prussian sentiments of the working population aroused but similar feelings took root in middle-class circles. Their reactions, however, were due not so much to national sentiment as to a growing realization that unification under Bismarck's aegis meant the spread of illiberalism over wider areas of Germany, a retrograde development not likely to be conducive to the liberal changes they expected in France.

The sense of frustration was turned inwards leading to increasing attacks on the regime and demands for political change. After 1866–7 Napoleon faced mounting difficulties at home, partly because of his failure to obtain territorial compensation and partly because of impatience at the pace of political change. By the end of October Thiers expressed a growing feeling that in two years when Austria was ready the moment would arrive for France to resist Prussian expansionism by force.

One can summarize this brief survey of popular attitudes by saying that between 1867 and 1870 anti-French feeling on the German side and anti-Prussian feeling on the French side became prominent features of Franco-German relations. These animosities found frequent expression in newspapers and books on both sides of the Rhine and helped create an atmosphere of mutual suspicion between Paris and Berlin, making possible the outbreak of war over a matter of 'national honour'. This does not mean that national feeling on either side of the Rhine was a prime determinant of war. But it did ensure for both governments that groundswell of popular support in moments of crisis without which modern war is a hazardous undertaking.

NAPOLEON III AND BISMARCK, 1866–9

It has been argued earlier that the dispute about the relative merits of the Primacy of Foreign Policy and the Primacy of Domestic Policy as rival explanations of the relationship between external affairs and internal affairs is sometimes carried too far by over-zealous partisans. In practice the two are closely interconnected; at times one element predominates, at times the other in the ever-shifting balance of factors determining foreign policy. Napoleonic France is a particularly apt illustration of this inter-relationship because of the emperor's function as an integrating figure in French society; both at home and abroad Napoleon's political survival depended on his ability to hold together disparate social groups.

Throughout the 1850s he enjoyed considerable success abroad. The Crimean War conferred immense prestige on the new empire. In 1859 French armies inflicted defeats on Austria, while in 1860 Napoleon rounded off the south-eastern frontier with the acquisition of Savoy and Nice. The 1860s, by way of contrast, were years of failure when Napoleon was outmanoeuvred by his opponents. As discontent began to show itself in France, a tyrant of the old school would have relied on police and army to stamp out every manifestation. But although Napoleon III will always remain something of an enigma, a man whose motives were complex and contradictory, it seems likely that he half-believed the myth he had created of his uncle as the great liberator. Even when he was at the height of his powers in 1860–1 Napoleon commenced to liberalize the political system through a modest increase in the powers of the Corps Législatif and some relaxation of the press regulations. Not, of course, that he ever intended to divest himself of the substance of power. When the opposition doubled its vote at the 1863 elections and thirty-two of them (seventeen Republicans and fifteen Monarchists) were returned to a chamber of 282 deputies, he expressed displeasure at the result – he was particularly incensed that the département of the Seine had returned eight Republicans and one Orleanist.

These modest beginnings simply increased opposition to the regime. By 1864 a third party appeared in the Corps Législatif which, while loyal enough to the emperor, campaigned for a completely free press, free elections and responsible ministers. Hitherto Napoleon had successfully maintained his authority by appealing to all groups in French society. Now he was being forced to take sides. To avoid that and to remain in control of the situation he needed to score a foreign political success. Precisely that eluded him. '*Les traités de 1815, n'éxistent pas*' he announced with characteristic élan. But his imaginative proposal in November 1863 for a great European Congress to scrap the settlement of 1815 and redraw the frontiers of the continent fell on deaf ears. Russia had no interest in an independent Poland and Britain had been suspicious of Napoleon's motives ever since the annexation of Savoy and Nice. And over Schleswig-Holstein Napoleon had encountered an opponent committed to a more drastic resolution of the German problem than was compatible with French power interests. Most of all, there was the Mexican adventure which typified the curious mixture of imagination, miscalculation and obstinacy characteristic of the emperor.

Originally Napoleon had planned to set up a Central American state as a centre of industrial activity and a barrier to North American penetration of that region. Then his interest shifted to Mexico where the anti-clerical regime of Benito Juarez had just suspended payment of its foreign debts. The outbreak of the American Civil War in 1861 encouraged Napoleon to intervene at first as part of a joint expedition with Spain and Britain to force Juarez to face up to his financial responsibilities. Misled by Mexican exiles and isolated when Britain and Spain withdrew their forces from Mexico, Napoleon attempted to restore monarchy to Mexico in the person of Archduke Maximilian of Austria. At the height of the campaign against Juarez France had 30,000 troops in the field. And Napoleon, who had fought alongside Italian nationalists, now found himself fighting against equally ardent Mexican patriots in order to impose a discredited foreign prince on them. When the American Civil War ended in 1865 Napoleon appreciated that the United States would not tolerate French interference in Central America. At home public opinion was sharply critical of the Mexican adventure. As the situation in Europe suddenly deteriorated, Napoleon had no alternative but to withdraw his troops from Mexico. Left to his own devices, Maximilian was captured and shot in 1867. The whole episode dealt a perhaps irreparable blow to the prestige of the regime.

Even before French troops were withdrawn the Prussian victory over Austria plunged France into a fresh crisis. Napoleon tried valiantly to argue that France had gained a great deal out of the war; the cause of Italian unification had been advanced by the cession of Venetia; Austria had been defeated for the second time in a decade; and the settlement of 1815 had been badly dented by the destruction of the German Confederation. And all this without a shot being fired from French guns. The problem, as we have already seen, was that the working population in town and country took a less altruistic view. And Napoleon always attached great importance to these elements, seeing in them the radical base of the regime. Now a sick man suffering from stones in the bladder for which he refused surgery, he was in a much weaker political position and felt obliged to support demands for territorial compensation in which he probably did not believe.

How best to secure this compensation was hotly debated in the imperial entourage. Austria had just asked the emperor to arrange an armistice with Italy. In return Austria ceded Venetia to France to be held in trust for Italy. Napoleon, anxious to extend the armistice to Prussia, approached King William on 4 July. The next day, however, the council of ministers decided on armed mediation to defend French interests. Foreign Minister Drouyn de Lhuys supported by War Minister Marshal Jacques Randon, Pierre Magne and the Empress Eugénie persuaded Napoleon that Prussia was now so strong militarily that she might refuse an armistice and continue the war. To prevent a further unwelcome shift in the balance of power, France would dispatch an observation corps of 80,000 men to the frontier at once, mobilize a further 25,000 men and, relying on the opposition of Austria and the southern states to Prussia, extract maximum benefit out of the situation.

Whether armed mediation would have been a more effective strategy is a matter of surmise. For it was abandoned almost as quickly as it was decided on through a combination of external developments and domestic pressures. Once the kings of Prussia and Italy agreed to an armistice the advocates of armed mediation were at a disadvantage. In addition their opponents – Marquis Charles de La Valette, Eugène Rouher and Jules Baroche, ably supported by Prince Jérome Napoleon – buttonholed the emperor after the council meeting and persuaded him that France was too weak to engage in a hazardous policy which could easily backfire if Prussia refused an armistice. To end up at war with Prussia and Italy could lead to charges of double-dealing in view of prior French promises to these countries. Finally, public opinion had suddenly swung from a belligerent to a pacific posture when war suddenly loomed on the horizon. This may well have been a decisive consideration. Years later Napoleon confided to the Spanish ambassador that 'It cost us a great deal to recognize the state of affairs which the battle of Sadowa created in Germany. We tolerated it, although not without regret. French public opinion was at that time very emphatic in favour of peace and I was resolved to respect that trend of thought.'[10]

But French opinion was equally insistent that France receive compensation for the dramatic shift in the balance of power. Thus, after the conclusion of the armistice Vincent Benedetti, ambassador to Berlin, sounded out Bismarck on the possibility of a secret convention giving France the 1814 frontier (i.e. the Saarland, Landau and part of the Palatinate) and Luxemburg. Bismarck's initial reaction was bellicose: in the face of such demands the king would probably refuse to sign the Nikolsburg peace agreement, continue the war and capture Vienna. Then, after consulting a map, he adopted a more congenial stance and remarked that 'for his part there would be no difficulty in establishing the frontier of 1814' always provided that the king and the Landtag agreed.[11] Nor did he object to the cession of Luxemburg. But finding compensation for the Dutch king might be difficult; perhaps he could have the Bavarian Palatinate, or perhaps France might settle for that territory in lieu of Luxemburg?[12] Belgium, too, was mentioned as an area where France might seek compensation.[13]

Naïvely the French took Bismarck at his word. On 5 August in addition to the 1814 frontier Benedetti demanded the Bavarian and Hessian Palatinate and the severance of all ties between Luxemburg and Limburg. Once the Nikolsburg peace preliminaries were signed Bismarck ceased to equivocate and declared vehemently to Benedetti that the surrender of German territory – especially the loss of Mainz – was out of the question. Neither the king nor the crown prince would countenance such exorbitant demands. Nor, he might have added, had he any intention of making Prussian expansion more difficult by alienating at a stroke National Liberals and South German rulers. Still, he pretended to leave the door open for negotiation. While refusing to accept Benedetti's main premise that the shift in the balance of power threatened France and justified compensation, he encouraged France to seek this in Belgium. But when Benedetti arrived back in Paris on 10 August to report to Foreign Minister Rouher he discovered that the whole city knew the details of his conversations with Bismarck. This because the minister–president had through an agent leaked them to the French correspondent of *Le Siècle* in order to emphasize the impossibility of any cession of German territory. These revelations produced angry outbursts in Germany where the bellicose liberal press demanded war with France rather than the surrender of German land. Napoleon quickly repaired the damage, informing the German ambassador in Paris that the convention project was all due to a 'misunderstanding'. With that retreat the first French attempt to obtain compensation ended ignominiously.

The second attempt, culminating in the Luxemburg crisis of 1867, had lasting effects on the attitude of both Prussia and France and deserves more detailed consideration.

The small but strategically important grand duchy of Luxemburg was handed over to the king of the Netherlands in 1815 as compensation for the loss of the duchy of Nassau. It had been a member of the German Confederation, and the confederate fortress in Luxemburg was garrisoned by the Prussians. French was the official language though the inhabitants spoke a German dialect. Some inhabitants were pro-French, others pro-German, but like most people throughout history what they really wanted was to be left alone to enjoy their independence.

The Luxemburg story commences in August 1866. After the first rebuff at German hands Drouyn de Lhuys, whose armed mediation policy was rejected on 6 August but who nevertheless had been obliged to stay in office and operate a policy which he rightly believed would not work, was replaced with effect from September by the Marquis Lionel de Moustier. While the latter was winding up his affairs in Constantinople, where he was ambassador, La Valette temporarily took over at the Quai d'Orsay. On 15 August Napoleon and Rouher agreed on a new approach to Prussia based on the nationality principle rather than on French strategic interests. Accordingly France would seek compensation in Belgium and Luxemburg.

Rouher instructed Benedetti to propose two agreements to Prussia. First, a secret treaty of alliance allowing France to acquire Belgium at some future date; in return the two powers would help each other if this led to war, for Rouher anticipated strenuous British opposition if France annexed Belgium. Secondly, a public treaty conceding the 1814 frontiers – a demand which Rouher knew was unacceptable and which Benedetti did not even bother to raise with Bismarck – and the right to acquire Luxemburg.

Bismarck encouraged Benedetti to believe that Prussia would not oppose French acquisition of Belgium and Luxemburg provided that France accepted final unification. Towards the end of August Benedetti drafted an agreement based on discussions with Bismarck.[14] In order to accelerate the negotiations Benedetti gave Bismarck a copy of the agreement but omitted to retrieve it after the London Conference. That copy was used by Bismarck in 1870 to discredit the French in the eyes of non-belligerents.

Historians are divided in their interpretation of Bismarck's motives in negotiating with Benedetti. Was this a genuine attempt to advance Prussian ambitions and avoid war by agreement with a powerful neighbour? Or was it simply a sophisticated exercise to lull the French into a false sense of security until the North German Confederation was founded? Or was Bismarck simply leaving his options open as he had done so often in the past?[15] The strong probability is that Bismarck was playing a double game and keeping the options open. Significantly he did nothing to help the French acquire Luxemburg. And, while readily agreeing that in the event of war France and Prussia would confer, he evaded references to a formal alliance; the harsh reality was that Prussia had not the slightest intention of fighting Britain to pull French chestnuts out of the fire. Writing to the French ambassador in Paris a few months later, Bismarck summed up his tactics in the autumn of 1866 succinctly: 'The French must retain hope and especially faith in our goodwill without our giving them definite commitments.'[16]

Taken ill at the end of September, Bismarck departed from Berlin and remained well out of Benedetti's reach until early December. When the ambassador eventually managed to see Bismarck, the latter, while still indicating nominal support for French plans, emphasized the difficulty of persuading the king to approve them. Significantly Bismarck now started to refer to the grand duchy as 'German territory'. By the end of that year he informed Goltz that Prussia could scarcely deliver 'Germans against their will and for no apparent cause to France'. An alliance would be 'too dearly bought' at the price of 'a humiliating injury to German national feeling'.[17]

As Prussian interest in the draft agreement waned in the winter of 1866–7, French anxieties increased. The domestic situation spurred Napoleon and his advisers to fresh action. In February 1867 the Corps Législatif was due to meet. Action was imperative to ward off the anticipated onslaught on the government for its manifest failure to obtain compensation. When Moustier instructed Benedetti to press Bismarck once more it was, as the foreign minister observed, because 'we must . . . give reply soon to the legitimate preoccupation of the country and to the great legislative bodies'.[18] But Benedetti could not move Bismarck.

Unable to make progress and deeply aware of mounting discontent at home, Napoleon attempted to defuse the situation with a measure of political change. In January 1867 the Corps Législatif was allowed to question ministers (but lost the right to vote an annual address); and all ministers were in future obliged to reply to interpellations (but ministers could not be members of the Corps Législatif). This cunningly balanced reform package did not save the government when Napoleon addressed the Corps Législatif on 15 February. Nailing his colours to the mast, he boldly declared his satisfaction with the recognition accorded the principle of nationality in Germany – an inevitable development in accordance with his uncle's (alleged) vision of a Europe of nation states. French prestige had been high enough to prevent Prussia absorbing all Germany. The speech was received coolly. Worse followed when Thiers delivered a devastating attack on the government on 15 March. To his mind the balance of power, not nationalism, was the only proper basis for foreign policy. By this criterion Great Powers had a perfect right to territorial compensation when the balance of power shifted significantly. The government had, however, failed miserably, dithering between intervention and non-intervention and ending up without a friend in Europe. He concluded with a savage comment on Napoleon's government: '*Il n'y a plus une seule faute à commettre.*'[19]

Rouher vainly attempted to retrieve the situation with the dubious argument that Germany was not stronger but weaker. The Germans were divided: twenty million lived in the North German Confederation, fifteen million in the southern states and thirty-three million in Austria. France was not isolated and friendless; on the contrary, she enjoyed the goodwill of all. Therefore '. . . it matters little whether France gains in width so long as she gains in stature'.[20] Rouher's apologia was ill received. On 19 March it was laughed to scorn when Bismarck suddenly revealed the existence of offensive–defensive alliances with the southern states. No doubt Bismarck hoped to warn the French against precipitate action. Yet domestic pressures were in his mind as much as in Napoleon's. Sharp criticism of the Nikolsburg preliminary peace was expected in the Constituent Reichstag where the National Liberals were likely to condemn Prussia for stopping at the river Main By revealing the existence of the treaties Bismarck hoped to deflect their wrath.[21] But the announcement completely discredited the French government, shattering the illusion that the Main would be a formidable obstacle to further Prussian expansion.

Meanwhile the French intensified their efforts to secure Luxemburg. Since mid February they had been negotiating directly with the Dutch. King William III was perfectly willing to sell his grand duchy for five million gulden and a French guarantee of the Netherlands and Luxemburg. However, Bismarck's announcement of the treaties combined with ominous Prussian troop concentrations on the Dutch frontier and a reference to Luxemburg in the Reichstag convinced the Dutch that Prussian agreement to the deal was essential. Accordingly the king approached his Prussian counterpart on 26 March.

Bismarck was far from displeased with this turn of events. Domestic concerns were still uppermost in his mind. Discussion of the draft constitution was entering the final stage in the Reichstag. Votes were due towards the end of March on the crucial issues of ministerial responsibility and the iron budget for the army. If external affairs could be pressed into service to secure a satisfactory outcome, so much the better.

The king of the Netherlands had played into Bismarck's hands by formally involving the Prussian government in the Luxemburg affair. Furthermore, while Bismarck had at an earlier stage encouraged the French to organize genteel demonstrations of pro-French feeling in Luxemburg, the French agents had encouraged large noisy demonstrations in favour of annexation which caused angry outbursts in Germany. Probably by pre-arrangement the Hanoverian politician Bennigsen asked Bismarck on 1 April 1867 what the government's intentions were towards Luxemburg, 'a German land from whose princely houses emperors of Germany have gone forth' and a land which the Dutch king had, therefore, no right to alienate from the fatherland. Secondly, Luxemburg was of strategic significance: 'We are not just defending a piece of German territory. We also have an important military position to protect for if this were to be lost when France acquired the territory both Belgium and the German Rhineland would always be exposed to an immediate threat.'[22] Thirdly, attempts by foreign powers to exploit the temporary weakness of the new Confederation must be vigorously resisted in order to prevent future interference. Regardless of party the German nation would support a strong policy on this issue – a remark greeted with rapturous applause.

Bismarck had for the first time succeeded in harnessing nationalism to the Prussian cause. Because liberals of all shades of opinion were united in face of the 'old enemy', they were much more accommodating over the power of the Reichstag, especially in respect of the military budget. It has rightly been observed that the decisions arrived at in this highly charged atmosphere left 'a permanent mark upon the institutional relationships of the Second Reich'.[23]

Simultaneously Bismarck used his domestic triumph as a launching-pad for an offensive against France. Public opinion was again pressed into service, this time to secure foreign political objectives.

In the face of such intense national feeling, what could Prussia possibly do about Luxemburg, he asked tongue-in-cheek. She could not even contemplate withdrawing her garrison, much less allow France to acquire the grand duchy. What mattered was not the intrinsic worth of the area: '. . . . Luxemburg in itself is hardly worth a war.' It was the nation's sense of honour which must determine Prussian policy.[24]

This was obviously a calculated ploy to scare the Dutch and French off the deal. War was never in his mind. In replying to Benningsen Bismarck carefully avoided inflammatory language, promising only 'to watch over the interests of the nation'. And while deepening the crisis he sought an avenue of escape from it. Already on 30 March he tried to mobilize Russian and British support. That met with little success. Russia left the initiative to Britain but Lord Edward Stanley, the British foreign secretary, thought the acquisition of Luxemburg by France would not upset the balance of power. Then on 3 April Bismarck informed the Hague that 'after the incitement of public opinion war would scarcely be avoided if the affair proceeds'.[25] War had never been in the Dutch king's mind either. Having inadvertently precipitated a crisis by appealing to Berlin, he de-escalated it by announcing on 5 April that he would not sign the treaty of cession.

The French were thoroughly mortified by this outcome. War was out of the question, as the council of ministers was well aware. Nor had France an ally on whom she could depend. How could she at least save face? Bismarck was most obliging. Once he had extracted the maximum benefit for Prussia out of the situation, he agreed to a British proposal for a meeting of the signatory powers of the 1839 treaty. At the London Conference in May 1867 a solution was found. The king of the Netherlands would remain ruler of Luxemburg; the grand duchy would enjoy autonomous status; Britain, France, Prussia, Austria and Russia guaranteed its perpetual neutrality; and the Prussian garrison was withdrawn and the fortress demolished.

In retrospect the Luxemburg crisis was an important milestone on the road to the war of 1870. The Mexican débâcle had been followed by complete failure to obtain compensation to offset a significant alteration in the balance of power. Influential sections of public opinion in the middle classes as well as in the working population were now hostile to Prussia. Some Bonapartists, fanatical right-wing Catholics who had the ear of the empress, military circles and Orleanists led by Thiers, believed war inevitable. Any attempt by Prussia to absorb South Germany by force would be the signal for a war in which they supposed – with reckless disregard for political realities – France would be actively supported by Austria and Italy while the South German states remained neutral.

That does not mean that the war of 1870 was in any sense inevitable. In the spring of 1870 the French government put on record its desire for peace. And a sizeable section of opinion – Radicals, Socialists and Conservatives – was still not prepared to believe that the final unification of Germany along Little German lines need lead to war. But one can say that the balance of opinion was such that in a crisis war was more likely to break out than before Sadowa.

BISMARCK AND SOUTH GERMANY, 1866–9

We turn now to Prussia. By expelling Austria from Germany Prussia had achieved her first objective of linking up her territories and becoming indisputably the dominant power in North and Central Germany. The decisive nature of her military victory opened up the possibility of absorbing the southern states and greatly extending her power base. In an age of *Realpolitik* when the Concert of Europe had manifestly broken down so far as major disputes between Great Powers were concerned, the continued independence of the southern states was likely to be precarious. Surrounded on three sides by powerful neighbours, the four states were likely to fall under the influence of one or other sooner or later. If Austria sought to reverse the defeat of 1866 – and it was not obvious at first that she would not seek to do so – South Germany was an ideal ally. Similarly for France these states formed a useful barrier against further Prussian expansion.

As for Prussia, the men in the corridors of power in Berlin including the king and the crown prince regarded the frontiers of the new Confederation as purely provisional. *Staatsrat* Gelzer, writing to the grand duke of Baden, observed that 'the Main line has to be observed for the time being out of concern for France and in order to allow the northern union time to consolidate. The complete union of North and South is, however, solely a matter of time . . . .'[26]

Gelzer was quite correct in thinking the diplomatic situation an important factor restraining Prussia in 1866 from precipitate action. Whenever major changes occur in the balance of power, other Great Powers are apt to intervene to safeguard what they suppose are their 'vital interests'. That happened in 1864, obliging Bismarck to manoeuvre adroitly at the London Conference to avoid a settlement of Schleswig-Holstein's affairs which would have tied Prussia's hands. Similarly, in 1866 the defeat of Austria might well have led to Great Power intervention.

Russia was the first to move. On learning of the Prussian peace terms, the tsar proposed the summoning of a European congress at which the signatory powers of the Treaty of Vienna could again try their skill at regulating Germany's affairs. When Russia persisted in this, Bismarck raised the bogey of revolution to scare her off. Outside interference, he announced, would compel Prussia to 'unleash the full national strength of Germany and the bordering countries'.[27] On 3 August, failing to drum up support in Paris and London, the tsar abandoned his proposal. But he remained uneasy about Prussian plans to annex territories in North Germany at the expense of the princes. Bismarck sent General Edwin von Manteuffel to St Petersburg to make it clear that attempts to pressurize Prussia would force her to proclaim the radical 1849 constitution. In Bismarck's famous phrase: 'If there is to be revolution, we would rather make it than suffer it.'[28] On 12 August the tsar assured the Prussian king that Russia would never be found on the side of Prussia's enemies. Bismarck's robust determination to use every means to ward off foreign intervention indicates his high degree of concern.

Of course, there were sound objective reasons why Russia did not intervene actively in German affairs at the end of the day which had nothing to do with Bismarck's bullying language. The real explanation for Russian inaction lay in the history of Russo-Prussian relations since the Crimean War. During the Polish Revolt of 1863 Prussia had actively aided Russia, offering in the Alvensleben Convention to return to the Russian authorities Polish insurgents who strayed on to Prussian soil. In view of the deepening antagonism with Austria in the Balkans, her defeat was a matter of some satisfaction in St Petersburg. The tsar's call for an international conference was a knee-jerk reaction quickly abandoned, as we have seen, when Britain and France showed no interest in it.

French intervention in the summer of 1866 was a much more serious possibility; Bismarck admitted in 1874 that this would have posed serious problems. Though the abandonment of armed mediation greatly reduced the danger, Prussia still had to handle Napoleon with great care. Though he did not hesitate to shake the mailed fist at Benedetti on 5 August, threatening to release the genie of 'national war' if the French persisted in demanding German territory, he did not, as we have seen, continue in this intransigent vein. He was flexible in other directions. In the draft peace treaty he had included a clause allowing for a future union between the new Confederation and the southern states. Bavaria at once lodged an objection. More important than that was Napoleon's mediation plan which guaranteed these states 'an independent international existence'. Bismarck's attempts to delete this from the final settlement failed. A further concession to French pressure was the promise to hold a plebiscite in North Schleswig, which Bismarck repudiated in 1879.

Although Austria obviously presented no immediate threat to Prussia, Bismarck was concerned to avoid unnecessary provocation likely to send her into the arms of the French. With the crown prince's help he restrained the exultant Prussian monarch from avenging Olmütz by staging a triumphal march through Vienna exacting a heavy indemnity and annexing some Austrian territory. The fact that Bismarck recognized the independence of the southern states helped to reassure Austria that, having won the struggle for mastery north of the Main, Prussia would not disturb the new status quo.

Secondly, as Gelzer remarked, for reasons of domestic policy Prussia could not possibly have absorbed the southern states in 1866. Her first task was to digest the annexed territories where Prussia was anything but welcome. Bismarck was deeply absorbed during these months with the task of drafting a constitution which would preserve the power of the monarchy and prevent the euphoric liberals from obtaining parliamentary government. Until these tasks were accomplished further extensions of Prussian power were excluded from the realm of practical politics.

Thirdly – a factor of great importance precluding union of north and south in the foreseeable future – was the attitude of the southern states towards Prussia. Three of them – Bavaria, Württemberg and Baden – were well established states. Though their boundaries and political structures dated only from Napoleonic times, their rulers had successfully consolidated them and enjoyed much popular support in these predominantly rural communities. Politically the consultative assemblies established after the Congress of Vienna had been in advance of anything north of the Main; in Bavaria taxpayers had the vote, while in Baden universal male suffrage with no tax qualification had obtained since the 1848–9 Revolution. In Prussia, by way of contrast, under the three-class system class 1 electors who comprised 47 per cent of all those entitled to vote chose the same number of *Wählmanner* (electoral college members) as class 2 (12.6 per cent) and class 3 (82.7 per cent) – though, of course, the introduction of universal male suffrage for the new Reichstag had brought Prussia into line with Baden and put it ahead of the rest of the south. Historically, liberalism had always been a more virile plant in Baden and Württemberg where liberals enjoyed much wider support than their Prussian counterparts. This was still the case in 1869, as will be seen later.

Another contrast between north and south lay in the strength of Catholicism in the southern states. Five million of the nine million inhabitants of these states were Catholic, the highest concentration being in Bavaria (71.2 per cent) and Württemberg (64.5 per cent). The south was also the heartland of political Catholicism or Ultramontanism. To this nineteenth-century phenomenon Bismarck remained bitterly hostile all his life. Writing to Leopold von Gerlach in 1854 he had described it as 'a hypocritical idolatrous papism full of hate and cunning, which conducts from the cabinets of princes and ministers right down to the mysteries of the marriage bed an unrelenting struggle with the most infamous weapons against the Protestant governments and especially against Prussia, the bulwark of the Gospel'.[29] Some words of explanation are called for about a political animal alien to the Anglo-Saxon world.

Political Catholicism was in essence the response of a Church which felt itself to be under siege because of its refusal to effect a reconciliation with the modern secular state emerging so rapidly in the middle of the century in Western Europe. The doctrinal intransigence characteristic of the post-Tredentine Church programmed Catholics to gravitate towards those of the same faith and to condemn as heretical all other denominations – an exclusive attitude heartily reciprocated by Protestants in the sixteenth and seventeenth centuries when theological differences were fiercely debated and deeply held on both sides. In the eighteenth century, the Age of Reason, interest in theological speculation declined and religious animosities diminished in intensity. In the nineteenth century, however, religious divisions between Catholics and Protestants deepened once more, introducing a new dimension into the political conflicts of the century. Before Napoleon's intervention in Germany the balance between Catholics and Protestants had been roughly equal. The abolition of the prince bishoprics and the drastic reduction in the number of states transformed the balance. By 1815 the majority of rulers were Protestant; the only Catholic dynasties were the Habsburgs and the Wittelsbachs. Furthermore, the Catholic populations in the Rhineland, Westphalia, Baden and Württemberg were now ruled by Protestant dynasties, while pockets of Evangelicals in Franconia, the Palatinate and Swabia were now under the Catholic Wittelsbachs.

These territorial changes need not in themselves have led to renewed tension between Catholic and Protestants. The really significant change was in the attitude of the Catholic Church towards state power whether exercised by Catholic or Protestant rulers. Pope Pius VII's resistance to Napoleon had greatly enhanced the status of the papacy and made it a rallying point for Catholics in the more centralized and Rome-oriented Church which emerged after the defeat of Napoleon. In some parts of Europe notably in France, Belgium, and Ireland, resistance to state attempts to control the Church led to the emergence of Liberal Catholicism, a movement highly critical of the 'Throne and Altar' mentality of extreme Bourbons such as Charles X of France. Liberal Catholics believed the time had come for the Church to recognize that close ties with monarchy had alienated it from the mass of the people. *'Libera chiesa e libero stato'* was their high ideal; a Church freed from the embrace of the state and able to fulfil her mission of evangelization. Liberal Catholicism did not take root in Germany, perhaps because German Catholics were little affected by the spirit of the Enlightenment so that in conflicts with the state the Church authorities could rely on the support of a loyal and obedient flock. What they borrowed from Catholic movements elsewhere was the technique of mass organization, not their outward-looking attitude.

The effects of this were first seen during the dispute with the Prussian government in 1837 over mixed mariages. The government introduced into its Catholic territories a regulation of 1825 whereby the father in a mixed marriage would determine the religion of the children. The Church insisted on the absolute right of the Catholic partner to decide and consequently came into conflict with the state authorities. During this contest – which ended very largely in a Catholic victory when Frederick William IV came to the throne – the Church enjoyed the support of liberals who argued that the Church as an independent association had the right to formulate her own regulations for her flock free of state interference. There was reciprocity in the alliance; in Württemberg Catholics supported liberals in their political struggle. However, these were exceptions. Elsewhere, especially in Bavaria, heartland of Catholicism, and in Austria popular Catholic movements gave active support to reactionary Catholic regimes which on occasion made life difficult for Evangelicals in those states.

A major confrontation between the Catholic Church and the new liberal philosophy was scarcely avoidable in the circumstances of the time. On the one hand an increasingly Rome-dominated Church clung more tenaciously than ever to an inward-looking and traditional theology. Neither Pope Gregory XVI nor his better-known successor Pius IX showed the slightest inclination to compromise with the secular world of expanding technology. On the other hand European liberals were not prepared to allow the churches to retain their near-monopoly in educational and matrimonial matters. Secular education and civil marriage were standard liberal demands fiercely resisted by the Church as unwarranted interference in an area which had been under her control from time immemorial.

Developments in Italy had a direct bearing on this clash of philosophies. Throughout the 1850s Rome was fighting a running battle with the Piedmontese government following the introduction of the Siccardi laws regulating relations between church and state to the disadvantage of the former. As Piedmont conquered more of

Northern and Central Italy in 1860–1 Pope Pius clung tenaciously to the Papal States, claiming that continued sovereignty over them guaranteed the independence of his spiritual office. When Italian troops occupied them the pope excommunicated Cavour and his colleagues. After the occupation of Rome in 1870 the intransigent old man retired into the Vatican and refused to recognize the new kingdom of Italy. Not until 1929 did Pope Pius XI heal the breach between Church and state.

Against this background the pope issued the encyclical letter *Quanta Cura* in 1864. Attached to it was the Syllabus of Errors, a forthright condemnation of liberalism and all its works with which – so the pope declared – the Church would not come to terms. It is hardly a coincidence that as the political bases upon which the Church rested began to crumble, her doctrinal intransigence increased; in 1854 the pope had proclaimed the doctrine of the Immaculate Conception of the Virgin Mary and in 1870 he was to declare at the First Vatican Council that the supreme pontiff when speaking *ex cathedra* on matters of faith and morals was infallible – propositions which only deepened the divisions between Catholics and Protestants. It was little short of tragic that the politico-philosophical conflict between the Church and liberalism was deepening at a crucial stage in the struggle between Austria and Prussia. Sadowa had tipped the balance decisively against Catholicism. In the old Confederation twenty-three million of the forty-three million inhabitants were Catholic, i.e. roughly 53.5 per cent. Once the twelve million Austrian Catholics were excluded Catholics became a minority in the new Reich. And as a Protestant state dominated the new Confederation, southern Catholics were not anxious to join it on religious grounds. Political Catholicism became a significant force after 1866 precisely because southern opposition to union with the north coincided with Catholic resistance to the attempts of liberal regimes to promote secular education and civil marriage.

Political Catholicism has had a bad press at the hands of the Little German historians – and others – who dismissed it as 'obscurantist', 'reactionary' and 'particularist'. No one would attempt nowadays to defend the excesses of clerical obscurantism or justify the dishonest electoral tactics employed on occasions by militant Catholics against liberal opponents. But one must distinguish between obscurantism and the natural desire of many German Catholics to defend the beliefs of their Church and the traditions of their *engere Heimat* against a state which from the time of Frederick the Great had been equated with militarism and *Kadavergehorsamkeit*. The ruthless treatment of defeated states in 1866, the disregard of dynastic rights and the minimal concessions made to liberal opinion in the new confederate constitution confirmed this view and strengthened the south in its opposition to the idea of union with the north.

The probability that France would take military action to prevent further Prussian expansion together with mounting opposition to Prussia in South Germany seemed certain to postpone the final stage in the creation of Little Germany to a date in the distant future. However, from the very beginning Bismarck did his best to even up the balance by establishing those 'national ties' between north and south envisaged in the Peace of Prague. His first limited success was the conclusion of offensive–defensive alliances with the southern states.

Bismarck had excluded them from the peace negotiations with Austria. Only when the latter were completed did he turn to the southern states. His peace terms were deliberately onerous : in addition to military alliances he demanded large indemnities and territorial cessions from Württemberg, Bavaria and Hesse-Darmstadt (but not from Baden, a state whose government was more favourably disposed towards Prussia.) The stick-and-carrot tactics worked. In return for a reduction in the size of the indemnity and the abandonment of most of the territorial demands, Württemberg agreed to a military alliance, as did Baden. The Bavarian foreign minister, von der Pfordten, turned in vain to France for support. Napoleon was hoist with his own petard : busily engaged in extracting territorial compensation out of Prussia, he was in no position to object to Bismarck's demands. Bavaria had no alternative but to accede to the Prussian request. In the offensive–defensive treaties the three states and Prussia guaranteed each other's territory and agreed in the event of war to place their railway systems and armies under the command of the king of Prussia. The first bridge had been built across the Main, 'the fruit of military victory and French rapacity, of southern isolation and the threat of a Draconian peace'.[30]

While pressure from Prussia was obviously a major factor in bringing about the alliances, strategic necessity would probably have forced the southern states into alliances. For as Baron Friedrich von Varnbüler of Württemberg commented:

Because it seemed to us to be very dangerous to be in an isolated position as a small state without the support of a Great Power even if one could assume that our neutrality is guaranteed by Europe – which in any case is hardly likely to happen – and as our experience with Austria make dependence on her the most thankless [option] imaginable and as reliance on France except in circumstances of exceptional necessity is contrary to national sentiment, we were obliged to conclude that the commitment entered into with Prussia corresponds to the interests . . . of Württemberg for it guarantees the integrity of the state.[31]

Incidentally, Bismarck did not demand that Hesse-Darmstadt conclude a military alliance with Prussia. As the province of Upper Hesse which lay north of the Main had become part of the new North German Confederation, a sizeable part of the grand duke's army was already under Prussian control. Prussia had not, however, annexed Upper Hesse so that the grand duke still exercised sovereign power over it as well as over Hesse-Darmstadt south of the Main where the remainder of the grand duke's small army was stationed. This territorial monstrosity, as even Baron Reinhard von Dalwigk, the leading minister, described it, was scarcely viable politically. Militarily Hesse-Darmstadt was in a most vulnerable position in view of French strategic plans for a thrust along the river Main in the event of war. So despite Dalwigk's well-known antipathy towards Bismarck, military necessity forced Hesse-Darmstadt to conclude a military convention with Prussia in April 1867 placing all Hessian troops under Prussian command. On 11 April, largely to please the National Liberals who controlled the government, Hesse-Darmstadt signed a military alliance with Prussia similar in format to those signed by the other states in the summer of 1866.

The offensive–defensive treaties did not remain paper agreements. Between 1867 and 1870 considerable progress was made towards the coordination of the military systems of the southern states with that of Prussia. Prussian discipline and techniques were introduced into the southern armies. In 1867 an exchange of military plenipotentiaries took place with Prussia. And in May 1868 Bavaria and Württemberg adopted the strategic plans of the Prussian general staff which required the concentration of the southern armies in the Palatinate to threaten the right flank of an invading force.

There was, of course, much popular opposition to the introduction of the three-year service system, the rigid drill and discipline of the Prussian army, as well as general resentment at mounting expenditure on armaments. Legislation on military reorganization had a difficult passage through the chambers in Bavaria, Baden and most of all in Württemberg in 1868. Southern governments shared with the opposition reservations about the corrosive effects of Prussian militarism. During the Luxemburg crisis Bavaria and Württemberg expressed alarm at the prospect of war. Varnbüler protested when Bismarck revealed the existence of the treaties and argued – much to Prussia's annoyance – that they were purely defensive agreements which left the southern governments free to determine the *casus foederis*. On the face of it a setback for Prussia. In fact, despite all their bluster Varnbüler and Prince

Chlodwig zu Hohenlohe-Schillingsfürst of Bavaria suspected that had it come to war Württemberg and Bavaria would have had no alternative but to fight. Certainly had they refused to join in 1870 their continued existence might have been problematical after a Prussian victory.[32] On the other hand, the persistence of anti-militarism in the south had one important consequence: it was a clear signal to Berlin that, in the event of war with France, Prussia must ensure that France be made to appear the aggressor in order to trigger off a wave of anti-French feeling which would carry the south into the fighting.

Prussia succeeded in establishing another bridge across the Main when the Customs Union was refounded in 1867. On the outbreak of war the customs treaties had lapsed technically, though in practice the economic ties were so strong that they continued as before and dues were paid out as usual at the end of 1866. During the peace negotiations Bismarck announced that within six months a new-style customs union would be founded to supersede the existing treaties (temporarily renewed in the peace treaties). On 15 February 1867 he proposed formal negotiations with the southern governments for a new union with a customs parliament as its central feature. That did not suit Württemberg and Bavaria, who preferred a looser association based on a federal council composed of representatives from the new Confederation and the southern states; its decisions would require ratification both by the Reichstag and by the southern chambers. That was totally unacceptable to the Prussians, who were determined to end the *liberum veto* in the old Customs Union.

The impasse was broken by Varnbüler. Anticipating trouble in persuading the chamber to pass the military reorganization bill, he hoped to swing the vote in favour through the renewal of the Customs Union. Bismarck was adamant: negotiations were dependent upon prior acceptance of a customs council and a customs parliament. The former would be composed of forty-two members of the federal council (*Bundesrat*) of the Confederation plus sixteen representatives from the southern states. The latter would consist of the members of the 297-strong Reichstag plus eighty-five members from the southern states elected by universal male suffrage. Decisions would be arrived at in both bodies by majority voting. Prussia would have seventeen of the fifty-eight seats on the council and would be the only state with a veto over decisions. She would convene and dissolve both bodies and preside over the customs parliament. In short, a structure reflecting the economic and military power of Prussia which by now controlled 90 per cent of German production in the mining and metallurgical industries and 50 per cent of textile production and employed two-thirds of all factory workers.

Baden and Hesse-Darmstadt agreed at once to renew on these terms. Bavaria and Württemberg were less easily persuaded. Dissatisfaction was loudly expressed in the lower chamber in Württemberg and in the upper house in Bavaria. Bismarck's threat in the autumn to dissolve the Customs Union forced the issue. The Bavarian upper chamber approved the treaty by thirty-five votes to thirteen; and reluctantly, the Württemberg chamber approved it by seventy-three votes to sixteen. For, as a contemporary observed, if Bavaria left the Customs Union 'one can say with mathematical certainty that such a storm would break out in Franconia, Swabia, the Rhineland Palatinate and here in Munich that any ministry of whatever complexion would have to give way'.[33] The simple truth was that manufacturers and merchants south of the Main did not want to create their own customs union. However strong their dislike of Prussia, economics in the final analysis determined the issue of union. Of course, whether the military and economic ties between north and south would on their own have brought about political union in the fullness of time is an open question on which historians are divided.[34] What can be said with assurance is that attempts by Prussia to build further bridges across the Main were frustrated by strong opposition in the south.

For a fleeting moment in the summer of 1866 the southern states were stunned by the extent of the Prussian victory. The high hopes entertained by von der Pfordten, Dalwigk and Beust that they could form a southern confederation with Austrian and French support were dashed overnight. On the other hand, National Liberals in the south were supremely confident that final unification would occur in the very near future. Their hopes, too, were dashed in the winter of 1866–7 as it became apparent that Prussia intended to be the dominant power in the new state and that the constitution drafted by Bismarck would severely restrict the effectiveness of the new Reichstag. Soon the liberal minister in Baden Roggenbach was referring contemptuously to the new state as 'the union of a dog with its fleas'.[35] Not only had liberal opinion grown sceptical about the type of union on offer. The rapid growth of Political Catholicism after 1866 created a new and formidable barrier to unification. Hence, Bismarck's attempts in the winter of 1866–7 to extend the authority of the Confederation over the southern states while allowing them to remain in control of their finances and armies were wrecked by Bavaria's staunch opposition. Similarly his attempt to facilitate the entry of Hesse-Darmstadt into the Confederation – as a means of attracting the other states to follow suit – ended in failure. Although Hessian members of the Reichstag as well as a majority in the Hessian Landtag favoured union, Dalwigk's stubborn opposition could not be overcome. In the midst of the Luxemburg crisis Bismarck was forced to agree to the military convention and lost the lever which he had hoped to use to secure her entry into the northern state.

Bismarck's hopes that economic ties might bind the south closer to the north were dashed by the outcome of the 1868 elections to the Customs Parliament. Southern National Liberals campaigned vigorously on the slogan 'From Customs Parliament to Union Parliament' (*Von Zollparlament zum Vollparlament*) in the confident expectation that the elections – the first to be held on the basis of universal male suffrage – would return candidates pledged to final unification. Yet only in Hesse-Darmstadt were nationalists elected to half of the (six) seats. Elsewhere anti-Prussian and anti-Protestant sentiment carried the day. In Bavaria the Progressive Party won only twelve out of forty-eight seats. The newly formed Bavarian Patriotic Party, drawing support from the rural population and petty bourgeoisie in the towns, won twenty-six seats. Even in Baden where nationalism was a strong force because of its proximity to France and nationalists won eight seats with 86,890 votes, their opponents who won six seats polled more votes (90,078). The greatest sensation was in Württemberg where the German Party was totally defeated. Ten seats were won by the Peoples' Party, which capitalized on the strong democratic and anti-Prussian feelings of the Swabians, and another ten by pro-government candidates. The oppositional mood of the electorate was encapsulated in a quip going the rounds during the campaign which summed up the essence of the Prussian spirit as: 'Pay up, join up and shut up' (*Steur zahlen, Soldat sein, Maul halten*). Considerable as the advantages of economic association with the north were, they were not great enough to overcome a visceral dislike of all things Prussian. The result was that forty-nine opponents of political union were returned to the Berlin parliament and only thirty-six supporters.

Bismarck had high hopes of the new-style Customs Union. 'Everything,' he commented, 'depends on the direction and swiftness with which public opinion develops in Southern Germany and a fairly serious judgement about this will first become possible through the Customs Parliament.'[36] Not that he would have welcomed a demand by that parliament for immediate union. That would have embarrassed him too much, for further Prussian expansion depended on a favourable international situation. What he did expect were indications of general support for the concept of final unification.

He was quickly disappointed. At the beginning of the first session, opened by the king of Prussia, the nationalists failed to carry a motion demanding that final unification be brought about through the Customs Union. This was defeated by 186 to 150 votes because Bismarck, having good reason to believe that Southern Catholics would stage a walk-out if the motion was carried, urged Prussian Conservatives to support an amendment that no vote be taken. Further nationalist attempts to introduce the unification issue into debates on purely commercial matters were frustrated by noisy interruptions. The point was not lost on Bismarck. Shortly before the session ended he observed that if unification was completed by the end of the century that would be a considerable achievement, if in five to ten years 'an unhoped-for gift of grace from God'.[37] Southern Catholics left Berlin rejoicing that they had 'brought the Prussian locomotive to a permanent halt on the Main', as one of them put it. The nationalists learned their lesson and did not attempt to raise the unification issue during the second session of the Parliament in June 1868. From now on the Parliament confined its deliberations to purely commercial matters. In general much good work was done in the three sessions to facilitate the progress of the Customs Union. Bismarck did not abandon hope that the political climate would change but consoled himself with the thought that 'we all have national unification at heart, but for a calculating politician the essential precedes the desirable, i.e. first build the house then extend it'.[38]

Nevertheless, on the eve of the Franco-Prussian War anti-Prussian sentiment in the south was, in fact, growing stronger, not weaker. The nature of this opposition varied from state to state. In Württemberg it was purely political. As the government had not come into conflict with Catholics over the sensitive areas of education and civil marriage, they did not form a separate party but continued to cooperate with the democratic Peoples' Party. At the Landtag elections in July 1869 the party secured twenty-three seats and the Greater German Party – for which most Catholics voted – twenty-two seats, giving the two parties a majority of twenty over the German party and the ministerial party. The success of the opposition was explicable in terms of mounting resentment at an impending increase of 30 per cent in taxation to cover the costs of military reorganization. In the autumn of 1869 the Peoples' Party launched a campaign and secured 150,000 signatures (i.e. 75 per cent of those who had voted in the last election) on a petition for a reduction in military expenditure. In March 1870 the two parties introduced a motion to cut expenditure and alter the period of service with the colours – a feature which was arousing intense popular resentment. The government, realizing that it could not secure the passage of the budget and fearful of the outcome of fresh elections, postponed the meeting of the chamber until the autumn. The opposition was further antagonized by a government reshuffle which strengthened the conservatives and by Varnbüler's statement in reply to a question in the chamber that he had been wrong when he declared in October 1867 that Württemberg had the right to determine the *casus foederis* under the offensive – defensive treaty. In the summer of 1870 the government attempted to conciliate the opposition by publishing new budget proposals cutting military expenditure slightly and reducing the period of service with the colours to twenty months. Whether the political crisis would have been resolved in the autumn of 1870 seems highly unlikely. The government was determined to make no more concessions on military expenditure, while the opposition was strengthened in its resolve by the promise of grass-roots popular associations to organize a tax boycott in support of the chamber.

In Baden and Bavaria where governments had attempted to curtail the activities of the Church, Catholic parties hostile to Prussia on both religious and political grounds came into existence. In Baden at the close of the 1860s Catholics clashed with the government over a range of issues: approval of a new archbishop to replace Archbishop Vicari (an implacable opponent of the liberal government); regulations requiring Catholic theological students to pass a state examination in secular subjects; the introduction of civil marriage; and the transfer of charitable institutions from Church to state control. In 1869 the Catholic Peoples' Party was founded in Heidelberg. It demanded the separation of Church and state, freedom for the Church to manage her own affairs; and the unification of Germany on a federal basis with the inclusion of Austria. It also stood for the introduction of universal male suffrage for it had dawned on Catholic leaders that a broad franchise would enable them to mobilize the rural population with the help of the clergy and swamp the urban base of political liberalism. Though only three members succeeded in being elected in 1869 to a chamber of fifty-one – not surprising under the prevailing system of indirect election – these members were constant critics of government policy.

But it was in Bavaria that Political Catholicism emerged as a major force, partly for political and partly for religious reasons. The appointment in 1867 of Hohenlohe-Schillingsfürst, a Catholic firmly committed to final unification, antagonized Catholics still nominally committed to the creation of Greater Germany – though in practice most realized that this was an impossible objective and concentrated instead on preserving Bavarian independence. Secondly, government measures reducing Church control over Catholic schools was bitterly denounced as 'godless liberalism'. In the winter of 1868–9 the Bavarian Peoples' Party or Patriotic Party was founded as the political arm of Bavarian Catholicism. After a bitter election campaign in May 1869 the Patriotic Party, which had the support of the rural population and the lower middle class in the towns, won an overall majority in the lower chamber.[39] After ten members were disqualified for electoral irregularities, the Patriotic Party and its opponents held seventy-two seats each. Following a bitter election campaign in October 1869 during which officials openly intervened in the government interest and the Catholic clergy acted as recruiting agents for the Patriotic Party, it was returned with eighty seats to a combined opposition of seventy-one.[40] The political crisis deepened in February 1870 when both houses of the legislature carried a no-confidence motion in Hohenlohe, who resigned feeling that he could not rely on King Ludwig's support should he follow Bismarck's advice to dissolve the chamber and create new peers to break the hostile majority.

The crisis deepened still further when a committee of the lower house proposed a cut of 2,200,000 gulden in the military budget and reduced the period of military service to eight months – clearly a first step towards the introduction of a militia system. In July 1870 the new minister–president and the finance minister both declared the proposals unacceptable. Had war not intervened, a head-on collision between the Bavarian government and the lower chamber would have been unavoidable.

The outbreak of war and the wave of anti-French feeling which swept through Baden and Württemberg and affected Bavaria (though to a lesser extent) has tended to obscure the fact that the two largest German states in which six and a half million of the 8,700,000 inhabitants of South Germany lived were in the grip of a political crisis in the summer of 1870 much more serious than that facing the Prussian government in 1862. In both states a significant polarization of opinion was taking place. The forces of 'law and order' – the crown, the military, and the bureaucracy supported by the National Liberal minorities – were coming together in one camp held together by the threat mass democracy posed to their privileged position and throughly resolved for that reason to resist cuts in military expenditure. Their opponents enjoyed wide grass-roots support which Prussian liberals had neither possessed nor really wanted, and they displayed a much greater degree of determination to win the struggle against the government.

It would be far too simplistic an interpretation of the complex relationship between external policy and domestic tensions to suggest that Bismarck plunged Prussia into war in 1870 to divert attention away from an internal political crisis, any more than it would be fair to Cavour to say that he invaded the Papal States in 1860 only in order to prevent Garibaldi's forces spreading radical ideas destructive of monarchy throughout the whole of Italy. But we know that Bismarck did regard the rapidly deteriorating political situation in South Germany with grave concern. Lord Loftus reported in mid February Bismarck's comment that in the event of serious complications in Bavaria the Prussian army would march into that state at once: *'Nous entrerons de suite, nous ne pouvons pas faire autrement.'*[41] In March after the fall of Hohenlohe it was rumoured that Prussia was contemplating military action against

Munich and Stuttgart and had designated three army corps for this purpose.[42]

Although Bismarck often cautioned against arbitrary interference in the course of history, remarking in a celebrated passage in 1869: '. . . we can put the clocks forward, but time does not on that account move any faster, and the ability to wait, while the situation develops, is a prerequisite of practical politics', he did not always follow his own advice.[43] In the early months of 1870 he was actively seeking to refloat the becalmed ship of unification. That is the significance of the Kaiser project. Early in January Bismarck investigated the possibility of obtaining for King William the title of emperor of Germany or perhaps emperor of the North German Confederation. Domestic considerations certainly entered into his calculations. He confided to the crown prince that the government needed favourable majorities in the forthcoming Reichstag and Landtag elections because on 31 December 1871 the Iron Budget arrangement would lapse, i.e. the compromise agreed to by the Constituent Reichstag in 1867 whereby for four years military expenditure – which accounted for 95 per cent of total expenditure – would be outside Reichstag control. Bismarck clearly hoped to make the Iron Budget a permanent feature of confederate finances but feared he might be plunged into a bitter struggle over budgetary control if the opposition got the upper hand. However, if an imperial title was conferred on the king this might help whip up enthusiasm for government candidates in the elections. The project did not become airborne. Reichstag approval of a title would be needed and the National Liberals demanded responsible government as a *quid pro quo* – for another disagreeable feature of the post-Königgrätz period from Bismarck's point of view was the liberal tendency to seek compensation for the failure to complete unification by laying greater emphasis on constitutional issues. The establishment of the Liberal Empire in France encouraged the belief that constitutional change should not be long delayed in Germany. To that Bismarck was adamantly opposed. When he turned to the princes whose consent to the title was obviously essential, he found no enthusiasm for the elevation of one of their number to the imperial purple.

Anxious as Bismarck was for action of some kind, it is equally clear that he had not the slightest intention of allowing the National Liberals to take the initiative. They were greatly depressed by the bleak prospect lying ahead of them and impatient at the slow progress Prussia was making. Bavarian National Liberals were under no illusion that if the 'German question' was not 'brought to life quickly and decisively then the disintegrating process will continue and in three years Bavaria will be completely in the hands of the priests'.[44]

In February 1870 in an attempt to break the impasse and force Bismarck's hand, Eduard Lasker moved his celebrated motion requesting the Reichstag to recognize the national aspirations of Baden and facilitate its entry into the Confederation as quickly as possible. The National Liberals calculated that if France tolerated the move, then the other states would join in, bringing Little Germany into being at last. If France chose to make the Baden motion a *casus belli* – which the National Liberals hoped they would – the southern states would either be swept into union by a wave of patriotic fervour during the 'national' war against the 'hereditary foe' or at the lowest estimate be intimidated into joining by the big battalions of Prussia.

Bismarck rejected the Lasker motion out of hand. He may well have feared that the incorporation of Baden would alienate Bavaria and Württemberg still further from the north so that in the event of war they might remain neutral, making Prussian expansion much more difficult. But he was probably just as anxious to prevent his liberal enemies dictating the pace of events in 1870 as they had tried to do in the winter of 1863–4. The fact that he spoke of 'national unification' did not mean he was working hand in glove with the National Liberals. His objective remained what it had been in 1862: the aggrandisement of the kingdom of Prussia. He was equally determined to uphold the power of the Prussian crown and may well have sensed that the entry of Baden into the Confederation at the request of the National Liberals would strengthen their resolve to seek to revise the 1867 constitution. And that constitution was not negotiable in Bismarck's view. It represented the maximum he was prepared to concede to liberalism and was intended to be a reassuring signal to the southern rulers that Prussia could be relied upon to resist demands for full-blooded parliamentary government.

Reference was made earlier to the argument that the economic and military ties between north and south were deepening every day despite political opposition, so that without any initiative from Berlin the southern rulers might in the fullness of time have concluded that there was little alternative to union. That is a matter for speculation. On the other hand, as one historian of the period has wisely commented:

> The chronological relationship between his [Bismarck's] adoption of the Hohenzollern candidacy, the resignation of Hohenlohe in Bavaria, the campaign to cut the military budget in Württemberg and the National Liberal revolt, all of which reached a climax in the same month, is more than suggestive. Although it would probably be impossible to demonstrate conclusively the interconnection among these events, to assume that they were mere coincidences stretches the limits of credulity too far.[45]

The war of 1870 did not come out of a clear blue sky but was preceded by a period of mounting international tension. From 1867 onwards the *cognoscenti* were convinced that war could not be long delayed. Writing at the turn of 1869–70 Ludwig von Gerlach remarked that: 'since 1866 Europe has been bracing itself nervously for a big war, so nervously that it is being said on all sides that commerce, trade and finance are suffering'.[46]

After Sadowa France, alarmed by the speed and efficiency of the Prussians, made strenuous efforts to re–arm. Napoleon's objective was a million–strong army to equal that of Prussia. This proved difficult to achieve, partly because of complacency in military circles and partly because of opposition in the Corps Législatif where some deputies feared that Napoleon might be tempted to use an enlarged army for a new Mexican-style adventure. Still, the 1868 law did bring about considerable improvements. Meanwhile, on the other side of the Rhine the Prussian general staff finalized their plans for war against France. By 1869 Britain had grown fearful that the new arms race would lead to war and, still worse, to revolution in France. To reduce the mounting tension Lord Clarendon, the British foreign secretary, acting on a suggestion from French Foreign Minister Count Napoleon Daru, proposed that both France and Germany reduce the annual intake of recruits. The Frenchman was only seeking to embarrass Bismarck, confident that the latter would reject the proposal out of hand, as indeed he did with the comment: 'We are surrounded by three great empires with arms as large as our own and which can at any time coalesce against us.'[47]

France tried with little success to forge alliances which would sustain her in her hour of need. It is unnecessary to discuss the intricate diplomacy of the late 1860s. Suffice to say that France failed to attain her objective. In part this was due to Bismarck's astute diplomacy as, for example, during the long drawn-out Cretan crisis when he played a part in preventing a rapprochement between France and Britain. Britain was further alienated from France by the Belgian Railways affair in 1869 when the French Eastern Railway with government encouragement signed agreements to acquire key Belgian railways. The Belgians were annoyed and, encouraged discreetly by Prussia, passed a law preventing the alienation of their railways. Whereupon the Paris press denounced Bismarck's suspected machinations and talked of war. The crisis blew over but added appreciably to the tension in Europe at the turn of the year.

Nor did desperate attempts to negotiate an *alliance à trois* with Italy and Austria get very far. As long as Napoleon was committed to a French garrison in Rome, any agreement would be operative only when war obliged Napoleon to remove the French troops. As for Austria, military circles led by Archduke Karl favoured war and Beust, a bitter enemy of Prussia, was ready to flirt with France and discuss plans for a new Germany of roughly equal states. But the Austrians were not prepared to enter into binding military commitments. The truth was that Austria was now more interested in seeking help against Russia, which was of no use to Napoleon. Furthermore, internal problems with Poles, Czechs and Magyars allowed her little room for manoeuvre; the balance of power inside Austria–Hungary was swinging towards the Magyars who were not in the slightest interested in a war of revenge in Central Europe. Certainly, a draft agreement was drawn up in May 1869 guaranteeing the status quo and promising to enter into an offensive–defensive alliance – but only in the event of war. All France could hope for was that when the conflict came Italy and Austria would overcome their hesitancy and join in.

THE HISTORIOGRAPHY OF THE WAR OF 1870

Finally, we turn to the immediate causes of the war of 1870. No historian today supposes that the Second World War was caused simply and solely by the megalomania of Adolf Hitler. That is not, of course to deny that Hitler's decision to attack Poland was a factor of crucial importance in September 1939. In the same way the leading figures on the French and German sides played a crucially important role in those events which constitute the proximate causes of the war of 1870.

For nearly a century Bismarck's role in the outbreak of war has been the centre of attention for historians. This was not so in 1870, when general opinion blamed the war on the reckless behaviour of Napoleon and his advisers who were said to have wantonly plunged Western Europe into a major conflagration for the sake of French prestige. The accused in turn blamed public opinion for driving them to war. Twenty years elapsed before suspicion fell on Bismarck who, at the time of the war, had informed the federal council tongue-in-cheek that he had learned of the Hohenzollern candidacy only on 3 July. But in the autumn of 1892, out of office and anxious to play up the importance of his role in the unification process, he claimed in an interview with a foreign journalist that he had manufactured the war and admitted that by omitting certain passages he had completely altered the tone of the Ems Telegram. In November Chancellor Count Leo von Caprivi sprang to the old man's defence, declaring in the Reichstag that Bismarck had done no more than carry out the king of Prussia's suggestion that he make use of the information in the telegram as he saw fit. What Bismarck did was, in Caprivi's opinion, thoroughly justified in face of provocation from France. Justification by omission was Bismarck's line in his reminiscences published in 1898; he observed that there had been no more effective way of overcoming the mistrust of the southern states 'than through a common national war against a neighbour who has been an aggressor for centuries'.[48] Many historians took a less charitable view of the ex–chancellor's actions and focused their attention on him as the chief suspect in the investigation into the origins of the war.

Interest in this question was kept alive by the attitude of the German foreign office, aided and abetted by successive chancellors. Scholars were systematically denied access to the secret files and heavy pressure was exerted on several scholars from Heinrich von Sybel to Hermann Oncken who came across incriminating evidence not to publish their findings. The emperor, Caprivi, Hohenlohe and Bethmann Hollweg all did their best to keep the documentation secret. Not that the Germans were exceptional in this matter of secrecy. At the beginning of the century it was only some thirty years since the Franco-Prussian war. And it was long after the end of the Second World War before the British government reduced the fifty-year rule to thirty years in the case of Britain's Public Records Office. Even now the government reserves the right to withhold any document it chooses from public scrutiny for much longer periods.

However, it was not just the natural conservatism of foreign office officials which made them conceal the truth for so long. Nor was it loyalty to the old man, whose resignation in 1890 was greeted with an audible sigh of relief in official circles. The real reason for the Wilhelmstrasse's reticence was a growing awareness that the outside world feared and mistrusted Bismarck's restless Reich. That made it mandatory to preserve as long as possible the image of Bismarck the 'honest broker' who had constructed an elaborate alliance system in the 1870s and 1880s with the object of preserving the peace. The truth about the Ems Telegram had unfortunately been revealed by the old man. All the more important to preserve the fiction that Bismarck knew nothing of the candidacy before 3 July 1870. The nearer Imperial Germany moved towards war in the second decade of the new century, the more urgent became the duty of concealing the truth. But as suspicion mounted in the outside world about the general objectives of German foreign policy, the more historians were inclined to see in Bismarck the real villain of the piece in 1870.

Foreign office and imperial government were fighting a losing battle. In 1894 when the second volume of the memoirs of King

Carol of Rumania – the younger brother of Leopold of Hohenzollern – were published it confirmed suspicions that Bismarck had known of the candidacy before 3 July.[49] Then, just before the First World War, the historian Hermann Hesselbarth, much to the chagrin of the foreign office, obtained from the private papers of the former head of the German chancery in Madrid copies of a damaging exchange of telegrams between Bismarck and Eusebio y Mazzaredo Salazar.[50] After the publication of Richard Fester's book (also in 1913) containing these telegrams as well as other material from the Spanish, German and French press it was abundantly clear that Bismarck had been involved at an early stage in the proceedings.[51] These revelations did not dampen the enthusiasm of most German historians for Bismarck. On the eve of war they were still arguing that the need to unify Germany and enable her to act as the guardian of the peace in Europe justified acts of duplicity on the old man's part.

After the defeat of Germany in 1918 the Wilhelmstrasse continued the battle. Two historians of the older generation, Walter Platzhoff and Karl Reinhold, reported on behalf of the foreign office that while publication would doubtless please scholars, it was politically inadvisable. As sole guilt for causing the war of 1914 had just been laid at Germany's door, could she afford to publish material which could be used to establish Bismarck's guilt?[52] The foreign office agreed and consequently the American historian Richard Howard Lord, whose book appeared in 1924 (and who argued that Bismarck had indeed 'manufactured' the war), was not given access to the secret files nor to the Sigmaringen archive.[53]

Not until after the Second World War were the archives at last completely open to scholars. In 1948 Jochen Dittrich used the documentation in the Sigmaringen archive in a doctoral dissertation published as a book in 1962.[54] Before its appearance Georges Bonnin, a Frenchman working in England on the captured German archives, had published the key foreign office documents and a selection from the Sigmaringen archive, though regrettably in English translation. At the end of the day with all the documents available to historians it is abundantly clear that Bismarck played a major role in promoting the Hohenzollern candidacy from February 1870 onwards.

This does not, of course, explain his motives for seeking to put a Hohenzollern prince on a Spanish throne. Because he concealed his part in the affair and re-edited the Ems Telegram, it does not follow that his objective from the outset was war. Broadly speaking, there are three possible interpretations of his actions in 1870. First, that he was without blame, did not seek war but had it forced on him by the trigger–happy French. Secondly, that he deliberately sought war, believing this to be the only way to achieve final unification, i.e. to extend the boundaries of Prussia down to the Bodensee. And thirdly, that he made use of the candidacy to try to out-manoeuvre the French; his intention was to score a diplomatic victory, throwing them into disarray, and to absorb the southern states when a favourable opportunity presented itself. Only when the manoeuvre misfired did Bismarck opt for war to escape an impasse.

The first position has been upheld by several historians, most notably in Germany, commencing with Sybel who exonerated Napoleon as well as Bismarck and laid all the blame at the door of the Duc de Gramont and warmongering journalists in Paris. A later variation suggested that Bismarck took up the candidacy only to protect Prussia against a threatening diplomatic combination between France, Austria and Italy. War broke out because the French refused to settle for the withdrawal of Prince Leopold.[55] Another variation suggested that Bismarck was simply seeking to enhance Prussian prestige by persuading a second Hohenzollern to accept a foreign crown as a kind of exercise in glorification by association.[56] Interestingly enough some French historians, notably on the political left – where the impressive organization of the German Social Democratic Party was greatly admired – were also ready to exonerate Bismarck. Ernest Denis and Jean Jaurès, for example, condemned the opposition of the French to German unification which they believed had forced Bismarck to fight in 1870. And even though Jaurès admitted that Bismarck acted provocatively in the final stages of the crisis, nevertheless he insisted that the stupidity of French diplomacy and the frivolity of the French people had contributed enormously to the outbreak of war.[57] Since the Second World War supporters of the 'not guilty' thesis have included Hans Rothfels, Ludwig Reiners, Werner Richter, Alan Taylor and most recently Eberhard Kolb.[58] Taylor states the case in characteristically blunt terms: '. . . there is not a scrap of evidence that he worked deliberately for a war with France, still less that he timed it precisely for the summer of 1870'.[59]

The second thesis, that of deliberate intent, was favoured by several French historians though only with significant qualifications. Thus Albert Sorel, Henry Salomon and Henri Welschinger, while conviced that Bismarck had planned the war, still attached much blame to blundering French diplomacy.[60] Since the Second World War supporters of this interpretation have included Charles Grant Robertson, Friedrich Darmstaedter, George Gooch, Georges Bonnin, Josef Becker and most recently George Kent.[61]

This school of thought attaches considerable weight to the damning comments certain highly placed contemporaries made about Bismarck's intentions. Grand Duke Friedrich of Baden, King William of Prussia's son-in-law, claimed in a statement (made, however, in 1901) that Bismarck's Spanish policy was intended 'to provoke war'. Roggenbach, the grand duke's minister, was convinced that Bismarck wanted war as much as the French. Prince Karl Anton, head of the Sigmaringen house, accused Bismarck in June 1871 of having used the candidacy 'in order to win an occasion for war with France'.[62] According to the memoirs of the Saxon minister of war, Bismarck declared early in 1870 that 'he regarded war with France in the near future as an unavoidable necessity'.[63] Finally, Bismarck himself had spoken in 1869 about the possibility of using the Spanish question or other issues to provoke war with France should an international crisis arise.[64]

Secondly, it is argued that Bismarck felt the only way to break the complete deadlock on unification was to take forward action calculated to lead to war. Thirdly, the law of probability suggests that a man who deliberately precipitated war with Denmark in 1864 and with Austria in 1866 was perfectly capable of doing so again and probably had done so.

The third thesis – that Bismarck aimed in the first instance at the diplomatic defeat of France – has been advanced in its most sophisticated form by Jochen Dittrich. Writing immediately after the Second World War when a devastated Europe had grown weary of national rivalries and a spirit of reconciliation was in the air, Dittrich exonerated both French and Germans from sole responsibility for 1870. War had broken out because Bismarck's cunning diplomacy, designed to outwit the French and complete German unification by peaceful means, had backfired. Only then did he decide on war and when he did the French were as eager for it as the Germans.

In so far as we can ever be certain about the motivation of this complex and sophisticated political operator, those biographers seem nearer the truth who maintain that he never committed himself whole–heartedly to any one approach to a political problem. In Otto Pflanze's words:'. . . it is safe to say that he had more than one possibility in mind. Whatever the result it would bring egress from the impasse of the German question.'[65] W.N. Medlicott refers to 'the skilful pursuit of alternative possibilities: either that France would acquiesce in the Hohenzollern election . . . or France would not, in which case there might be war, for which he was ready'.[66] One of the latest biographers, Lothar Gall, goes further: 'a warlike culmination, a peaceful agreement, a clear diplomatic defeat of one side over the other or a surprising resolution of the whole problem as a consequence of internal developments in Spain – all this seemed possible until the very last'. For the special quality of Bismarck's diplomacy was its extraordinary flexibility. It 'ran on several lines taking into account all possibilities, not simply in terms of the final result but in the same breath [these became] starting–points for quite new activities and in particular for new configurations'.[67]

THE HOHENZOLLERN CANDIDACY

In September 1868 Queen Isabella of Spain was forced off the throne by revolution. As her son, Alfonso Prince of the Asturias, was unacceptable to the new government and as King Ferdinand of Portugal refused the crown, the Spaniards looked outside Spain for a new ruler whose connections with one or other of the Great Powers would enhance the standing of Spain in Europe. The candidates who were seriously considered were: Duke Antoine of Montpensier, a son of the French Citizen King and married to a daughter of ex–Queen Isabella; Duke Amadeo of Aosta, third son of the king of Italy and likely to succeed to the Italian throne as the crown prince was childless; and Duke Thomas of Genoa, a nephew of the Italian king.[68] A fourth candidate whose name was actively considered from the very beginning was Prince Leopold of Hohenzollern–Sigmaringen, a junior branch of the royal house. A Catholic married to Princess Antoinette Infanta of Portugal, his claims were enhanced by the possibility that his wife or her children might succeed in Portugal, thus uniting the Iberian Peninsula as it had been from 1580 to 1640.

In April 1869 the Spanish government put out feelers to the Hohenzollern–Sigmaringens via Count Philippe of Flanders who was married to Princess Marie of Hohenzollern. The count wrote to Karl Anton suggesting that if Leopold presented himself as a candidate he might well have prospects of success. Rumours in March of the Spanish interest in Leopold alarmed Napoleon III. When Benedetti saw the undersecretary of state, Hermann von Thile on 31 March (in Bismarck's absence) he made it plain that 'such an eventuality interested the Emperor's government too directly for it not to be my duty to call attention to its dangers in the event of there being grounds for believing that it might come to something'. Thile replied that 'there had not been and never would be a question of the Prince of Hohenzollern for the Crown of Spain'.[69] Still dissatisfied, Benedetti saw Bismarck on 8 May. The chancellor admitted that the Hohenzollern–Sigmaringens had been sounded out but declared that Karl Anton with the king's approval had declined the offer.[70] In September the Spanish envoy Salazar made the first formal approach to the Hohenzollern–Sigmaringens. Although Karl Anton and Leopold avoided commitment, Salazar formed the impression rightly that they were interested but that rather than take the initiative they wanted King William to order Leopold (a serving officer) to accept the crown. That Karl Anton was well aware of the French dimension is evident from his insistence that a (hypothetical) candidacy must first be cleared in direct negotiations between the French emperor and the Prussian king.

Enough had been said by the French for Bismarck to have realized that France was concerned about the issue and that active support of Leopold's candidacy would lead to dangerous complications. Nevertheless when Salazar appeared at the Weinburg on the Bodensee in February 1870, this time with a firm offer of the Spanish crown, Bismarck began to advocate acceptance of the offer. King William, however, strongly opposed the candidacy feeling that the unruly Spaniards would soon send a foreign king packing – a shrewd comment as events were to prove. Bismarck bombarded the old man with a variety of arguments: Spain was strategically important; under a Hohenzollern ruler it would be well placed to check French ambitions and help to keep the peace or, if war did break out, France could be intimidated into keeping one or two army corps on the frontier. There would also be trade benefits for Germany. Moreover, was it not essential to prevent Spain becoming a republic and a hotbed of revolutionary activity inimical to the cause of monarchy everywhere? Nor was it in Prussian interests to allow the Bavarian Wittelsbachs to secure the crown, for that would strengthen southern opposition to final unification. Indeed, any candidate other than a Hohenzollern was likely to veer towards France, Austria and the Papacy. And finally, a Spanish crown would bring lustre to the house of Hohenzollern.

These were arguments *ad hominem*. To take Bismarck at his word and suppose that he had no ulterior motives in urging the king to allow acceptance of the candidacy but, like any good diplomat, was merely seeking to exploit the situation in the interests of his country without any thought of war, is naïve.[71] The impasse over final unification, the mounting political crisis in South Germany and the forthcoming elections in the North German Confederation weighed too heavily on his mind for him to have overlooked the diversionary effects the candidacy would have. There can be little doubt that he appreciated that support of the candidacy entailed a very considerable risk of war. Highly placed circles in Berlin anticipated trouble. Karl Anton told Bismarck that he expected 'a wild outcry from anti–Prussian Europe'.[72] Bismarck had also read too many reports from ambassadors not to know that France was likely to act violently if the candidacy was accepted. The newspaper–reading public appreciated this too, for on 1 May a Viennese paper carried a report that Napoleon had told the Spanish ambassador that a successful Hohenzollern candidacy meant war. Of course, one must go on to say that Bismarck was too sophisticated an operator completely to exclude peaceful outcomes equally beneficial to Prussia. He was fond of suggesting that statesmen were not free agents but were utterly dependent on the forward thrust of events. 'No one will charge me with making history,' he said on one occasion (admittedly not without a touch of sarcasm). 'That, gentlemen, I could not even do in company with you . . . we cannot make history, we can only wait until it fulfils itself.'[73] What he omitted to point out was that when an opportunity presented itself to accelerate the pace of events or turn the tables on an opponent, he could be relied upon to take it. This pragmatic approach coupled with a conviction that war would almost certainly be the outcome of the operation is the key to his tactical manoeuvring in the summer of 1870.

At first Bismarck failed to persuade King William to support the candidacy. On 22 April when Bismarck was ill at Varzin Leopold declined the candidacy, as did Friedrich, his younger brother. When Madrid was informed of this on 4 May, the affair seemed at an end. However, the Spaniards had not lost interest in the Hohenzollerns. Neither, it would seem, had Bismarck. His agents, Lothar Bucher and Major Maximilian von Versen, were busy at work reviving the candidacy with the help of Bismarck's new–found ally, the crown prince. Once Karl Anton and Leopold renewed their interest, Bismarck sprang into action, assuring them that it was in Prussian interests that the Hohenzollerns obtain the crown. Significantly he succeeded in persuading Karl Anton and King William to drop the request for negotiations with Napoleon to secure French agreement – another sign that he was not averse to trouble with the French.[74] Grudgingly the king acquiesced in the candidacy. On 21 June Salazar sent a telegram to Manuel Zorilla, president of the Cortes, informing him that he (Salazar) would arrive back in Madrid 'about 26' bringing with him the formal letter of acceptance. 'About 26' was a code phrase which meant that if he indicated a date before 1 July the Cortes should be kept in session to elect Leopold at once and present Europe with a *fait accompli*. A cipher clerk in the Madrid embassy decoded the phrase incorrectly as 'towards the 9th'. On receipt of this news Zorilla prorogued the Cortes on 23 June. By the time Salazar arrived in Madrid on 28 June he found the deputies already departed to their homes. On 2 July, when news of Leopold's candidacy was reported in the Paris press, the crisis broke.[75]

To understand the French reaction we must look at internal developments in France since the Luxemburg crisis. It was soon apparent that the cat–and–mouse reforms in January 1867 were totally insufficient to stifle growing criticism of the regime. At the elections in May 1869 – freer than any since 1849 – government supporters polled 4,438,000 votes and opposition candidates

3,355,000. The rural areas were still supportive of the government, though not the towns. But the government faced a new political situation because over half the members of the Corps Législatif consisted of official candidates who had rejected the official ticket and campaigned for constitutional reform. Emile Ollivier, a leading liberal of centre–right inclinations, organized a group of 116 members to support an interpellation requesting the government to concede the principle of ministerial responsibility. With some help from the Left this group commanded a majority of nine in the chamber. Napoleon read the signs correctly and in July 1869 made further concessions: the Corps Législatif was allowed a share in initiating legislation; it could now elect its own officers, vote on the budget, amend government bills and question ministers. At last Napoleon dropped the old guard – Rouher and Baroche resigned and a caretaker government took over. After months of negotiation the Ollivier government was formed in January 1870. Finally, in May 1870 a plebiscite was held on the new constitution drawn up to formalize the political changes. A total of 7,358,786 Frenchmen (67.5 per cent) voted for, 1,571,939 against and 1,900,000 abstained. This significant victory for the government was a reassuring sign to Napoleon that he still enjoyed considerable popular support.

The 1870 constitution was a curious hybrid mixture of authoritarianism and parliamentary government. Napoleon remained head of state and commander–in–chief of the armed forces; he appointed all ministers, presided over their deliberations, retained the right of veto on legislation and his right to appeal to the people via the plebiscite. On the other hand, he had now agreed to rule 'with the cooperation' of ministers and parliament and to share the initiative in legislation with both houses of parliament. Ministers were 'responsible' – as was the emperor – but to whom they were 'responsible' was left undefined. And although the powers of the Corps Législatif had been increased, these were carefully counterbalanced by provisions that the Senate (still a nominated body) should have a veto over legislation and that the constitution could be altered only by a plebiscite held on the emperor's initiative. Emile Ollivier, the spiritual father of the new arrangements, was an old–fashioned liberal who, deploring the excesses of both Jacobin–style democracy and Bonapartist dictatorship, had constructed a system analogous to that of seventeenth–century England where the king shared some of his power with the people. One authority has rightly pointed out that the 1870 constitution was no half–way house on the road to full–blooded parliamentary government but should be compared to the constitutional arrangements of 1814, 1848 and 1958 which combined strong government with respect for civil liberty and democratic principles. Ollivier's political philosophy coincided more or less with Napoleon's desire to retain as much real power as possible while swimming with the tide.

What would have happened had the Liberal Empire lasted longer is an intriguing question. If urban opposition had become more strident, might Napoleon have yielded to the prompting of reactionaries among whom the empress was a leading light and emerged as the *rocher de bronze* 'restoring order' as in 1851? Possibly. But, on the other hand, a man with his political perception would scarcely have acted in that way unless the dynasty was in deep trouble. More likely, given his mercurial temperament, he would have soldiered on, responding to *'la force des choses'* but always striving to slow down the pace of change as much as possible and retaining the substance of power as long as he could.

Paradoxically enough, the establishment of the Liberal Empire did not, as one might suppose, lessen the risk of war. On the contrary, it increased it because of a significant shift in the relationship between public opinion and the government. The French ambassador in Karlsruhe observed very shrewdly that any attempt by the Prussians to cross the Main would lead much more easily to war than in the past because previously Napoleon had had to move cautiously abroad to avoid the accusation that he was waging war for dynastic reasons and in order to divert attention from discontent at home. That danger no longer existed. If the new cabinet went to war to defend France's honour, it would enjoy the whole–hearted support of the French people. Thus when Foreign Minister Daru was replaced on 15 May by Duc Agénor de Gramont, former ambassador in Vienna and a staunch opponent of Prussia, Bismarck concluded correctly – and no doubt with satisfaction – that the chances of war were considerably increased.

Nor was the attitude of Emile Ollivier, Napoleon's chief minister, conducive to the preservation of peace. True, he declared his wish for peace with Germany so that he could concentrate all his efforts on building up the Liberal Empire. He did not subscribe to the old balance–of–power notion that a weak and divided Germany was the only guarantee of French security. On the contrary, he believed a united Germany would be the friend of France and a bulwark against autocratic Russia. In theory he was not disposed to regard the formal union of North and South Germany as a legitimate reason for war; had not the Customs Union and the offensive – defensive alliances brought them together already? These rational sentiments were far outweighed by his extraordinary sensitivity to any slight, real or imagined, to the honour of France. A man who would not have dreamed of waging war for balance-of-power considerations was perfectly prepared to contemplate it to obtain satisfaction for some insult to the national pride of the French. Equally dangerous and irresponsible was his extraordinary belief that if the whole of the French nation wanted war that would be a sufficient cause for conflict. Lord Loftus summed up Ollivier's views succinctly in January 1870, stating that (Ollivier):

> . . .was particularly alive to the importance of not exposing France to the appearance of being slighted: in fact he would not conceal from me that under present circumstances a public rebuff from Prussia would be fatal – "un échec (he said) c'est la guerre". We who have to render an account to Parliament and the country are less than the former government able to put up with any wound to the national pride. Our main object is peace (he added) but we must also show firmness and spirit or we shall not be able to cope with Revolution and Socialism at home.

Yet another indication of the interaction between foreign and domestic policy so characteristic of France in these years.[76]

On 2 July several Paris newspapers reported that a Hohenzollern prince had been offered the Spanish crown. Though uneasy about the situation and inclined to see a Prussian plot behind the candidacy, the editors seemed prepared to wait upon government reactions. It had good reason to be concerned about the strategic implications of a Hohenzollern on a Spanish throne. For in the event of war an entire army corps would have to be stationed along the Pyrenees to keep the Spaniards quiet. But what mattered most to the policy–makers in Paris was not the strategic but the symbolic significance of the candidacy. Was this not a further unpleasant reminder of the extent to which France had forfeited the international status she had enjoyed in 1856? France ought to have been consulted on this issue and had not been. Was this not a slight on her honour? Only a ruling élite thinking primarily in terms of prestige politics could have escalated the crisis the way the council of ministers did in the next fourteen days.

A cooler and more level–headed cabinet might have exerted heavy pressure on Spain to force her to reconsider the offer; if one power wishes to intimidate another it is well advised to choose one of the weaker brethren. However, although Prussia was technically uninvolved, the French government decided – quite correctly – that without prior Prussian approval Leopold would never have accepted the candidacy. It was not, therefore, unreasonable to put out feelers in Berlin. But the French ought surely to have adopted a conciliatory stance and sought via confidential negotiations to persuade Prussia to drop the candidacy without too great a loss of face. There were distinct possibilities of success given King William's known distaste for the candidacy. Instead of that, Gramont, an impetuous and abrasive ex–diplomat, chose a highly dangerous course with the full consent of Napoleon and Ollivier. They were bent not on conciliation but on securing for France a resounding diplomatic victory over Prussia. This they hoped to achieve by a public declaration expressing their concern and threatening to use force unless the candidacy was withdrawn.

As a first step Paris sought information from Berlin about the extent of the Prussian government's involvement. On 4 July the French chargé d'affaires was assured by Undersecretary Thile (acting in Bismarck's absence) that Prussia had no knowledge of the candidacy. This non–commital reply was totally unsatisfactory to Gramont who was only too ready to see the hand of Bismarck behind the whole affair. Whereupon on 6 July the council of ministers unanimously approved a declaration drawn up by Gramont to be read in the Corps Législatif. The council was in a euphoric mood, buoyed up firstly by the conviction that the army could easily defeat Prussia in the event of war, and secondly by high (and misplaced) hopes of active assistance from Italy and Austria–Hungary.

It is difficult to assess the influence of the press and of public opinion in general on the government's decision to seek confrontation. One can safely say that opinion was divided in July, though the exact balance is hard to determine. On the right wing Legitimists, Catholics and Orleanists, and on the left wing Republicans were anti–Prussian, while some radical–democratic papers were pro–Prussian, and financial circles were generally against war. Nor, despite underlying concern about France's deteriorating position in Europe, did the war spirit manifest itself at a popular level until late on in the crisis. One must conclude that the council of ministers entered upon their policy not through pressure from press or public opinion but because they knew they could rely on signficant sections of opinion to support a tough line. In reply to an interpellation later that day in the Corps Législatif, Gramont read the declaration. The gist of it was that any attempt to place a foreign prince on the throne of Emperor Charles V – an emotive phrase inserted by Ollivier and calculated to arouse passion – might upset the European balance of power and would certainly jeopardize the interests and honour of France. He concluded with the bellicose remark that if the candidacy was not withdrawn '. . . we shall know how to do our duty without faltering or weakening'. [77] This remark, received by right–wing deputies with rapturous applause, was intended to appease critics of the government and reassure their supporters that the government would pursue a tough line with the Prussians. That does not mean that Napoleon, Ollivier or even Gramont was deliberately seeking war at all costs. To calm the fears of left–wing deputies, Gramont neatly encapsulated government policy in the words '. . . peace if that is possible; it is war if that is inevitable'.[78] Peace with honour was the objective, Ollivier assured the chamber on the same occasion, but war was certainly preferable to another Sadowa. However, this does give an air of coherence to French policy which it probably lacked. As one French historian shrewdly observed: 'The government was not prepared either to negotiate or go to war; it had no clear intentions nor any agreed plan of action'.[79] An emotional spasm, not the dictates of cold logic, lay behind the declaration of 6 July.

This maladroit piece of megaphone diplomacy without precedent in the annals of diplomatic history set France on a collision course with Prussia. A purely dynastic affair was transformed overnight into a make-or-break issue for a great country. European chancelleries were filled with foreboding, aware, if the ruling élite in Paris was unaware, that France had placed herself in an untenable position should Prussia refuse to retreat. On receiving the news at breakfast in Varzin on 8 July, Bismarck is reported as exclaiming in surprise: 'that certainly looks like war. Gramont would not have used this unrestrained language unless war had been decided on. We ought now to mobilize the whole army and attack the French.'[80] That was not a serious suggestion; it would have been difficult to persuade the king to approve a pre-emptive strike; nor could he have rallied the southern states if Prussia appeared to be the aggressor. But, recovering quickly from his surprise, he instructed Bucher to stir up the German press against the French, especially against Empress Eugénie who was to be accused of seeking a new war of the Spanish Succession.

Gramont's next step was to instruct Benedetti to visit King William who was taking the waters at Bad Ems. He was to request that the king advise Leopold to withdraw the candidacy. On 9 July Benedetti had the first of several meetings with the king spread over the next few days. William made it clear that he had authorized acceptance of the offer not as king of Prussia but as head of the Hohenzollern house. But because he had approved Leopold's candidacy only reluctantly, he was much more conciliatory than Bismarck would have been. Unlike Thile, William admitted that the Prussian government had been informed of the candidacy, thus destroying the fiction that it had been a purely dynastic affair. Moreover, while he refused to try to influence the Hohenzollern–Sigmaringens, he was conscious of the excitement in France and had therefore asked them whether they still intended to go ahead with the Spanish project – a step he had taken, incidentally, without informing Bismarck. He went on to say that if the family did decide on withdrawal, he would certainly approve such a step and inform Benedetti accordingly. They parted company on good terms. The ambassador dined with the monarch and visited the theatre in his company afterwards. Benedetti informed Paris that King William hoped the candidacy would be withdrawn. At the same time common prudence in an experienced diplomat obliged him to add that the interview could be a delaying tactic to allow Prussia to mobilize her forces.

Gramont's declaration on 6 July had aroused high expectations in Paris that Prussia would soon be cut down to size. When Benedetti's telegram arrived on 9 July much of it was indecipherable due to atmospheric conditions in the Rhine valley during transmission. What was legible was alarming: the king had indeed endorsed the candidacy and refused to ask Leopold to withdraw; furthermore, Benedetti had warned that this might be a delaying tactic. Ollivier was greatly alarmed, fearing that France now faced either a humiliating defeat or war. He and the colleagues he hurriedly called together considered it essential to obtain a clear answer from the king. Napoleon was also worried and commenced to take preliminary military measures.

Gramont ordered Benedetti to try again.[81] On 10 July the king encountered the ambassador by chance during an evening stroll and told him that he had not heard from the Sigmaringens. Benedetti seized his chance to request an interview to explain in detail why his government, on the eve of making another statement in the chamber, would be in great difficulties if the king had not replied to him. King William readily agreed to see Benedetti the next day.

When the ambassador saw the king on 11 July he requested that William ask Leopold to withdraw in order to satisfy the French government and French public opinion. The king refused; he repeated that he was involved in the affair only as head of the Hohenzollern house, not as king of Prussia – a claim Benedetti contested. In any event, the king saw no earthly reason why a few days' delay should affect the issue. Taking the offensive, the king observed that if the French refused to wait he would have to assume that they were seeking a pretext for war. And in view of rumours circulating in Germany about French military measures, he wanted to make it absolutely clear that Prussia would not stand idly by. However, the interview ended on a more conciliatory note, for the king said that he expected news from the Hohenzollern–Sigmaringens that very evening and asked Benedetti to inform Gramont of this.[82] Anxious to the very last for a peaceful outcome, the king, immediately after the interview – and again without consulting Bismarck – sent Baron Karl von Werther, the German ambassador, to Paris to assure the government there of Prussia's peaceful intentions.

On 12 July the crisis took a turn for the better, followed almost immediately by a turn for the worse. The good news was the withdrawal of the candidacy. Karl Anton, frightened by the prospect of war, withdrew the candidacy on behalf of Leopold, temporarily incommunicado on an Alpine walking tour. On receiving the news the king at once informed Benedetti who was lunching with him and added that written confirmation would arrive the next day. That evening Benedetti dined with the king confident that once William had informed him officially, the crisis would be over. The euphoric mood did not last. Returning to his hotel, he found fresh instructions awaiting him from Gramont which filled him with gloom. The foreign minister now ordered Benedetti to ask William not as head of the Hohenzollerns but as king of Prussia for 'the assurance that he shall not again authorize this candidacy'.

Why did Gramont escalate the crisis? After all, diplomatic opinion in Paris believed France had won a significant victory. Even Thiers, a bitter critic of the government, commented that '. . . we emerge from an embarrassing dilemma with a victory; Sadowa is almost avenged'.[83] Was it because of the pressure of public opinion? Certainly feelings were already running very high in both Senate and chamber; the fact that the father and not the son had made the renunciation statement did not inspire confidence in it. Many deputies were strongly critical of the government's handling of the situation, considering Gramont's announcement on 13 July that the candidacy had been withdrawn and negotiations were proceeding with Prussia totally inadequate. Clément Duvernois inquired what guarantees the government intended to secure from Prussia against a renewal of the candidacy. Anticipation of serious trouble for the government unless he went much further may have swayed the decision. But this was really a secondary issue. Basically Gramont believed that if France was to score a really resounding diplomatic victory over Prussia, either the king in person or the Prussian government would have to announce the withdrawal. That Gramont was able to make the running at this point reveals much about the ambiguous relationship between the council of ministers and the emperor. Napoleon possessed very real power and ministers were much more dependent on him than on each other. That was how Gramont was able to take a step of the utmost gravity without consulting his colleagues. Initially Napoleon had been satisfied with the news of the withdrawal though, like Gramont, he was soon worried by adverse public reaction. But he quickly succumbed to Gramont's arguments, which were supported by the empress who was openly seeking war. With Napoleon's approval but without consulting Ollivier, Gramont drafted new instructions for Benedetti. On the other hand, when Ollivier met him late that night at the foreign office the prime minister readily agreed to the new course of action. On the basis of a letter from Napoleon confirming his decision prime minister and foreign minister sent off yet another telegram to Benedetti ordering him to obtain guarantees. That three emotionally unstable people should have been thrown together in positions of power at this crucial juncture was a tragedy for France and a revealing comment on the decision–making process in July 1870.

Significantly, Gramont's colleagues were much less enamoured by his policy. When the council of ministers met on 13 July, according to Ollivier four ministers wanted to drop Gramont's demand entirely but the minister of war, General Edmond Leboeuf, conscious of mounting tension, urged the calling–up of reservists.[84] During the debate on Leboeuf's motion Napoleon suddenly informed the meeting of a message from the British ambassador, Lord Richard Lyons, expressing Britain's deep concern at the new demands. This evidence of a change in the British attitude from sympathy to hostility may have been decisive. Certainly Leboeuf's motion was defeated. Finally the council agreed by eight votes to four on a weak – and dangerous – compromise. In principle they supported the request for a guarantee of non–renewal but they insisted that it not be treated as an ultimatum. If the king of Prussia gave the guarantee, well and good; if not, so be it. Either way the affair of the Hohenzollern candidacy would be deemed to be at an end.

On 13 May Benedetti requested an audience with the king. As William had already left for his usual two–hour walk in the Kurgarten, Benedetti contacted Prince Anton Radziwill, the king's equerry, who, along with Prince Albrecht, had accompanied the monarch on his walk. Benedetti asked Radziwill to inform the king that the French ambassador requested an audience in order to obtain a declaration for use by the French government when it had to face the chamber later in the day. Radziwill returned with the message that the king would receive Benedetti some time in the afternoon.

Benedetti's reference to a declaration may well have put King William on his guard. Now in receipt of warning messages from Bismarck, the king probably intended to see Benedetti only after consulting Count Fritz zu Eulenburg, due to arrive in Bad Ems later that morning from Berlin. In accordance with the advice from Berlin the king intended to confine himself to the bare statement that Leopold's decision had been announced to the Paris and Madrid governments. However, the king was handed a copy of the *Kölnische Zeitung* containing news of the withdrawal. Probably acting on sheer impulse the king sent Radziwill with the paper to Benedetti. After reading the passage Benedetti handed back the paper with thanks, and for the king's benefit handed Radziwill a telegram stating that Karl Anton had informed the Spanish government the previous evening of the withdrawal. Whether Benedetti was encouraged by the royal gesture to believe he could presume on the king's good nature and obtain the necessary declaration on the spot we do not know. Perhaps he simply felt the matter so urgent that it brooked no delay. At all events, he stationed himself at the park gate as the king left, clearly hoping for just such an encounter.

The king, out of politeness, took the initiative at this famous meeting which occurred at 11.30 a.m. on 13 July and is still marked by a commemorative stone. *'Eh bien, voilà donc une bonne nouvelle qui nous sauve de toutes difficultés'*, he remarked jovially to Benedetti.[85] He then thanked the ambassador for the news that the French government knew of the withdrawal, remarking light–heartedly that Benedetti was better informed than he was as he the King had received the news only by private telegram. But thankfully, the affair, which might have landed both countries in difficulties, was now over. And he assured Benedetti that when he received the official communication from Karl Anton he would inform the ambassador at once.

Benedetti seized his opportunity to advance the new demand: Karl Anton's declaration was insufficient; would the king authorize him to inform Paris that he would use his royal authority to prevent any renewal of the candidacy in the future? The king replied that such a guarantee was out of the question. What would happen, he inquired, if one day Napoleon thought the prince the most suitable candidate? That would never happen, interjected Benedetti; indeed, public opinion in France was deteriorating hour by hour and a calamity might occur if the king refused to make the necessary declaration. To which William retorted that just as Napoleon could never say that he would not approve Leopold's candidacy, so he (the king) could not say that Karl Anton's declaration had settled the matter for ever. Benedetti pressed harder still: could he then inform his government that the king would never permit a renewal of the candidacy? At this William bridled and declared that he had made it abundantly clear that he could not make that sort of declaration. As a crowd had begun to gather making further discussion unseemly, the king raised his hat and walked on.

While Benedetti, back at his hotel, was reading the latest telegram from Gramont emphasizing the extreme urgency of obtaining the declaration,[86] Radziwill appeared, to inform him that Leopold had officially withdrawn according to a letter received at 1 p.m. Benedetti reminded the equerry that he still expected to be received in audience to explain in detail the reasons for the new demand. In fact, after receiving Karl Anton's letter the king discussed with Eulenburg whether or not to go ahead with the audience. William's instincts were against it for he felt morally affronted by the demand. Clearly Eulenburg told the king of Bismarck's dissatisfaction with William's conciliatory attitude and counselled sterner tones in view of German public opinion.

But when Radziwill conveyed Benedetti's renewed request to the king, the latter wavered once again. In his reply, while reminding

Benedetti of what he had said in the Kurgarten about the impossibility of making a declaration, he did authorize the Frenchman to inform his government that the king of Prussia entirely approved of Leopold's withdrawal 'in the same sense and in the same degree in which he had given his approval to the acceptance'. At long last the king had conceded what had been the main French demand. Nevertheless, in desperation Benedetti repeated his request for an audience. Before replying to the ambassador's renewed request the king received most unwelcome news: Werther reported from Paris that Ollivier and Gramont had demanded a personal letter of apology from the king addressed to Napoleon in order to pacify French public opinion. Whereupon a highly indignant monarch told Benedetti through Radziwill that he flatly refused to grant him an audience and that, if he wished to pursue the matter further, he should address himself to the Prussian minister–president.

The by now thoroughly dejected ambassador made one final attempt on 14 July to reach the king. Fresh instructions had arrived from Gramont – who did not yet know of William's refusal – urging Benedetti to secure the guarantee. Realizing that the king was virtually certain to refuse him an audience, Benedetti raised the matter with Eulenburg. In vain. Eulenburg reported back to Benedetti that the king had refused. As Benedetti had by now been ordered back to Paris with or without the guarantee, he sought to take formal leave of the monarch. King William was due to leave by the afternoon train for Koblenz. On the platform of Ems railway station Benedetti met the king for the last time. William reiterated that he had nothing to add to his previous statement but repeated that, if desired, negotiations could be continued at government level. Friendly to the last, the king parted from Benedetti with the words: *'nous deux, nous resterons amis'*.[87]

While the king of Prussia had been genuinely affronted by the French demand with its clear implication that a king's word was not his bond, his resistance – as we have seen – had been stiffened by Bismarck's intervention. The chancellor was deeply concerned by the king's conciliatory stance, especially by the damaging admission that the Prussian government had known of the candidacy. Bismarck felt that the time had come to return to Berlin. On the evening of 12 July, while still sitting in his coach outside the foreign office, he learned to his dismay of Leopold's withdrawal. Since Gramont had elevated the affair into a make–or–break issue on 6 July, the withdrawal signified a loss of face for Prussia.

This was the moment of truth for Bismarck. Thoughts of resignation may have flashed through the head of this highly strung individual who habitually lived on his nerves. If so, he quickly suppressed them and set about plucking victory out of defeat. War was now a near certainty, for he could not expect the French to climb down after their initial triumph. As far as King William was concerned, Bismarck launched an immediate damage–limitation exercise. Further exchanges between the adroit French diplomat and the well–meaning but politically naïve monarch had to be avoided at all costs. Bismarck repeated the advice first tendered on 12 July: the king should not receive Benedetti. If William had to say something, he was urged to confine himself to the bare comment that Leopold would inform the Spanish government of his decision.

Originally Bismarck had intended to proceed at once to Bad Ems. Instead he stayed in Berlin and sent Eulenburg to see the king. Physical exhaustion may have played a part, but it is obvious that from Berlin he could more easily sound out diplomatic opinion and work with might and main to extricate himself from the impasse. To prevent a sense of anti–climax from dampening down the crisis, he instructed Busch to stir up the German press: Leopold's withdrawal must be presented as the result of advice from London and Brussels, certainly not pressure from Prussia – that would not have been possible after Gramont's provocative demands to which the king had no intention of agreeing. Busch was also to spread the story that the Reichstag would soon be recalled. This was part of a scheme forming in his fertile mind on 12–13 July: as reports were coming in of threatening military movements in France and of the fresh demands the French were likely to make, Prussia had every right to demand an explanation. If France refused to give a guarantee of her peaceful intentions and to withdraw Gramont's impertinent demands, then a reconvened Reichstag would be informed of the situation – a step certain to inflame national feeling and make war inevitable. On 13 July Bismarck telegraphed the king to return to Berlin to help draw up an appropriate ultimatum to France. Meanwhile diplomatic soundings confirmed Prussia's favourable position: Austria would certainly remain neutral; Britain and Russia were both critical of France; and Bavaria declared that in the event of war she would be on Prussia's side, relieving Bismarck of his anxieties about South German reactions.

Nothing came of the ultimatum project because at 6.05 p.m. on 13 July a telegram arrived from Bad Ems containing a report of the king's encounter with Benedetti in the Kurgarten. In his notoriously unreliable reminiscences Bismarck gave posterity a highly coloured and mendacious account of the origins of the so-called 'Ems Telegram'. According to Bismarck, he was dining with Moltke and Roon, and all were in despondent mood when the telegram arrived. After reading it, Bismarck asked the generals if Prussia was ready for war. On receiving an affirmative reply he quickly deleted passages from the telegram so as to present the interview as a calculated insult to German national pride. When this version was given to the press and to all Prussian embassies abroad it would, he calculated, act as a 'red rag to the Gallic bull'.

On hearing Bismarck's version Moltke exclaimed: 'It has a different ring; it sounded like a parley, now it is like a flourish in answer to a challenge.'[88]

The truth is quite different. Bismarck and his companions were far from despondent around the dinner table. On the contrary, they were eagerly planning a counter-offensive against France. The telegram simply provided Bismarck with a better pretext for war than the ultimatum project. The original telegram, drafted by Heinrich Abeken on behalf of the king, was short and to the point:

> His Majesty the King writes that Count Benedetti stopped me on the promenade to demand of me in a very importunate manner in the end that I should authorize him to send a telegram at once to the effect that I would bind myself in perpetuity never again to give my consent to the Hohenzollern's renewal of the candidature. I declined in the end somewhat sharply for one should not *à tout jamais* undertake such commitments nor is it possible to do so. Naturally I told him that I had still received nothing and as he had better information via Paris and Madrid than I did, he would surely realize that my government was not involved in the affair. His Majesty has since then received a letter from the prince [Karl Anton]. As His Majesty told Count Benedetti that he was awaiting word from the prince, All Highest decided in view of the above-mentioned demand and on the advice of Count Eulenburg and myself not to receive Count Benedetti any more but to let him know through an adjutant that His Majesty had now received confirmation from the prince of the news Benedetti had already had from Paris and that he had nothing further to say to the ambassador. His Majesty leaves it to Your Excellency to decide whether our ambassadors and the press should be informed of Benedetti's new demand.[89]

The Ems Telegram with passages scored through in pencil by Bismarck does not exist, and never did. Bismarck simply dictated a shortened version for press consumption which ran as follows:

> After the news of the renunciation of the Prince of Hohenzollern had been communicated to the Imperial French Government by the Royal Spanish Government the French ambassador made a further demand of His Majesty the King at Bad Ems that he should authorize him to send a telegram to Paris to the effect that His Majesty undertook in perpetuity never again to give his consent should the Hohenzollerns once more renew the candidature. His Majesty the King thereupon refused to receive the ambassador again and through his adjutant informed the ambassador that he had nothing further to say.[90]

Between them Bismarck and Abeken had turned the truth completely upside down. All references to the king's conciliatory gestures had been excluded from the final version and the Kurgarten encounter had been transformed into a brusque confrontation between an ambassador who had overstepped the bounds of propriety with his importunate demands and a highly incensed monarch who had rightly refused further dealings with him. Thus was born the 'Ems legend'. It is significant that Bismarck elaborated upon the alleged rudeness of Benedetti as the crucial point when speaking to the Spanish and Russian ambassadors. He also ensured that the press drove home the same point, so much so that on 14 July even the *Times* correspondent in Berlin wrote that Benedetti's 'insolence' was possibly intentional. After such an 'insult to national honour', to use the parlance of the day, the German public would expect diplomatic relations to be broken off, which was precisely the impression Bismarck sought to convey. By 9 p.m. at his instigation a special supplement to the *Norddeutsche Allgemeine Zeitung* containing only the text of the doctored Ems Telegram printed in large type and suitable for display in public places was being distributed free on the streets of Berlin. It had the desired effect: noisy crowds, infuriated by the 'insolence' of the French ambassador, gathered before the royal palace on Unter den Linden cheering the king and shouting 'To the Rhine. Let us all defend it! [91]

Whether war would break out still depended on French reactions. As the debate in the corridors of power in Paris swayed backwards and forwards, the doubt and uncertainty felt by the principal actors in the drama is painfully apparent. When news of the king's explicit approval of the withdrawal arrived late on 13 July, Napoleon and Ollivier were greatly relieved. Even Gramont, who – encouraged by sharp criticism of government policy in both Senate and chamber and despite the council of ministers' decision – had beavered away to obtain the guarantee at all costs, had to admit that *'approbation entière et sans reserve'* was a big step forward. That was also the view of foreign diplomats in Paris who believed that France had won a considerable victory.

When news of the Ems Telegram arrived, the mood changed abruptly. Its blunt language stung the French to the quick. Gramont burst in on Ollivier, thrust the telegram into his hands and declared dramatically that this was an affront to national honour which France could not tolerate. Ollivier had to admit that the efforts the Germans were making to publicize the telegram through their embassies suggested that they were deliberately driving the French to war. He called in several colleagues and requested that the emperor call a council meeting that afternoon. Against a background of angry street demonstrations the council met at 12.30 p.m. on 14 July. Gramont, always one of the first to respond excitedly to the popular mood, threw his briefcase on to the table and declared dramatically that no foreign minister who opposed war was worthy to remain in office. Leboeuf, reflecting in his self-confidence the martial and ebullient mood of the army, demanded the immediate call-up of reservists so that France could exploit fully the fifteen days' lead the army allegedly had over the Germans. However, Gramont did not have it all his own way. Several members wanted to defer action, pointing out that the telegram from Benedetti describing the encounter did not reveal any discourteous conduct even though the Ems Telegram published in Berlin was most certainly an affront to France. One of the opposition, more perceptive than most of the council, turned to Napoleon and observed prophetically: *'Sire, entre le roi Guillaume et vous la partie n'est pas égal. Le roi peut perdre plusieurs batailles; Pour Votre Majesté la défaite, c'est la Révolution!'*[92] But the council was persuaded by Leboeuf's arguments and decided at 4 p.m. on mobilization.

After Leboeuf departed for the war ministry to draft the necessary mobilization order, Benedetti's telegram arrived containing details of the final meeting with King William on Bad Ems railway station. Once again the 'native hue of resolution' was 'sicklied o'er with the pale cast of thought'. So the king had not broken off diplomatic relations after all, as the Ems Telegram implied. An unidentified member of the council suggested that the king's assurances ought to be accepted and the question of future guarantees turned over to a European congress which would hopefully enable France to save face by agreeing to exclude members of princely houses related to the rulers of Great Powers from accepting crowns going a-begging. Napoleon, with a sudden vision of playing host to a glittering assembly of plenipotentiaries as he had done in the good old days, seized upon the suggestion with alacrity, as did Ollivier. At 5 p.m. the council finally agreed to make a statement along these lines the next day. Symptomatic of the muddled thinking in high places was their failure to rescind the decision to call up the reservists. Characteristically Napoleon wrote a note to Leboeuf suggesting that military measures were not as urgent as had been supposed earlier in the day.

As Leboeuf was on the point of dispatching orders to military commands all over France, he urged the emperor to decide the issue one way or another at a reconvened council meeting. Within a few short hours the pendulum swung back to war. Napoleon and Ollivier had already had second thoughts about the congress proposal. The empress warned Napoleon against the proposal while Ollivier's family and friends, much to his surprise, denounced the proposed declaration when he read it out to them. And as public indignation mounted and crowds clamouring for war demonstrated on the streets, it dawned on both of them that the proposal would be howled down in the chamber.

Though the accounts of the meeting of the reconvened council of ministers held at 10 p.m. conflict, it seems that three considerations were decisive in burying the congress proposal. First, reports were coming in of considerable troop movements in Prussia. Secondly, in what was clearly a concerted campaign to turn opinion against France, the Berne and Munich embassies reported that the Prussian government was informing all other governments of the contents of the Ems Telegram with the addendum that Benedetti had deliberately insulted the king. Quite obviously Bismarck was determined to turn the Kurgarten episode into an official matter. Finally, Werther had informed Gramont that he was going on indefinite leave, an ominous sign that Prussia was probably clearing the decks for action. All thought of calling for a congress was abandoned. At 11 p.m. the decision to recall the reservists was upheld – though no formal vote was taken because of absences. Ollivier and Gramont were charged with the preparation of a new declaration to be discussed next morning before presentation to the chamber. Characteristically the council still did not agree on a declaration of war although it was painfully apparent that war could not now be avoided. As Napoleon ruefully reflected: 'You see in what a situation a government can sometimes find itself. Even if we had no admissible reason for war we should now be compelled to declare it to obey the will of the country.'[93]

The new declaration was approved by the full council after a brief meeting at 9 a.m. on 15 July. To carry the chamber into war, Ollivier and Gramont presented Prussian behaviour in the worst possible light. No reference was made to King William's genuine search for an accommodation and, although grudging reference was made to his approval of the withdrawal, the phrase *'entière et sans reserve'* was deliberately omitted. Heavy emphasis was laid on the refusal to grant Benedetti an audience, the communication of the Ems Telegram to other governments, the recall of the Prussian ambassador and, finally, on Prussia's military measures. The declaration ended:

> In these circumstances to make a further attempt at conciliation would have been neglectful of dignity and imprudent. We have neglected nothing to escape war; we are preparing to wage the war that is presented to us, leaving each side the share of responsibility that falls upon it. Yesterday we called up our reserves and with your concurrence are going to take at once the measures necessary to safeguard the interests, the security and the honour of France.

Napoleon enthusiastically applauded the declaration and the council agreed unanimously on a declaration of war.[94]

The declaration was received with enthusiasm in the Senate, but in the chamber the government encountered some opposition. No one in that body doubted for an instant that France would win if it came to war. The left feared, however, that in the event of victory Napoleon would set aside the Liberal Empire. War must, therefore, be avoided if at all possible. Criticism was levelled at the government for refusing to be content with the withdrawal of the candidacy. What proof was there that France had really been insulted, the critics wanted to know. Thiers, arguing forcefully that the government had brought the war on itself, demanded that the chamber be informed of the content of the dispatches between the government and the ambassador. The demand was rejected by 159 votes to 84. Nevertheless, in order to mollify the government's critics a commission was hastily set up to look in confidence at this documentation. In practice little attempt was made to get at the truth. Gramont, called to give evidence, easily persuaded the commission that the government had demanded withdrawal of the candidacy and guarantees of non-renewal simultaneously and not – as the left suspected – one after the other. Gramont's economical use of the truth was well illustrated at the close of his testimony. When asked what allies France had, he implied that conversations with the British and Russian ambassadors – which he claimed he had broken off to appear before the commission – told their own story. The most notable omission of all was the failure to call Benedetti (now in Paris) to give a first-hand account of the events of 13 July. The commission's report, which broadly endorsed the government's position, was debated in the chamber. In the end war credits were voted by 245 to 10 votes, a decision greeted with roars of approval and shouts of '*à Berlin*' by large crowds outside the chamber. On 15 July when news reached Potsdam that the war credits had been voted, King William, who had resisted the entreaties of Bismarck, Roon, Moltke and the crown prince for immediate mobilization, now agreed to give the necessary order. This was read out to wildly cheering crowds by the crown prince the same day. The French declaration of war was not, in fact, sent to Berlin until 17 July and handed to Bismarck by the French ambassador on 19 July. That was a mere formality. The war machines on both sides of the Rhine were already on the move.

To sum up on the origins of the war of 1870. This, like the war of 1866, was in essence a power struggle fought to determine who should be master in Europe. In one corner stood Prussia who, having consolidated her power north of the Main, wanted to extend her political control over the South German states. In the other corner was France whose objective was the negative one of preventing this drastic alteration in the balance of power and of arresting the gradual decline in France's standing in Europe. The difference from 1866 was that in 1870 nationalism played a significant role in the outbreak of war. When Austria and Prussia went to war Prussia was almost totally isolated in Germany and did not have National

Liberal support. Only after the victory over Austria did many nationalists become whole-hearted supporters of Prussia because a further extension of her power – about which there were few illusions – happened to coincide with their desire to create a Little German Reich. In the process they confidently expected that Bismarck would be swept along on a tidal wave of national feeling so that the new Reich would be a more liberal state than the North German Confederation. This feeling, which had a pronounced anti-French orientation, remained on the surface after 1866 sustained by the activities of the National Society and buoyed up by popular festivals so that it was a formidable psychological force which could be mobilized and manipulated by the Prussian government in 1870. No crowds had gathered outside the royal palace in Berlin in June 1866 when Bismarck declared the German Confederation at an end. Four years later noisy crowds, inflamed by the doctored Ems Telegram, demanded war against the 'hereditary foe'.

It is important to realize that Bismarck had taken good care to ensure that the causes of war were located in French demands for hegemony in Europe (in effect), not in a German demand for final unification. Only subsequently did Little Germany come into being as a consequence, not a cause, of war. If the National Liberals had been the makers of policy, war would almost certainly have occurred but it would have been fought over the unification issue, over either Luxemburg or the admission of Baden to the North German Confederation. The international dimension was never far from Bismarck's thoughts. A war fought purely and simply to complete the unification of Germany or to expand the frontiers of Prussia (much the same thing in Bismarck's eyes[95]) might have led to international complications. By shifting the responsibility for war on to France through his exploitation of the Hohenzollern candidacy, turning a dynastic dispute into a matter of national honour, Bismarck effectively tied the hands of the Great Powers. Only later in the century did the decisive alteration in the balance of power consequent upon the defeat of France begin to worry them.

Similarly in the case of France, the balance of research suggests that national feeling did not drive the government into confrontation with Prussia. But the existence of strong anti-Prussian sentiments at a popular level ensured massive support for the government when war was declared. Indeed, arguably, the council of ministers' decision for war preceded the largest and most vociferous demonstrations. By 1870 on both sides of the Rhine governments could rely on large sections of their urban population, aided and abetted by the press, to support whole-heartedly a view of international relations which substituted for rational discussion of disputes the ethos of the duelling match. 'Honour' had been 'outraged'; 'satisfaction' was demanded; and when an 'apology' was not forthcoming, 'trial by combat' was welcomed as the only 'honourable' way of resolving the matter. Without the prevalence of that attitude a dispute about guarantees to prevent a German prince who had withdrawn his candidacy to a foreign throne from ever renewing it could not possibly have become an 'acceptable' reason for a major war.

THE WAR, THE PEACE OF FRANKFURT AND ITS SIGNIFICANCE

On past form the French were the favourites to win the war. Their victories in the Crimea and Northern Italy suggested they were formidable opponents. The *furia francesa* when charging French infantry overwhelmed the Austrians in Italy was a quality which the Prussians recognized and respected. It was also confidently expected in government circles in Paris that Austria and Italy would fight alongside France, making possible a grand offensive into South Germany where it was also supposed the French would be favourably received. Furthermore France had reorganized her forces since 1866 and possessed new weapons superior to those of Prussia: the *chassepot*, a rifle capable of accurate fire up to 1600 yards compared with the needle gun's 600 yards; and the *mitrailleuse*, a rudimentary machine gun which fired 150 rounds a minute and was effective up to 2000 yards.

The reality was very different. Neither Austria nor Italy joined in, frightened off finally by the Prussian victories on 6 August. And despite past glory in Russia and Italy, the French army was in poor shape. Her officers were poorly trained and lacked the social status of the Prussian officer corps – in the eyes of the French aristocracy the army symbolized Napoleon 1 whom many of them heartily detested while the middle class, busily enriching itself, detested it as a barbarous and costly institution. Only under Napoleon III had the army's reputation revived. Even so, the general staff was woefully inferior to that of the Prussian army, as indeed were all general staffs at this time. And although France had invented the concept of the 'nation in arms' with universal conscription as its characteristic feature, since 1815 she had maintained a small army (because of her legislators' desire to curtail expenditure) and limited the number of recruits by employing a ballot system to select them. In the 1860s the army was only 288,000 strong.

At first French soldiers consoled themselves with the thought that Napoleon 1 had regularly defeated superior forces with even smaller numbers. But after Sadowa desperate efforts were made by Napoleon and his generals to remedy this situation despite strong opposition from the Corps Législatif. The 1868 army law was designed to produce an army of 800,000 by 1875 supplemented by a Garde Mobile (a type of Landwehr) of 500,000. Unfortunately the organizational structure remained pitifully weak. The ruling principle remained as before: *le système D: on se débrouillera toujours*. At the outbreak of war mobilization was so chaotic that when Leboeuf arrived at imperial headquarters in Metz, confident that France could take the offensive, he found that only 200,000 of the 385,000 reservists had reported for duty. On these grounds an offensive across the Rhine was ruled out. Instead the French were forced to hold a defensive line running roughly from Metz through Saarbrücken (taken by the French in a rare offensive action) to Strassburg. Nor did they have any clear plan of campaign, partly because they had expected to go on to the offensive and partly because of conflicting views between Napoleon, commander-in-chief of the French armies, the war council in Paris and Marshals François Bazaine and Patrice MacMahon who commanded the army of the Rhine and the army of Châlons respectively.

The Germans were greatly surprised by the French failure to cross the Rhine. But, recovering quickly, Moltke ordered three armies into Lorraine: on the right flank the first army, 50,000 strong, commanded by General Karl Friedrich von Steinmetz; in the centre the second army, 134,000 strong, commanded by Prince Friedrich Karl; and on the left flank the third army, 125,000 strong, commanded by the crown prince. Moltke's hopes of repeating the Sadowa victory by dealing a devastating blow at the French in a battle of encirclement north of the Saar failed because of the third army's slowness in advancing and Napoleon's failure to attack. But battles at Weissenburg and at Wörth on 4 August and Spichern on 6 August – into which the German first and third armies blundered contrary to Moltke's wishes – revealed the edge the Germans had over the French. The latter might have the *chassepot* and the *mitrailleuse* but since 1866 the Prussian artillery had improved out of all recognition and more than cancelled out the new weaponry on the French side. These early and bloody engagements finally ended all lingering hopes the French had of carrying the war into Germany.

As Bazaine fell back on Metz, he was surrounded by the Germans after a series of bloody but indecisive engagements on 16 August at Vionville and Mars-la-Tour and on 18 August at Gravelotte and St Privat. When Marshal MacMahon attempted to raise the siege of Metz, where Bazaine's army was now imprisoned, he was trapped between the Meuse and the Belgian frontier.

There followed on 1 September the decisive battle of Sedan. Surrounded by the German third army and pounded by 500 Prussian guns, surrender was the only course open to Napoleon, who had taken his stand with MacMahon. The emperor passed into genteel captivity at Wilhelmshöhe while 104,000 French soldiers were taken prisoner together with 419 cannon. The army of Châlons had ceased to exist. It was also the end of the Napoleonic regime. On 4 September Paris rose in revolt and a republic was proclaimed.

The war was not over. On the contrary, it now assumed the proportions of a national struggle. On the German side news of early victories released a tidal wave of national sentiment. Because of this, as well as the fact that the French declaration of war was a clear *casus foederis*, the southern states had gone to war promptly. Bavaria and Baden mobilized on 16 July and Württemberg on 17 July. Their contingents, incorporated in the third army, fought on the battlefield as enthusiastically as the Prussians. Demands were soon made in the German press for the punishment of the 'wicked' French; moral condemnation of the enemy and demands for her complete humiliation now became a regular feature of the total war situation in which people were pitted against people. It was accompanied by demands for territorial compensation in the shape of Alsace-Lorraine to secure Germany against future 'aggressors who have ravished German soil for the past two hundred years'.

Similarly, on the French side national feelings were aroused. The government of National Defence promptly declared that France would fight on rather than yield 'an inch of her soil or a stone of her fortresses' to the Germans. When Bismarck informed Foreign Minister Jules Favre that Germany must have Alsace, part of Lorraine and Strassburg the government determined on *guerre à outrance*. Leon Gambetta, escaping from Paris by balloon, threw himself into the task of raising new armies. He also encouraged the formation of partisan bands – the *francs-tireurs* – a doubtful asset to any side in war time. Their attacks on German troops simply led to savage reprisals, adding a new horror to what was already a bloody conflict.

France was not lacking in manpower but the hurriedly raised and largely untrained Armies of National Defence were no match for disciplined German soldiers. On 28 September after bombarding and assaulting Strassburg, the city capitulated to the Germans. On 29 October Metz was starved into surrender and Bazaine's army of the Rhine, 154,000 men in all, surrendered. The siege forces were now free to join the two armies which had cut Paris off from the outside world on 20 September. French attempts to relieve Paris during the next three months all failed. Bismarck, anxious to end the war before international complications arose, insisted on the bombardment of the capital city. This began on 5 January. An attempt by 90,000 troops to break out of the city on 19 January failed. On 22 January Paris asked for an armistice. When this came into force on 28 January the Franco-Prussian war had effectively ended. Peace negotiations commenced and peace preliminaries were agreed on 26 February and ratified on 3 March.

The main feature was the cession by France of the provinces of Alsace and Lorraine, an area once part of the Holy Roman Empire but gradually absorbed by France in the seventeenth century. After the victory at Sedan demands for the annexation of these provinces multiplied very rapidly in the German press. Bismarck encouraged them - another example of his manipulation of national feeling - though, as usual, his motives were not nationalistic. The fact that Alsace and part of Lorraine spoke a German dialect was of little interest to him, though he used the argument when it suited his book. Strategic reasons were decisive. Firmly believing that France was bound to remain an implacable foe, he insisted on securing the fortresses of Strassburg and Metz to protect France in the event of a war of revenge. The military agreed that it was essential to secure the Alsace-Lorraine salient; only because Germany mobilized more quickly than France had a French invasion of Baden been frustrated in July 1870. The popular demand for the provinces was yet another factor that turned the war – which could have ended with the overthrow of the Napoleonic regime – into a bitter national struggle. In the end France had to surrender the whole of Alsace and one-third of Lorraine (the so-called 'German' part). But she retained the fortress of Belfort commanding the road from the Jura to the Vosges, although only on condition that she allowed the Germans to march in triumph through Paris, which they did in March 1871.

In addition France was saddled with an indemnity of 5000 million francs, 1000 million to be paid in 1871 and the remainder within three years. German occupation forces were to be progressively withdrawn from most of France when 2000 million francs had been paid. Troops would remain in six departments and in the fortress of Belfort until the last 3000 million francs had been paid. In fact, France paid the indemnity in full by 1873 and all French territory was evacuated.

No account of the war of 1870–1 would be complete without some reference to the last stage in the creation of Little Germany. In July 1870 the wave of anti-French feeling which swept through the cities and towns of South Germany forced the governments – whether they wanted to or not–to order mobilization. In fact, South German troops played their part in the campaign with as much enthusiasm as the North Germans. After Sedan it was clear to the southern states that they would have to come to terms with the new political situation. Baden and Hesse-Darmstadt were ready to join the new Reich, the former with enthusiasm, the latter reluctantly but well aware that with one province already in the North German Confederation she had little option. Predictably Württemberg and Bavaria were much less eager to join. Instead they hoped to create a southern confederation only loosely associated with North Germany. To schemes of this sort Bismarck was adamantly opposed and, employing his usual tactics of intrigue, pressure and blandishments, he forced them in the end to abandon these ideas. By the end of November after difficult negotiations, all four states had signed treaties of accession to the new state.

Bismarck was obliged to make a number of concessions to the southern states. The authority of the federal council was extended in formal matters; for example, its consent was now required for declarations of war. Bavaria and Württemberg were allowed to keep their own railway network and postal and telegraph systems. And while the Württemberg armed forces became part of the Prussian army, the king retained the right to appoint the commander and all officers. Bavaria did even better; her king remained in complete control of the Bavarian army which would pass under Prussian command only in war time. In addition she kept her diplomatic corps; and she was to preside over a special foreign affairs committee of the federal council on which Württemberg and Saxony had permanent seats. Although these concessions limited Prussian power they did not seriously weaken it and were a useful foil against the Reichstag whose power Bismarck was determined not to extend.

Once the treaties of accession had been concluded Bismarck arranged for King William to be offered the imperial title. This was in Bismarck's view essential to give cohesion and lustre to Little Germany. The senior German prince, King Ludwig II of Bavaria, was prevailed upon to make the offer in return for a bribe of 300,000 marks a year, a secret arrangement which came to light only years later after King Ludwig's death and after Bismarck had left office. King William was extremely reluctant to accept a title which might diminish his standing as king of Prussia. Accordingly he held out to the bitter end in his usual obstinate manner for a form of words which subordinated the imperial to the royal title: 'by the grace of God King of Prussia chosen emperor of Germany'. Just as firmly Bismarck insisted on a formula which gave precedence to the imperial dignity and would on that account be more acceptable to the south: 'by the grace of God German emperor and King of Prussia'. The issue was resolved only at the very last moment on 18 January when the German empire was proclaimed in the Hall of Mirrors at Versailles in a ceremony attended by princes and by 500 officers from the army which had besieged Paris, but from which the Reichstag delegation was carefully excluded.[96] Grand Duke Friedrich I of Baden, the highest-ranking prince present in the absence of the three kings, had the honour of greeting the king with his new title. As neither king nor minister would give way, the grand duke dodged the issue with his own salutation: 'Long live his imperial and royal majesty Emperor William!' A furious sovereign ignored his chancellor and shook hands with the other dignitaries. However, he soon made up his petty quarrel with a minister who had become that rare political animal, an indispensable adviser, and who was to preside over the destinies of the new Reich for twenty years and was to outlive his royal master by ten.

NOTES AND REFERENCES

1. Quoted in Rudolf Buchner, *Die deutsch–französische Tragödie 1848–1864* (Würzburg, 1965), p. 118.
2. Quoted in R. Poidervin/J. Bariéty, *Frankreich und Deutschland* (Munich, 1982),p. 73.
3. Quoted in Rudolf Buchner, op. cit., p. 16.
4. Paul Henry, 'La France et les nationalités en 1848. D'après les correspondances diplomatiques' *Revue historique* 188–9 (1940) pp. 244–5.
5. F. Valsecchi, 'Das Zeitalter Napoleon IIIs und Bismarcks 1854–1870', *Historia Mundi* Bd. X (Bern, 1961), p. 59.
6. E. Ollivier, *L'empire libéral* 3, p. 537.
7. Quoted in Lynn M. Case, *French opinion on war and diplomacy during the Second Empire* (Philadelphia, 1954), p. 178.
8. Ibid., p. 205.
9. Ibid., p. 213.
10. Ibid., p. 210.
11. Quoted in W.A. Fletcher, *The mission of Vincent Benedetti to Berlin 1864–1870* (The Hague, 1965), p. 109.
12. Nationalist historians indignantly repudiate the suggestion that Bismarck could have offered to cede German territory. That was not the crown prince's impression. Cf. Heinrich Otto Meisner, *Kaiser Friedrich III: Tagebücher von 1848 bis 1866* (Leipzig, 1926), p. 458 entry 8 July 1866.
13. Writing to Goltz on 8 August he remarked: 'I do not consider Belgium a viable state in the long run; and we can tolerate the increase in the power of France through French Belgium because it does not disturb our position in Germany and does not render impossible a friendly relationship between Germany and France as a cession of German territory would.' *GW* 6, no. 539.

14. The terms of the agreement were as follows:
(i) France would recognize the conquests made by Prussia and the establishment of the North German Confederation.
(ii) The king of Prussia promised to facilitate French acquisition of Luxemburg by negotiating with the king of the Netherlands. The French would pay compensation to him.
(iii) The French emperor would not oppose a federal union between the North German Confederation and the southern states provided that it respected the latter's sovereignty.
(iv) In the event of French troops being sent to Belgium, the king of Prussia would render assistance to France against any power intervening against her.
(v) France and Prussia would conclude an offensive–defensive alliance. APP 8, no. 10.

15. M. Stürmer, *Das ruhelose Reich : Deutschland 1866–1918* (Berlin, 1983), p. 153, believes that Bismarck toyed with the idea of compensation; L. Gall, *Bismarck: Der weisse Revolutionär* (Propyläen, 1980), argues that there was no proof (pp. 406–7); Otto Pflanze, *Bismarck and the Development of Germany: The Period of Unification 1815–1870* (Princeton, 1963), p. 375, believes Bismarck kept his options open.

16. *GW* 6 no. 684, Bismarck to Robert von Goltz, 15 February 1867.

17. *RKN* 2 no. 323, 19 December 1866; no. 355, 13 January 1867.

18. *OD* XIV no. 4014, Moustier to Benedetti, 7 January 1867.

19. E. Ollivier, op. cit., p. 280.

20. Ibid., p. 294.

21. 'The treaties would serve us as a weapon for repelling attacks on the Main line which will not fail to be made in the Reichstag'; *APP* 8 no. 288, Bismarck to the missions in Munich, Stuttgart and Karlsruhe.

22. Hermann Oncken, *Rudolf von Bennigsen: Ein deutscher liberaler Politiker. Nach seinen Briefen und hinterlassenen Papieren*, II (Stuttgart and Leipzig, 1910), p. 36.

23 O. Pflanze, op. cit., p. 380.

24. *GW* 6 no. 740, Telegram to Karl von Werther, 3 April 1867.

25. Ibid. no. 738, telegram to Count Perponcher.

26. Quoted in R. Wilhelm, *Das Verhältnis der süddeutschen Staaten zum Norddeutschen. Bund (1867–1870)* (Husum, 1978), p. 17.

27. *GW* 6 no. 515, Bismarck to Robert von Goltz, 31 July 1866.

28. *GW* 6, telegram to Baron von Manteuffel, 11 August 1866.

29. *GW* 14 no. 486, Bismarck to Leopold von Gerlach, 20 January 1854.

30. O. Pflanze, op. cit., p. 371. A surprising feature of the treaties was the absence of any time limit in duration or of any provision for a state to contract out.

31. Quoted in Gustav Roloff, 'Bismarcks Friedenschlüsse mit den Süddeutschen im Jahre 1866', *HZ* 146 (1932), p. 32.

32. R. Wilhelm, op. cit., pp. 163–4.

33. Ibid., p. 164.

34. Ibid., p. 163 thinks they would have done so, whereas M. Stürmer, op. cit., p. 160. disagrees.

35. Quoted in Werner Richter, *Bismarck* (London, 1962), p. 142.
36. *GW* 6a, Bismarck to Baron von Flemming, 13 November 1867.
37. *GW* 7 no. 201, Bismarck to General von Suckow, 11 May 1868.
38. Ibid.
39. The Patriotic Party won seventy-nine seats, the liberals fifty-five and the ministerial party twenty.
40. After by–elections in the spring of 1870 the Partriotic Party won an additional three seats.
41. Veit Valentin, *Bismarcks Reichsgründung im Urteil englischer Diplomaten* (Amsterdam, 1937), p. 409.
42. Quoted in J. Becker, 'Zum Problem der Bismarckischen Politik in der spanischen Thronfrage 1870', *HZ* (212), June 1971, FN pp. 539–40, from the diary of the Baden foreign minister, Freydorf, 3 March 1870 after a conversation with Grand Duke Friedrich of Baden. Bismarck offered military assistance to Stuttgart; R. Wilhelm, op. cit., p. 183, Spitzemberg to Varnbüler, 23 March 1870.
43. *GW* 6b no. 1327, Bismarck to Georg von Werthern, 26 February 1869. It has to be remembered in this context that he was concerned to allay Bavarian fears about a forward Prussian policy.
44. *GW* 6b no. 1459, Bucher to Georg von Werthern, 10 December 1869.
45. G. Windell, *The Catholics and German Unity 1866-1971* (University of Minnesota, 1954), p. 246.
46. Quoted in J. Becker, 'Der Krieg mit Frankreich als Problem der kleindeutschen Einigungspolitik Bismarcks 1866–1870' in M. Stürmer, *Das kaiserliche Deutschland:Politik und Gesellschaft 1870–1918* (Düsseldorf, 1970), p. 75.
47. Quoted in M. Stürmer, *Das ruhelose Reich*, p. 162.
48. *GW* 15, p. 309.
49. *Aus dem Leben des Königs Karl von Rumänien. Aufzeichnungen eines Augenzeugen*, vol. 2, passim.
50. H. Hesselbarth, *Drei psychologische Fragen zur spanischen Thronkandidatur Leopolds von Hohenzollern. Mit Geheimdepeschen Bismarcks, Prims usw*, (Leipzig, 1913).
51. R. Fester, *Briefe Aktenstücke und Regester zur Geschichte der Hohenzollernischen Thronkandidatur in Spanien* (Leipzig and Berlin, 1913), Hefte 1 and 2.
52. Although they believed French hostility to German unification was the real cause of the war, they had to admit that ' . . . it is possible to draw the conclusion that he [Bismarck] wanted to create a *casus belli* and provoke the conflict'. G. Bonnin, *Bismarck and the Hohenzollern candidature for the Spanish throne : The documents in the German diplomatic archives* (London, 1957), p. 34.
53. Richard Howard Lord, *The Origin of the War of 1870. New documents from the German Archives* (Cambridge, Mass, 1924).
54. Jochen Dittrich, *Bismarck Frankreich und die spanische Thronkandidatur der Hohenzollern* (Munich, 1962).
55. Hans Delbrück in several articles in the *Preussische Jahrbücher*: 'Der Ursprung des Krieges von 1870', vol. 10; 'Das Geheimnis der Napoleonischen Politik im Jahre 1870', vol. 17. Delbrück admitted that Bismarck's strategy had an offensive – but not a belligerent –

flavour, whereas Fester considered it purely defensive in *Neue Beiträge zur Geschichte der Hohenzollernschen Thronkandidatur in Spanien* (Leipzig, 1913).

56. H. Hesselbarth, op. cit., p. 60.

57. Ernst Denis, *La fondation de l'empire allemand 1852–1870* (Paris, 1906); Jean Jaurès, *La guerre franco–allemande* (Paris, 1908).

58. H. Rothfels, *Bismarck und der Staat. Ausgewählte Dokumente* (Darmstadt, 1958); L.Reiners, *Bismarck* (Munich, 1956–7) ; W. Richter, *Bismarck* (London, 1964); Eberhard Kolb, *Der Kriegsausbruch 1870: Politische Entscheidungsprozesse und Verantwortlichkeiten in der Julikrise 1870* (Gottingen, 1970) ; A.J.P. Taylor, *Bismarck: The man and the statesman* (London, 1955).

59. A.J.P. Taylor, op. cit., pp. 115–6.

60. A. Sorel, *Histoire diplomatique de la guerre franco–allemande* (Paris,1875); Henri Welschinger, *La guerre de 1870, causes et responsabilité* 2 vols (Paris, 1910); Henry Salomon, *L' Ambassade de Richard de Metternich à Paris* (Paris, 1930).

61. C. Grant Robertson, *Bismarck* (London, 1947); F. Darmstaedter, *Bismarck and the Creation of the Second Reich* (London, 1948); J. Becker, 'Zum Problem der Bismarckischen Politik in der spanischen Thronfrage 1870', *HZ* 212, June 1971; George Kent, *Bismarck and his times* (South Illinois University Press, 1978).

62. H. von Holborn (ed.), *J.M. von Radowitz : Aufzeichnungen und Erinnerungen aus dem Leben des Botschafters* (Berlin, 1925), I, p. 228.

63. H. von Friesen, *Richard Freiherr von Friesen : Erinnerungen aus meinem Leben. Aus dem Nachlass* (Dresden, 1910), III, p. 106.

64. *GW* 6b no. 1334, Bismarck to Prince Reuss, 9 March 1869.

65. O. Pflanze, op. cit, p. 447.

66. W.N. Medlicott, *Bismarck and Modern Germany* (London, 1965), pp. 18–2. Cf. O. Pflanze, op.cit., p. 449: 'Bismarck's goal . . . was a crisis with France. He deliberately set sail on a collision course with the intention of provoking either a war or an internal collapse.'

67. L. Gall, op. cit., p. 425; ibid., p. 426. The exception is E. Engelberg, *Bismarck Urpreusse und Reichsgründer* (Berlin, 1985), p. 726 : while agreeing that Bismarck had begun 'silent aggression' in encouraging the candidacy, Engelberg goes on to say that Paris and Berlin were both set on war. Nevertheless 'historically France put herself in the wrong by opposing the national unification of Germany'. This judgement is explicable in terms of the Marxist–Leninist belief that the economic consequences of unification, i.e. the emergence of a German industrial proletariat, formed an essential step on the road to socialism.

68. In November the duke of Savoy was elected king but abdicated in February 1873. In 1874 the prince of the Asturias finally became king as Alfonso XII.

69. *OD* XXIV no. 7368, Benedetti to Marquis de La Vallette.

70. Karl Anton asked King William in April to give his permission for the Hohenzollern–Sigmaringens to decline the offer, which the king was only too happy to do.

71. Eberhard Kolb arrives at this conclusion by assuming that, as the possibility of war is not mentioned in the diplomatic correspondence, there is no reason to suppose it was in Bismarck's mind.

72. G. Bonnin, op. cit., p. 64, Karl Anton to Bismarck, 25 February 1870. And to Abeken he wrote on 8 July – admittedly at the height of the crisis – 'I not only dimly sensed but clearly foresaw that the whole business would touch France to the quick' ibid., p. 230.

73. *GW* II no. 12, to the Reichstag of the North German Confederation, 16 April 1869.

74. When a worried Karl Anton asked Major von Versen on 19 June whether the candidacy would not lead to complications with France, the latter replied : 'Bismarck says that is just what he is looking for.' G. Bonnin, op. cit., p. 278; but cf. Eberhard Kolb, op. cit, p. 48.

75. Too much should not be made of the clerk's mistake. Had the Cortes elected Leopold, France would still have reacted angrily to the news.

76. T. Zeldin, *Emile Ollivier and the Liberal Empire of Napoleon III* (Oxford, 1963), p. 174.

77. E. Ollivier, op. cit., 14, p. 110.

78. Ibid.

79. A. Sorel, *Histoire diplomatique de la guerre franco–allemande* (Paris, 1875), I, p. 86.

80. Robert von Keudell, *Fürst und Fürstin Bismarck : Erinnerungen 1848–1872* (Berlin, 1901), p. 429.

81. It is indicative of Gramont's excitable and euphoric frame of mind that in a private letter to the ambassador he wrote : 'If the king won't advise the prince of Hohenzollern to renounce, well, it's immediate war and in a few days we'll be on the Rhine.' *OD* XXVIII no. 8382.

82. On 10 July the king sent Colonel Karl von Strantz to inform Karl Anton of French military preparations; though as determined as ever not to influence the Hohenzollern–Sigmaringens, the king was clearly doing all he could to force a withdrawal out of them.

83. Quoted in L. Steefel, *Bismarck, the Hohenzollern Candidacy and the Origins of the Franco–German War of 1870* (Cambridge, Mass., 1962), p. 146.

84. Esquirou de Parieu, Charles Plichon, Charles Louvet and Emile Ségris. As there are no protocols of the council's proceedings, we are dependent on the divergent recollections of those participants who subsequently put pen to paper.

85. *GW* 6b no. 1613, Telegram to Georg von Werthern, 13 July 1870 FN2.

86. After the council deliberations of 13 July Gramont had, of course, no right to take this line.

87. W.A. Fletcher, op. cit., p. 259.

88. Otto von Bismarck, *Gedanken und Erinnerungen Reden und Briefe* (Berlin, 1951), p. 231.

89. Heinrich Abeken, *Ein schlichtes Leben in bewegter Zeit* (Berlin, 1898), p. 231. It is not certain whose suggestion it was that the press be informed. It may possibly have been Eulenburg. As early as

8 July the king thought that Gramont's declaration should be publicly repudiated. What is odd is the suggestion that the press be informed about negotiations not yet ended.

90. *GW* 6b no. 1612.
91. The *Times* correpondent, commenting on the effect of the supplement, wrote: 'It was hailed by young and old alike: it was welcome to fathers of families and to beardless youths; it was read and reread by women and girls, and, in an outburst of patriotism, turned over finally to the servants. There was but one opinion concerning the manly and dignified conduct of the king ; there was a unanimous determination to follow his example and pick up the glove that had been thrown in the face of the nation . . . . It was the explosion of long-restrained wrath.'Quoted in Emile Ollivier, *The Franco–Prussian War and its Hidden Causes* (London, 1913), p. 290.
92. Le Lautcourt, *Les origines de la guerre de 1870 : la candidature Hohenzollern 1868–1870* (Paris, 1912), pp. 498–9.
93. Emile Ollivier, op. cit. 14, p. 373.
94. Pierre de la Gorce, *Histoire du Second Empire* (Paris, 1903), VI, p. 301.Whether the ministers who opposed war on 14 July were now
completely converted or merely thought discretion the better part of valour is an open question.
95. He commented in his reminiscences : 'The Gordian knot of the German situation cannot be dissolved in mutual love by dualism but only hacked through by military means. The important point was to win the king of Prussia and the Prussian army consciously or unconsciously for the national cause. Whether one considered the main issue from a Borussian angle to be the leading role of Prussia or from a national angle to be the unification of Germany, both objectives coincide.' *GW* 15, p. 198.
96. The king, surrounded by princes and generals, received this thirty–strong delegation on 18 December when Simson (who had played the same role on behalf of the Frankfurt Parliament in April 1849) petitioned him to accept the imperial crown.

BIBLIOGRAPHY

PRIMARY SOURCES

Historische Reichskommission (ed.), *Die auswärtige Politik Preussens 1858–1871* (Munich, 1932–45), 9 vols. Vol. 7 (March to August 1866) was never published. Nor were the three volumes covering the period after 1866.

Heinrich Ritter von Srbik (ed.), *Quellen zur deutschen Politik Österreichs 1859–1866* (Oldenburg, 1934–8), 5 vols.

Hermann von Petersdorff et alia (eds), *Fürst Otto von Bismarck: Die gesammelten Werke (Berlin, 1923–35)*, 15 vols.

Ministère des Affaires Etrangères, *Les origines diplomatiques de la guerre de 1870/1, Recueil des documents officiels* (Paris,1910–32), 29 vols.

Emile Ollivier, *L'Empire libéral: études, récits, souvenirs* (Paris, 1895–1916) 16 vols.

Hermann Oncken (ed.), *Die Rheinpolitik Kaiser Napoleon IIIs von 1863 bis 1870 und der Ursprung des Krieges von 1870–71* (Berlin, 1926), 3 vols. Oncken claims that the key to Napoleon's policy was an obsessive desire to gain part of the Rhineland.

Harald Jørgensen (ed.), *Statsraadets forhandlinger 1848–1912* Copenhagen, 1954–72), includes ministerial conferences as well as Statsraadet meetings. Vols 8 and 9 cover the period December 1859 to July 1864. This official publication replaces Aage Friis's edited extracts in *Statsraadets forhandlinger om Danmarks Udenrigspolitik 1863–1879* (Copenhagen, 1936).

SECONDARY SOURCES

The following works were found useful in the preparation of the text.

214

GENERAL TEXTS

Heinrich Lutz, *Zwischen Habsburg und Preussen:Deutschland 1815–1866* (Berlin, 1985), puts the Austrian case; T. Nipperdey, *Deutsche Geschichte 1806–1866: Bürgerwelt und starker Staat* (Munich, 1987), a mine of information on social and economic conditions; James J. Sheehan, *German History 1776–1866* (Oxford, 1989), an excellent survey.

MONOGRAPHS

Much has been written about Bismarck. The modern biographies include: Ernst Engelberg, *Bismarck: Urpreusse und Reichsgründer* (Berlin, 1985), by a GDR historian; Lothar Gall, *Bismarck: Der weisse Revolutionär* (Propyläen, 1980); A. Hillgruber, *Bismarcks Aussenpolitik* (Freiburg, 1972), a perceptive analysis; George Kent, *Bismarck and his times* (South Illinois University Press, 1978); W.N. Medlicott, *Bismarck and Modern Germany* (London, 1965); W. Mommsen, *Bismarck: Ein politisches Lebensbild* (Munich, 1959); Otto Pflanze, *Bismarck and the Development of Germany: The Period of Unification 1815–1871* (Princeton, 1963); F. Stern, *Gold and Iron: Bismarck, Bleichröder and the Building of the German Empire* (London,1977), for his financial dealings; A.J.P. Taylor, *Bismarck: The Man and the Statesman* (London, 1955), readable as always: On the international background: W.E. Mosse, *The European Great Powers and the German Question 1848–1871* (Cambridge, 1958), primarily British and Russian policy; A.J.P. Taylor, *The Struggle for Mastery in Europe 1848–1918* (Oxford, 1954).

Important symposia on unification and its problems: H. Bartel/E.Engelberg, *Die grosspreussisch-militärische Reichsgründung 1871: Voraussetzungen und Folgen* (Berlin, 1971), 2 vols. for a GDR perspective; Josef Becker/Andreas Hillgruber, *Die deutsche Frage im 19 und 20 Jahrhundert* (Munich, 1983); Helmut Boehme, *Probleme der Reichsgründungszeit 1848–1879* (Cologne, 1968); T. Schieder and E. Deuerlein, *Reichsgründung 1870–71: Tatsachen, Kontroversen und Interpretationen* (Stuttgart, 1970).

Work on the origins of nationalism is a growth industry. Important studies include: P. Alter, *Nationalismus* (Frankfurt a/M, 1985); John Breuilly, *Nationalism and the State* (Manchester, 1982), a brilliant analysis of the legitimization function of nationalism; Otto Busch and James J. Sheehan (ed.), *Die Rolle der Nation in der deutschen*

Geschichte und Gegenwart (Berlin, 1978); O.Dann, 'Nationalismus und sozialer Wandel in Deutschland 1806–1850', in O.Dann, *Nationalismus und sozialer Wandel* (Hamburg,1978); Karl W. Deutsch, *Nationalism and Social Communication: An inquiry into the Foundation of Nationality* (Cambridge, Mass., 1966), a basic study; Dieter Düding, *Organizierter gesellschaftlicher Nationlismus in Deutschland (1808–1847)* (Munich, 1984), the first thoroughly researched study of mass organisations; Michael Hughes, *Nationalism and Society in Germany 1800–1945* (London, 1988), a perceptive commentary; Hagen Schulze, *Der Weg zum Nationalstaat: Die deutsche Nationalbewegung vom 18 Jahrhundert bis zur Reichsgründung* (Munich, 1985), the latest German account; James J. Sheehan, 'What is German History? Reflections on the role of the nation in German history and historiography', *JMH* (53), 1981, thought-provoking; H.A. Winkler (ed.), *Nationalismus* (Königstreu/Ts, 1968), contains important essays.

On liberalism: Eugene N. Anderson, *The Social and Political Conflict in Prussia 1858–1864* (Lincoln, Neb., 1954), exaggerates the degree of popular support for liberalism; M. Gugel, *Industrieller Aufstieg und bürgerliche Herrschaft: sozio-ökonomische Interessen und politische Ziele des liberalen Bürgertums in Preussen zur Zeit des Verfassungskonflikts 1875–1867* (Cologne, 1975), goes to the other extreme and underestimates the liberal desire for change; an early work on the National Society is Le Mang, *Der deutsche Nationalverein* (Berlin, 1909); an important article by Lenore O'Boyle, 'The German Nationalverein', *J. Cent. E. Affairs* (16), 1956/7, is critical of Anderson; James J. Sheehan, *German Liberalism in the nineteenth century* (London, 1982), is a standard work; H.A. Winkler, *Preussischer Liberalismus und deutscher Nationalstaat 1861–1866* (Tübingen, 1964), believes resistance to liberalism was greater in Germany because of the power of local dynasties.

On conservatism: Arno J. Mayer, *The Persistence of the Old Regime: Europe to the Great War* (New York, 1981), emphasizes the dominant role of aristocracy down to 1914; J. Weiss, *Conservatism in Europe 1800–1945* (London, 1977).

On public opinion and the press there are only: Kurt Koszyk, *Deutsche Presse im 19 Jahrhundert: Geschichte der deutschen Presse Teil II* (Berlin, 1966); and Eberhard Naujoks, *Bismarcks auswärtige Pressepolitik und die Reichsgründung* (Wiesbaden, 1968).

On the Schleswig-Holstein Question for the pre-1848 period, see W. Carr, *Schleswig-Holstein 1815–1848: A study in National Conflict* (Manchester, 1963); Manfred Jensen-Klingenberg, *Schleswig-Holstein in der deutschen und nordeuropäischen Geschichte: Gesammelte Aufsätze von Alexander Scharff* (Stuttgart, 1969), contains perceptive essays by a former professor at Kiel University; P. von Linston, 'Bismarck Europa og Slesvig-Holsten 1862–1866', *HT* 78 (1978), is important; on Schleswig Lorenz Rerup, *Slesvig og Holsten efter 1830* (Copenhagen, 1982), is an excellent survey; Keith A.P. Sandiford, *Great Britain and the Schleswig-Holstein Question 1848–1866: A Study in diplomacy, politics and public opinion* (Toronto and Buffalo, 1975); Lawrence Steefel, *The Schleswig-Holstein Question* (Cambridge, Mass., 1932); Johannes H. Voigt, 'Englands Aussenpolitik während des deutsch–dänischen Konflikts 1862–1864', *ZGSHG* 90 (1965).

For the Danish perspective: Troels Fink, *Deutschland als Problem Dänemarks: Die geschichtlichen Voraussetzungen der dänischen Aussenpolitik* (Flensburg, 1968); Erik Møller, *Helstatens Fald*, 2 parts (Copenhagen, 1958), is a detailed study, but cf. review *ZGSHG* 85/86 (1961), pp. 351–9; N. Neergaard, *Under Junigrundloven: En Fremstilling af det danske Folks politiske Historie fra 1848 til 1866*, 2 vols (Copenhagen, 1892–1916), another detailed study still of great value; Johannes Nielsen, *1864: Da Europa sik af lave* (Odense, 1987), describes the 1864 War; Vagn Skovgaard Petersen, *Tiden 1814–1864*, vol. 5 of *Danmarks Historie* (Copenhagen 1977–85) and Roar Skovmand, *Folkestyrets Fødsel 1830–1870* (Copenhagen, 1964), vol. 11 of *Danmarks Historie* by John Danstrup and Hal Koch are the latest general histories.

On the conflict between Austria and Prussia: C.W. Clark, *Francis Joseph and Bismarck before 1866: The diplomacy of Austria before the war of 1866* (Cambridge Harvard, 1934); H. Friedjung, *Der Kampf um die Vorherrschaft in Deutschland 1859 bis 1866*, 2 vols (Stuttgart and Berlin, 1912), is a classic account hostile to Prussia but also highly critical of Austrian leaders; the revisionist case in Heinrich Lutz und Helmut Rumpler, *Österreich und die deutsche Frage in 19 und 20 Jahrhundert: Probleme der politisch-staatlichen und sozial-kulturellen Differenzierung im deutschen Mitteleuropa* (Vienna, 1982); on the Habsburg monarchy C.A. Macartney, *The Habsburg Empire 1790–1918* (London, 1968).

On the economic rivalry between Austria and Prussia: Helmut Boehme, *Deutschlands Weg zur Grossmacht: Studien zum Verhältnis von Wirtschaft und Staat während der Reichsgründungszeit 1848–1881* (Cologne and Berlin, 1966), a pioneer work though less original than the author claims; Hans-Werther Hahn, *Geschichte des Deutschen Zollvereins* (Göttingen, 1984), is the latest account of the Customs Union superseding W.O. Henderson, *The Zollverein* (London, 1939). A veritable treasure trove of material on economic and social development in Theodore S. Hamerow, *The Social Foundations of German Unification 1858–1871*, vol. 1, *Ideas and Institutions* (Princeton, 1969); vol. 2, *Struggles and Accomplishments* (Princeton, 1972); a comparison of the Prussian and Austrian economies in H. Kernbauer/E.März, 'Das

Wirtschaftswachstum in Deutschland und Österreich von der Mitte des 19 Jahrhunderts bis zum ersten Weltkrieg', in W.H. Schröder und R. Spree, *Historische Konjunkturforschung* (Stuttgart, 1980), pp. 47–59; material on Austrian development in Herbert Matis, *Österreichs Wirtschaft 1848–1913: Konjunkturelle Dynamik und gesellschaftlicher Wandel im Zeitalter Francis Joseph I* (Berlin, 1972); W. Zorn, 'Wirtschafts und Sozialgeschichtliche Zusammenhänge der deutschen Reichsgründungszeit 1850–1879', *HZ* 197 (1963), pp. 318–42.

On the military side of the war of 1866: G. Craig, *The Battle of Königgrätz: Prussia's victory over Austria 1866* (Princeton, 1964).

On German Catholicism, a subject rather neglected by historians: George G. Windell, *The Catholics and German Unity 1866–1871* (University of Minnesota Press, 1954); and J. Sperber, *Popular Catholicism in nineteenth-century Germany* (Princeton, 1984).

On Franco-German relations: Rudolf Buchner, *Die deutsch-französische Tragödie 1848–1864* (Würzburg, 1965); Alan Mitchell, *Bismarck and the French Nation 1848–1870* (New York, 1971); Raymond Poidevin, Jacques Bariéty, *Frankreich und Deutschland. Die Geschichte ihrer Beziehungen 1815–1975* (Munich, 1982).

On France: Mary Barker, *Distaff Diplomacy: Empress Eugénie* (London, 1957); J.P.T. Bury, *Napoleon III and the Second Empire* (London 1964); T. Zeldin, *The political system of Napoleon III* (Oxford, 1958);idem *Emile Ollivier and the Liberal Empire of Napoleon III* (Oxford,1963).

On public opinion in France: A. Armengaud, *L'opinion publique en France et la crise nationale allemande en 1866* (Paris, 1962); E.M. Carroll, 'French Public Opinion in the war with Prussia', *AHR* 31, 1929 pp. 679–700; Lynn M. Case, *French Opinion in war and diplomacy during the Second Empire* (Philadelphia, 1954); Irene Collins, *The government and the newspaper press in France 1814–1881* (London, 1959); Elisabeth Fehrenbach, 'Preussen-Deutschland als Faktor der französischen Aussenpolitik in der Reichsgründungszeit', *HZ Beiheft 6* (Munich, 1980).

On the Hohenzollern candidacy: Josef Becker, 'Zum Problem der Bismarckischen Politik in der spanischen Thronfrage 1870', *HZ* 212,1971, puts the blame for war on Bismarck; idem, 'Der Krieg mit Frankreich als Problem der kleindeutschen Einigungspolitik Bismarcks 1866–1872', in M. Stürmer, *Das kaiserliche Deutschland: Politik und Gesellschaft 1870-1918* (Düsseldorf, 1970); Georges Bonnin, *Bismarck and the Hohenzollern candidature for the Spanish throne* (London, 1957), contains an important selection of documents from the Sigmaringen archives; Jochen Dittrich, *Bismarck Frankreich und die spanische Thronkandidatur der Hohenzollern* (Munich, 1962), contains an appendix of documents from the Sigmaringen archives in the original German; Eberhard Kolb, *Der Kriegsausbruch 1870. Politische Entscheidungsprozesse und Verantwortlichkeiten in der Julikrise 1870* (Göttingen, 1870), puts the blame back on the French: cf. trenchant criticism in William S. Halperin, 'The Origins of the Franco-Prussian war revisited: Bismarck and the Hohenzollern candidature for the Spanish throne', *JMH* 45 (1973); a series of essays on the international context of the war in Eberhard Kolb, *Europa vor dem Krieg von 1870: Mächte Konstellation-Konfliktsfelde-Kriegsausbruch* (Munich, 1987); William S. Langer, 'Red rag and Gallic bull: the French decision for war 1870', in Otto Brunner/Dietrich Gerhard (ed.), *Europa and Übersee. Festschrift für Egmont Zechlin* (Hamburg, 1964), unravels some confused chronology; R.H. Lord, *The Origins of the War of 1870: New documents from the German archives* (Cambridge, 1924); Lawrence D. Steefel, *Bismarck, the Hohenzollern candidacy and the Origins of the German War of 1870* (Cambridge, Mass., 1962).

For the military events: Michael Howard, *The Franco-Prussian War: The German Invasion of France 1870 –1871* (London, 1961).

MAPS

1. The German Confederation in 1815

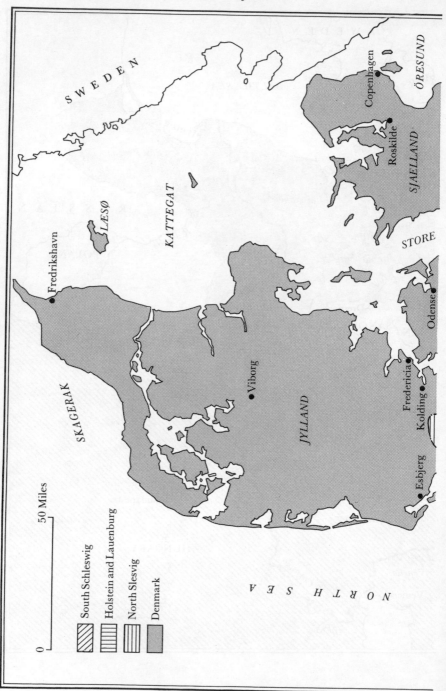

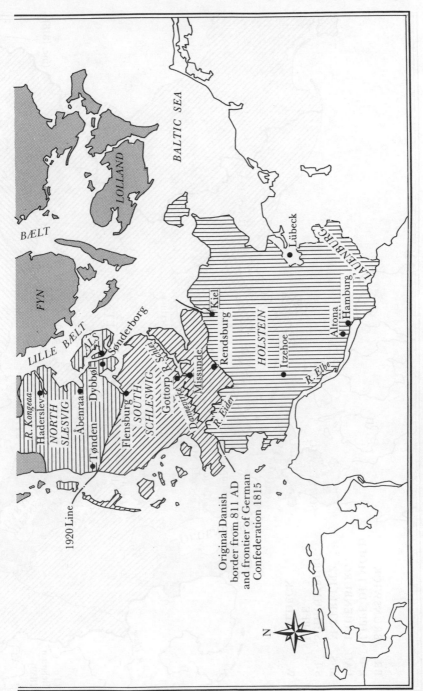

2. The War of 1864: Denmark and the Elbe Duchies

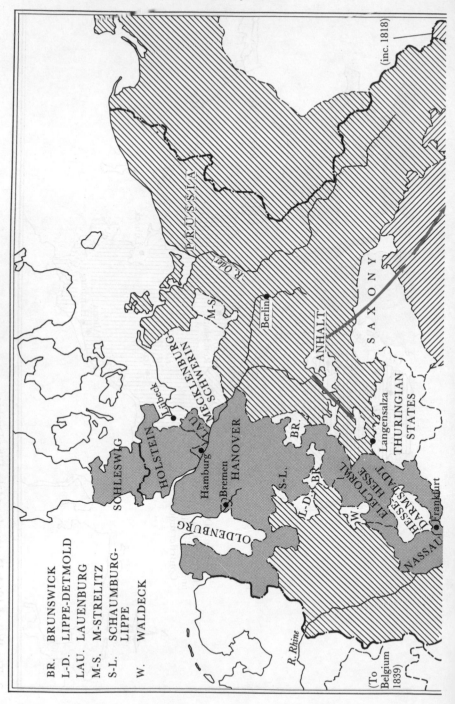

(inc. 1818)

R. Oder

PRUSSIA

Berlin

SAXONY

M-S

ANHALT

Langensalza

THURINGIAN
STATES

Lübeck

MECKLENBURG

HOLSTEIN

MECKLENBURG
SCHWERIN

HANOVER

BR.

Hamburg

Bremen

S-L.

L-D.

BR.

W.

ELECTORAL
HESSE

HESSE
DARMSTADT

Frankfurt

SCHLESWIG

OLDENBURG

R. Rhine

NASSAU

(To
Belgium
1839)

BR.   BRUNSWICK
L-D.   LIPPE-DETMOLD
LAU.   LAUENBURG
M-S.   M-STRELITZ
S-L.   SCHAUMBURG-
        LIPPE
W.   WALDECK

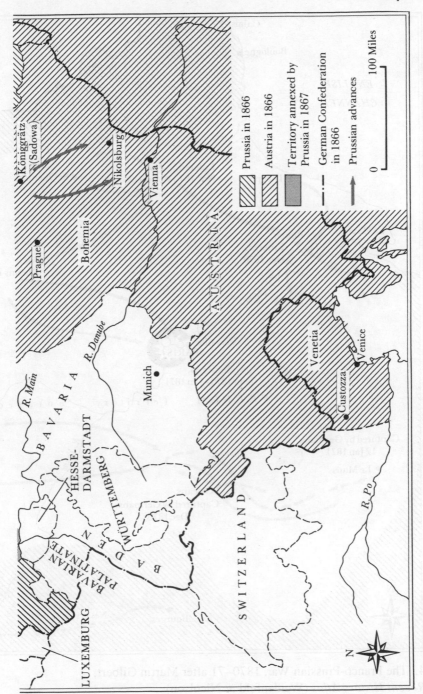

3. The War of 1866

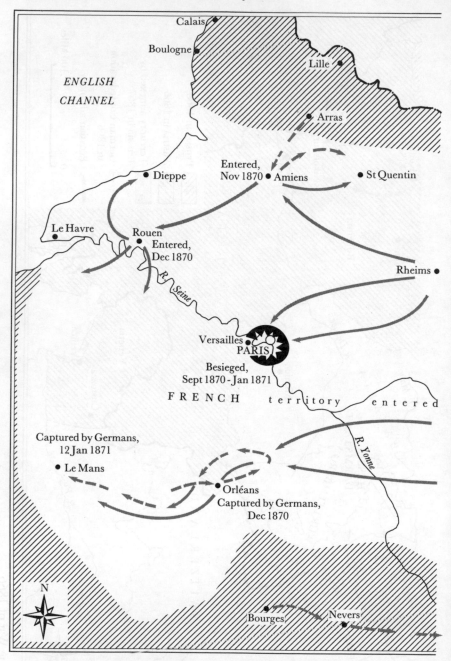

4. The Franco-Prussian War, 1870–71 after Martin Gilbert,
Recent History Atlas (Weidenfeld & Nicolson)

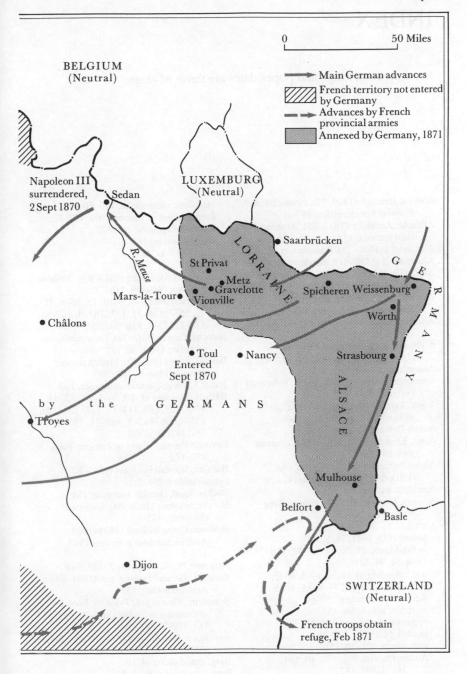

Scale: 0 — 50 Miles

Legend:
- → Main German advances
- ▨ French territory not entered by Germany
- ⇢ (dashed) Advances by French provincial armies
- ▓ Annexed by Germany, 1871

BELGIUM (Neutral)

Napoleon III surrendered, 2 Sept 1870 — Sedan

LUXEMBURG (Neutral)

Saarbrücken

LORRAINE

St Privat
Metz
Gravelotte
Mars-la-Tour
Vionville

Spicheren   Weissenburg

GERMANY

Wörth

Châlons

Toul — Entered Sept 1870

Nancy

Strasbourg

ALSACE

by the GERMANS

Troyes

Mulhouse

Belfort

Basle

Dijon

SWITZERLAND (Netural)

French troops obtain refuge, Feb 1871

R. Meuse

INDEX

For emperors, kings and popes dates are those of reigns